The Language of S

The Language of Social Media

Identity and Community on the Internet

Edited by

Philip Seargeant
The Open University, UK

and

Caroline Tagg
University of Birmingham, UK

First published 2014 by
PALGRAVE MACMILLAN

Palgrave Macmillan in the UK is an imprint of Macmillan Publishers Limited,
registered in England, company number 785998, of Houndmills, Basingstoke,
Hampshire RG21 6XS.

Palgrave Macmillan in the US is a division of St Martin's Press LLC,
175 Fifth Avenue, New York, NY 10010.

Palgrave Macmillan is the global academic imprint of the above companies
and has companies and representatives throughout the world.

Palgrave® and Macmillan® are registered trademarks in the United States,
the United Kingdom, Europe and other countries.

ISBN 978-1-349-44013-9   ISBN 978-1-137-02931-7 (eBook)
DOI 10.1057/9781137029317

This book is printed on paper suitable for recycling and made from fully
managed and sustained forest sources. Logging, pulping and manufacturing
processes are expected to conform to the environmental regulations of the
country of origin.

A catalogue record for this book is available from the British Library.

A catalog record for this book is available from the Library of Congress.

Typeset by MPS Limited, Chennai, India.

Transferred to Digital Printing in 2014

Contents

List of Figures and Tables

Figures

Tables

Notes on Contributors

Ana Deumert is Associate Professor in Linguistics at the University of Cape Town, South Africa. She has worked, taught and researched on three continents: Africa, Europe and Australia. Her research programme is located within the broad field of African sociolinguistics and has a strong interdisciplinary focus. She is one of the co-authors of *Introducing Sociolinguistics* (2000/2009), has edited books on language history and language contact, and published a monograph on the sociolinguistic history of Afrikaans (*The Dynamics of Cape Dutch*, 2004). Her present work focuses on digital communication and she is currently working on a book titled *Sociolinguistics and Mobile Communication*.

Henna Jousmäki is preparing her doctoral dissertation on the discourse aspects of Christian metal music and identity in the Department of Languages, University of Jyväskylä. Her research interests include the sociology of language and religion, language and identities in popular culture, as well as new media discourses.

Samu Kytölä is a post-doctoral researcher in the Department of Languages, University of Jyväskylä. His research areas include multicultural/multilingual football (soccer) discourses, sociolinguistic diversity in Finland, non-native and non-Standard Englishes, multilingualism *vis-à-vis* societal and individual inequalities, and the ethnography of ways of writing, particularly internet writing. He has recently worked in three projects: 'The Centre of Excellence for the Study of Variation, Contacts and Change in English', 'Multilingualism as a Problematic Resource', and 'Language and Superdiversity: (Dis)identification in Social Media'. Besides co-authoring the *National Survey on the English Language in Finland: Uses, Meanings and Attitudes* (2011), recent publications have appeared in *Routledge Critical Studies in Multilingualism* and Palgrave Macmillan's *Language and Globalization* series.

Carmen Lee is Assistant Professor in the Department of English at the Chinese University of Hong Kong. Her research interests lie mainly in language and literacy practices in new media. She has published and carried out research projects specifically on text-making practices, multilingualism and code choice on the internet, especially on Web 2.0 sites. She is also interested in the interaction between online and offline linguistic practices in everyday lives.

Aoife Lenihan recently completed her doctoral studies at the School of Languages, Literature, Culture and Communication, University of Limerick, Ireland. Her doctoral research is titled: 'The Interaction of Language Policy, New Media and Minority Languages'. Her research is primarily situated in the field of sociolinguistics, her overall interest being in language and popular culture, and her research interests include media discourse, language and globalization, the commercialization of minority languages and multilingualism. Recent publications include '"Join our community of translators": language ideologies and/ in Facebook', in Thurlow and Mroczek's *Digital Discourse: Language in the New Media* (2011).

Sirpa Leppänen is a Professor in the Department of Languages at University of Jyväskylä, Finland. With her research team (www. socialmediadiscourses.fi), she investigates the ways in which resources provided by languages and discourses are used by individuals and groups in social media and the ways in which such resources are used for the collaborative creation, negotiation and appropriation of a participatory social and cultural reality offline and online. In her own work, she has approached these questions within a framework provided by sociolinguistics, discourse studies, ethnography and cultural studies, and looked at a range of social media settings and discourses. Particular questions investigated by her have included (1) the impact of globalized translocal social media on language choice and use, (2) linguistic and discursive heterogeneity as a semiotic resource for social interaction and cultural production in social media, (3) constructing and regulating identities and communality online, and (4) interventions and parody as a means for discrimination, social critique and activism. In addition, with the research team, Research Unit for Variation, Contacts and Change in English (www.jyu.fi/varieng), she has conducted a nation-wide survey on Finns' uses of and attitudes to the changing sociolinguistic situation in Finland, and the role of English in this change.

Frank Monaghan is Senior Lecturer and Staff Tutor in the Centre for Language and Communication at The Open University, UK. His interest in Liverpool Football Club began in the mid-1960s when, as an 8-year-old boy, it was possible to wander into the team's training ground and changing room, gawp at your heroes and collect their autographs. Modern football is very different and fans' efforts to assert an alternative identity to the consumerist role globalizing corporatism seeks to ascribe to them provide rich evidence of both their collective creativity and their semiotic savvy. An applied linguist by trade, Frank is keen to explore language and football and to promote fans' creative use of newer technologies and multimodal resources as a significant and somewhat overlooked research area. He is currently researching fans' banners as markers of identity and sites of creativity.

Ruth Page is a Reader in the School of English at the University of Leicester. Her research interests include storytelling, sociolinguistics and social media. Her publications draw on literary-critical and discourse-analytic approaches to narratives in conversational, fictional and online contexts. She is author of *Stories and Social Media* (2012) and *Literary and Linguistic Approaches to Feminist Narratology* (2006).

Saija Peuronen is a junior researcher at the Department of Languages, University of Jyväskylä. Combining sociolinguistic, ethnographic and discourse-analytic approaches, her research explores how linguistic, discursive and semiotic means are drawn on to build socio-cultural affiliations and identifications both in social media spaces and offline settings. Particularly, in her ongoing PhD research, she examines the ways in which Christian extreme sports enthusiasts construct participation in their online/offline communities through heteroglossic language practices.

Philip Seargeant is Senior Lecturer in Applied Linguistics in the Centre for Language and Communication, The Open University. He is author of *The Idea of English in Japan: Ideology and the Evolution of a Global Language* (2009), *Exploring World Englishes: Language in a Global Context* (2012) and *From Language to Creative Writing* (with Bill Greenwell, 2013); he is also editor of *English in Japan in the Era of Globalization* (2011) and *English in the World Today: History, Diversity, Change* (with Joan Swann, 2012).

Caroline Tagg is Lecturer in English Language and Applied Linguistics in the English Department at the University of Birmingham. Her research interests are in language and creativity, and in the application of corpus linguistics and discourse analysis to the investigation of digital communication. She is author of *The Discourse of Text Messaging* (2012), co-editor (with Ann Hewings) of *The Politics of English: Conflict, Competition, Co-existence* (2012), and has published articles in journals such as the *Journal of Sociolinguistics*, *World Englishes* and *Writing Systems Research*.

Toshie Takahashi is Professor in the School of Culture, Media and Society, Waseda University, Tokyo. She was appointed faculty fellow at the Berkman Center for Internet and Society at Harvard University, 2010–2011 and, before that, visiting research fellow at the Department of Education in the University of Oxford. Her current research is an ethnography centred on cross-cultural research into youth and digital media in the US, the UK and Japan.

Camilla Vásquez is an Associate Professor in the Department of World Languages at the University of South Florida. Her research centres on discourse and identity in various social, professional, and online domains. Her recent work has appeared in *Narrative Inquiry*, *Journal of Pragmatics*, *Research on Language and Social Interaction* and *TEXT & TALK*.

Elina Westinen is currently a junior researcher in the Department of Languages, University of Jyväskylä and in the 'Language and Superdiversity: (Dis)identification in Social Media' research project (funded by the Academy of Finland, 2012–2016). Combining insights provided by sociolinguistics (of globalization), discourse studies and ethnography, her research looks into multilingual language use, discursive practices and (dis)identifications in popular culture, particularly in (translocal) hip hop cultures. In her PhD thesis, she explores how Finnish rap artists construct authenticity in their lyrics and interviews via linguistic and discursive repertoires, on several scale-levels and orienting towards various centres of norms.

Michele Zappavigna is a Lecturer in the School of Arts and Media at the University of New South Wales. Her major research interest is in the language of social media and how users engage in ambient affiliation online. She is author of *Discourse of Twitter and Social Media* and *Tacit Knowledge and Spoken Discourse* (2012), *Researching Language and Social Media* (with Ruth Page, Johann Unger and David Barton, forthcoming) and *Discourse and Diversionary Justice: An Analysis of Ceremonial Redress in Youth Justice Conferencing* (with J. R. Martin and Paul Dwyer, forthcoming).

Introduction: The language of social media

Philip Seargeant and Caroline Tagg

1 Early links in the chain

In 1929, the Hungarian author Frigyes Karinthy wrote a short story called 'Chain-links' in which a group of friends discuss the fundamental interconnectedness of the modern world:

> Let me put it this way: Planet Earth has never been as *tiny* as it is now. It shrunk – relatively speaking of course – due to the quickening pulse of both physical and verbal communication. This topic has come up before, but we had never framed it quite this way. We never talked about the fact that anyone on Earth, at my or anyone's will, can now learn in just a few minutes what I think or do, and what I want or what I would like to do. (2007[1929], p. 21)

The character who makes this speech goes on to argue that everyone in the world is related to everyone else though a series of chains of acquaintance, and that no-one is more than five acquaintances away from anyone else on the planet. Every individual is only six degrees of separation away from any other.

Karinthy's story is not a scientific hypothesis – it is more of a thought experiment – but the underlying idea became the basis for a great deal of the research and theorizing that has been conducted into the social networks that people form, and the way that society as a whole is structured around such networks. Part of Karinthy's argument was that changing patterns of social relations are a product of the ways in which technologies – such as the telegraph and telephone in the 1920s – 'shrink' our notions of time and space: the fact that ever-evolving

1

communications technologies allow us to stay in touch even when we are scattered across distant parts of the globe, rendering geographical boundaries increasingly less important. In other words, globalization changes our social and cultural relations; and communications technologies are a major driver behind such change.

Almost 80 years after the publication of 'Chain-links', Karinthy's idea was used as the name for what is often described as the first social network site: SixDegrees.com (boyd & Ellison, 2008).[1] Launched in 1997 – less than ten years after the invention of the World Wide Web – SixDegrees.com did not last very long itself, but the model it developed was adopted and modified by other influential sites: first by Friendster, then MySpace, and then Facebook. By the end of the first decade of the 2000s, social network sites had become an integral part of modern life the world over, and figured as paradigmatic examples of the increased social-orientation of online activity. The shift that occurred in the nature of the web in the early years of the new millennium – the move from the idea of Web 1.0 to Web. 2.0 (O'Reilly, 2012 [2005]) and the rise of social media – saw an explosion in online interactivity and user participation. The web was no longer a place where you went predominantly to consume content and information. It became a place where you participated; a dynamic space that was shaped (both intentionally and inadvertently) by your own actions and contributions. And social network sites, purpose-built to facilitate social interaction, grew to become amongst the most used sites on the web (Pew Internet and American Life Project, 2012).

One of the results of the rise of sites such as Facebook is that they have transformed the ways in which people can interact. They do not simply offer an alternative way of engaging in the same forms of communicative interaction that were available prior to their emergence; they also provide a number of notably different communicative dynamics and structures. Just as the telegraph and telephone before them introduced new possibilities for the way people could communicate – and with this altered both communicative practices and patterns of social relations – so online social media are having a profound effect on the linguistic and communicative practices in which people engage, as well as the social groupings and networks they create. The aim of this book is to critically examine these effects, and investigate the implications that emergent online practices are having for an understanding of language use in society. To this end, it brings together a collection of studies exploring the linguistic and communicative practices being used on social media in order to shed light on this important new form of communication and some of the influential roles it is playing in contemporary society.

2 Sharing, connecting and commenting: definitions of social media

This introduction has a twofold purpose: to outline the language and communication issues that exist for social media; and to delineate the topics, contexts and problems that the book addresses. The concept of social media is an extremely broad one. The focus of the book is primarily on those internet-based sites and platforms which facilitate the building and maintaining of networks or communities through the sharing of messages and other media. Social network sites (SNSs) such as Facebook and Line and microblogging sites such as Twitter have this as their primary function and thus figure as a central focus for the book. Yet other forms of social media, such as YouTube and TripAdvisor, also increasingly feature social network capabilities, and thus also give rise to important issues concerning communication and language use which will be covered in the book. Given the broad scope of the concept of 'social media', and in order to begin drawing out the nature of the communicative and sociolinguistic issues it presents, it is worth first giving a brief overview of its development and definition.

A number of competing terms have been used to highlight different elements of the changes that have taken place in the web over the last decade or so. Michael Mandiberg, in his introduction to the *Social Media Reader*, lists various names and phrases that have been used to refer to the phenomena that constitute this phase in the use and development of the internet (Mandiberg, 2012). As well as 'Web 2.0' (given currency by Tim O'Reilly), these include: 'user-generated content'; 'convergence culture' (coined by Henry Jenkins); 'the people formerly known as the audience' (coined by Jay Rosen); 'participatory media'; and 'peer production' (coined by Yochai Benkler). Each of these defines the general phenomenon from a slightly different perspective, reflecting the particular interests of the analyst who coined or employed the term. What they all have in common, with the exception of the first, is an acknowledgment of the *social* nature of practices that constitute modern online activity. In other words, the users of the services and sites which make up the modern web are themselves central to its nature – the audience or consumer is actively engaged in production (and not solely passively engaged in consumption) – and thus previous dichotomies such as author/audience and amateur/professional are becoming porous.

The first term in the list, 'Web 2.0', indicates a new stage in the ongoing development of the web. It is a metaphor which has been adopted in other contexts (for example, Wael Ghonim's *Revolution 2.0*, which documents the role played by social media in the Arab Spring of 2011), and its use from the mid-2000s onwards was meant to signal that a new model was in operation which had replaced the first phase of internet development (which can symbolically be marked as ending with the bursting of the dot-com bubble in 2001).

Scholars such as Leppänen *et al.* (this volume) define social media as including any digital environment which involves interaction between participants (see also Barton & Lee, 2012, p. 3), and it is this broad definition that we adopt in this book. The essence of social media, therefore, is a focus on the facilitating of participation and interaction, with the result that the 'content' of what is developed and shared on the internet is as much a product of participation as it is of traditional creative and publishing/broadcast processes. The expectation therefore becomes that this content is less regulated, more fluid, and more diverse, and that the dividing line between private or personal communication and publishing or broadcasting can be increasingly blurred.

The sites and platforms on which this happens are various and widespread, and increasingly applications and services which have a different primary purpose (e.g. the selling of books, the swapping of music) also include and make extensive use of commenting or sharing capabilities which allow users to interact with each other. Thus, for example, media sharing sites such as Flickr and YouTube have networking features, and, in a broad sense, have become social network sites themselves. Also in this category are wikis – websites produced collaboratively by users – which, despite their focus on content rather than connections, bring people with shared interests together. More traditional websites where content is posted for user consumption – such as newspaper sites and the TED website, which streams short conference talks – now also enable users to comment on the content posted there and thus to interact with each other. Furthermore, there is a growing tendency towards interconnecting different services, so that, for example, sharing options via Facebook or Twitter are integrated into operating systems (e.g. Apple's iOS), thus allowing any activity performed in any application to be linked to the social networks managed through these sites. The result is that the ability to share the details of one's interaction with the internet, and through this to connect to people and organizations, has become a fundamental part of the architecture of the online world.

3 Sociolinguistics and social media: changing concepts of identity and community

Although sociolinguistic research into these new media has been slow to get off the ground (Androutsopoulos, 2006a), there are many reasons why social media (and particularly social network sites) are – or should be – of interest for socially oriented linguistics. On a basic level, there is a clear connection: social network sites (along with other forms of social media with networking capabilities) are a major and relatively novel form of communication, and therefore the study of social language use will want to explore their nature and use. Of particular relevance to sociolinguistics, however, are two fundamental social dynamics at the heart of social network site (SNS) use: the presentation of self (i.e. issues that pivot around notions of *identity*), and the building and maintenance of networked relationships (i.e. issues relating to concepts of *community*). This is especially evident in SNSs such as Facebook which, as boyd and Ellison (2008) point out, comprise three main elements: the facility for: (1) constructing and presenting a member profile; (2) establishing (a network of) links with other members; and (3) viewing and searching the networked links of members in your network.[2] Brought together, these three different elements allow users to establish, maintain and access extensive social networks, and to do so in a visible way. And this visibility – the display of an individual's identity as indicated through their social connections – in turn becomes part of the act of communicating and relating. In this section, therefore, we look in turn at the concepts of *identity* and *community* as these are enacted via social media, and consider how they present questions of particular interest for sociolinguistic study. The following section then details how the chapters in the book, building upon detailed empirical studies of social media communication, explore and extend the theory and research which is emerging around these issues.

3.1 Identity

Identity is now predominantly understood, in sociolinguistics as in other disciplines, to be not a stable, pre-determined property of an individual, but rather a set of resources which people draw upon in presenting and expressing themselves via interaction with others (see, for example, Bucholtz & Hall, 2005). People therefore actively and repeatedly co-construct and negotiate their identity (within the constraints afforded by a range of social and individual factors), and present themselves in different ways depending on the particular contextual circumstances in which they are operating. As Lee (this volume) suggests, rather than talking of 'identity' singular, therefore, a more accurate characterization of people's actual experience may be the plural notion of an individual's 'identities', at least in the sense that different aspects of a person's identity may be foregrounded or sidelined at given times. The use of social media as a means of communication is interesting in this respect for two reasons; firstly, because the circumstances in which people perform identity online, and the resources they have with which to do this, are in many respects different from offline situations; and, secondly, because the novelty and distinctiveness of online interaction bring to the fore many of these contemporary constructivist ideas about the nature of identity. Despite this, as Androutsopoulos (2006a, p. 423) has noted, sociolinguistic research into identity on social media remains somewhat sparse. There is also, as Vásquez (this volume) points out, a tendency in the literature to explore online identity through member profiles (the sections on social media sites where users are able to provide short demographic and other personal information), rather than by examining the ways in which identities are discursively and dialogically performed in interaction.

On social media, to use Goffman's (1959) terms, both the identity cues that are 'given' – through deliberate and conscious management – and those which are 'given off' – less consciously revealed in interaction – are mediated not through face-to-face co-presence, but primarily through language use. As Vásquez (this volume) puts it, 'words, language, and discourse continue to serve as key resources in the presentation of self online and in the construction of identities in social media'. boyd's (2001, p. 119) suggestion that identities on social media are about 'writing oneself into being' is particularly apt, as it highlights the fact that they are, in many cases, performed not through the spoken word but predominantly through the written. This makes available for identity construction a particular set of visual resources, including typography (Vaisman, 2011), orthography (Tagg, 2012) and the creative combining of different scripts (Palfreyman & Al Khalil, 2007; Su, 2007; Tagg & Seargeant, 2012). And with the continued integration of multimedia affordances into social media platforms, these visual semiotic resources extend to the use of photos and images (both moving and still) (Androutsopoulos, 2010), which are becoming an increasingly important aspect of self-representation. Indeed, a fundamental component of the success of Facebook over earlier SNSs such as Friendster was that it was developed at the same time as digital photography saw a popular breakthrough, and was thus able to offer photo sharing capabilities

(Kirkpatrick, 2010). At the same time, however, the disembodied nature of text-based social media interactions means that other physical attributes related to identity – from tone of voice, facial expression and gesture to gender, age and accent – are less salient, if accessible at all. This disembodied, largely text-based aspect to social media-based communication allows for a selective approach to what is presented. It also, in some cases, allows for a certain amount of anonymity, although not necessarily, as Kennedy (2011) points out, the extreme degree of anonymity and complete freedom to reinvent oneself documented in earlier studies of online communication (Danet, Rudenberg-Wright & Rosenbaum, 1997; Reid, 1991; Turkle, 1995). A number of more recent linguistic studies have explored the ways in which individuals and groups draw on the affordances of social media to foreground certain aspects of their identity and to present themselves in ways that reflect the new online situations in which they find themselves (Jones, 2011; Page, 2012; Tsiplakou, 2009). The informal and unregulated situations in which this happens often tend to be perceived as global rather than local (one can converse with people all across the globe), and public rather than private, and factors such as these have an impact on the way in which people negotiate their identity online. One finding, for example, is that groups whose members would not normally express themselves in English do so online as a means of 'translating local cultures' and local identities to an audience with global potential (Barton & Lee, 2012, p. 10; Seargeant, Tagg & Ngampramuan, 2012).

A factor that is often seen as crucial to identity management across online situations is the notion of authenticity – the extent to which an online persona is seen by interlocutors to relate to the person behind it – as well as the social value placed on this perceived authenticity. Expectations about the perceived connection between the online persona and the offline self become very evident when people's sense of authenticity is violated, as happens in cases of online impersonations and scams (see Page, this volume). One of the reasons that authenticity is considered such an important issue on social media is that it provides an anchor for communication. Communication operates as a sort of contractual transaction: interlocutors agree to co-operate with each other in exchanging information, be this interpersonal or ideational. They invest in the interaction in terms both of emotion and personal disclosure, and do this on the basis of a belief that the interlocutor is likewise agreeing to the contract (Grice, 1975). Authenticity thus acts as a baseline from which this belief can be built, and plays a pivotal role in the way that people interact.

As well as expectations of authenticity, performances of identity on social media are further constrained by the perceived nature of the online audience. In this respect, the notion of 'context collapse' is important. This term (first coined by Michael Wesch in his *Anthropological Introduction to YouTube* video) refers to the almost infinite audience that is possible online, and the way that the different local contexts which give individual utterances of other semiotic acts their meaning all run together in communication via the social web. As Wesch (2008) writes, with reference to videos being made for uploading to YouTube:

> The problem is not lack of context. It is context collapse: an infinite number of contexts collapsing upon one another into that single moment of recording. The images, actions, and words captured by the lens at any moment can be transported to anywhere on the planet and preserved (the performer must assume) for all time. The little glass lens becomes the gateway to a blackhole sucking all of time and space – virtually all possible contexts – in upon itself.

Wesch's notion of context collapse has been used by boyd to describe the phenomenon on social network sites whereby a user's potential audience may be drawn from across the various people that make up their Friends list, and where the exact composition of an audience for any one post is therefore unknowable (boyd, 2001; Marwick & boyd, 2011). The implications this has for identity construction are that people must negotiate ways of communicating while presenting themselves in the same way to a variety of potential audiences simultaneously (Jones & Hafner, 2012, p. 152). This is often then further complicated by their awareness of the potential permanence and replicability of their message (Marwick & boyd, 2011) – that is, the fact that a post or video can persist indefinitely online, often in copied or remixed form. The potential conflict here is between simultaneously coming across differently to different people whilst projecting an identity that everyone can judge to be authentic (Ellison, Steinfeld & Lampe, 2011). As we show in our study of Facebook (Tagg & Seargeant, this volume), people thus develop strategies for distinguishing between different strands of the potential audience, and for presenting themselves in ways which target certain individuals and groups and exclude others. In this sense, self-presentation through social media can seem a more complex and nuanced process than in face-to-face (or one-to-one) situations – or, rather, the relative novelty of the online situation (where norms of interaction are not yet stable) makes particularly salient the actively discursive and selective nature of the identity performances in which people engage in offline as well as online interactions.

In sum, if identities are discursively (and semiotically) constructed and dialogically performed, then nowhere is this more evident than on social media, where people have relative freedom to choose how they wish to present themselves, have the opportunity to address new, diverse and potentially global audiences, and have at their disposal a novel set of resources for doing so. This is not to say that anything goes, however, or that a clean divide can be made between who you are offline and how you present yourself online. In fact, given the lack of the type of identity cues that are available in offline interactions, as well as the diverse and unknown nature of the online audience, people may have to work harder in some online environments to perform an identity which others can recognize as authentic.

3.2 Community

Identities both online and off are also partially performed by aligning oneself with different groups, opinions and cultural issues. As Leppänen *et al.* (this volume) put it, identities are 'constructed in active processes of identification and self-understanding, seeking or eschewing commonality, connectedness and groupness'. In this sense, identity performance cannot be discussed in isolation from the communities with which individuals align themselves and the ways in which those communities establish and maintain the relationships that comprise them. On social media, which is predicated on notions of connectedness and the establishment of social networks, these acts of alignment are very much to the fore, and affordances for realizing and displaying connections with others are built into the infrastructure of the applications people use to communicate. These affordances include, amongst other things: the visible display of one's network of followers or friends; the ability to 'like' posts and for this information to be shared amongst your network; the capacity to comment; and the way one can congregate around issues or concepts by using conventions such as the hashtag in Twitter. A long tradition of research into new media communication (e.g. Rheingold, 1994; Herring, 2008; Parks, 2011) has focused on determining the extent to which users exploit these structural affordances to form 'virtual communities', which may or may not be judged to meet the prerequisites of offline communities (i.e. a shared set of cultural references, a regular pattern of interaction, some sense of belonging). The chapters in this book, however, are interested less in the structural elements of community formation, or the extent to which online communities compare to offline ones, and focus instead on the ways in which social media users imagine and discursively construct online communities, and what the consequences of this are for the way people communicate via social media.

Offline social networks have traditionally been a foundational site of exploration for sociolinguistics, and thus the ways that SNSs (and other social media with social networking capabilities) operate are necessarily of interest for the discipline (Androutsopoulos, 2006a). In the 1960s, the sociolinguistic notion of the 'speech community' embodied the assumption that people form mostly homogeneous, immobile, stable groupings based on a shared history, a common 'native' language, and geographical proximity. This allowed sociolinguists to contextualize language features by linking them to social structures and uses. Since then, however, the notion of the community in sociolinguistics has undergone substantial developments – as have the phenomena it is used to refer to. Work on the concept of 'communities of practice' (Lave & Wenger, 1991; Wenger, 1998), for example, has shown how people can simultaneously belong to different groups which are characterized not by geographical proximity or shared histories but by the mutually structured and goal-oriented endeavours of their members. Within contexts such as these, shared language practices are an important part of the broader range of shared social practices which comprise group membership. Social network theory, meanwhile, has offered more nuanced ways of understanding how relationships within and across communities shape language patterns. Social networks in this context are defined as the patterns of relationship that people contract through interaction, be that socializing, communicating for work purposes or through shared interests or experiences (Meyerhoff, 2006). These patterns vary according to the frequency and nature of that interaction (i.e. there can be stronger or weaker links), and the extent to which everyone within a network knows each other or not (the extent to which networks are 'dense' or 'loose'). Within sociolinguistics, the foundational work of James and Lesley Milroy in Northern Ireland revealed how language change correlates with the patterns of social connections which make up social networks, and the Milroys thus argued that these networks are as important as larger social variables such as class or gender for explaining how variation occurs within a community (Milroy & Milroy, 1992).

Recent work by scholars such as Blommaert (2010), building upon and extending the examination of different types of social organization and their relationship to language practices, has stressed the fact that communities and social networks should not be conceptualized as static entities, especially within the era of globalization. Factors such as mobility, the range of different affiliations people have, and the dynamic nature of language use in general, all play a part in people's language practices. It is these contemporary conceptions of community – as the product of networked connections, and as flexible, shifting, and interactively constructed – that are confirmed and extended through consideration of social media alignments.

Online social networks operate in a context where a number of important factors have altered the nature of social reality, and thus the kinds of communities that people form. Firstly, notions of space have been radically changed by digital technologies. Distance is no longer an issue of such importance as it was in the pre-internet age. Where previous technologies partially overcame distance, or did so in a particular way (the telephone allowed for long distance calls, letters can travel over distance, but take time), modern digital technologies have almost completely removed this as a factor. Notions of time have similarly been changed, with communication being instantaneous to almost any destination without difficulty or prohibitive expense. In addition, access to communications technology is now ubiquitous, provided one has a computer or mobile device with an internet connection. Increasingly, social media are accessed via mobile devices, a capability which both increases the extent to which social media-related practices are integrated into the everyday routines of life – it intensifies the 'always on' (Baron, 2008) culture which exists for anyone who has a smartphone or other mobile device with an internet connection – and also alters the ways in which location and the local environment relate to people's communication practices. These factors enhance people's ability to manage their communication; they can choose not to respond immediately, they can carry on multiple conversations at the same time; or they can pretend to be offline and thus incommunicado. Finally, as mentioned earlier, there is the integration of different modes and different types of communication, with everything being accessible via the same platform. One-to-one and one-to-many communication are both possible via the same medium, and this lowers the overheads for people to come together.

These factors have important consequences for the types of communities that people are able to form. A first consequence is that online communities are often bounded not so much by geographical proximity and shared background, as by shared interests. That is, social alignments online involve the development of new social relations with strangers around particular topics or experiences. A number of sites specifically focus on particular activities and thus the networks that are developed around them have this shared cultural interest as their pivot – from eating disorders (Stommel, 2008), television soaps (Baym, 2000), photography (Barton & Lee, 2012; Thurlow & Jaworski, 2011) and political involvement (Monaghan, this volume) to gaming (Ensslin, 2012; Newton, 2011) and wiki collaboration (Myers, 2010; Pentzold, 2010). Other forms of social media are either purposefully structured around or become associated with shared social variables such as nationality, age, religion, sexual orientation, and language. Examples range from the German-based diaspora forums discussed by Androutsopoulos (2006b) to SNSs for older people such as Eldr (with its tagline 'Celebrate aging!'). Others, such as the Japanese housewives' chatroom discussed by Katsuno and Yano (2007), the Finnish Christian extreme sports enthusiasts described by Leppänen *et al.* (this volume) and the Irish Facebook translators discussed by Lenihan (also this volume), combine both. Such sites enable both the development of communities of practice in the more traditional sense of the concept, as well as those that are more diffuse and casual.

Related to the above are 'hashtag communities' of the sort which form on micro-blogging sites such as Twitter, where people have an 'ambient affiliation' (Zappavigna, 2011) to a topic or issue around which they interact (see Zappavigna, this volume). This is a case of there being a shared, transitory virtual space which allows people to identify a particular interest which they can then comment on. Ambient affiliation is, however, less of a 'community' in the sense of a group with shared practices and culture – beyond the shared affiliation itself, that is – and sustained interaction and levels of engagement will be lower than in traditionally conceived communities (Parks, 2011).

SNSs are also used for the continuation of pre-existing offline social networks, which can be maintained across time and space in a way that would not be possible without this new technology. A point of interest here, though, is that while geographical location is no longer of importance for the maintenance and performance of these community relations (i.e. they allow for globally dispersed members to retain connections), a sense of 'local' shared knowledge persists whatever real-world contexts/affiliations the participants may also have at the time. This takes the form of the shared culture that is indexed in the interactions people have – i.e. in the way that, despite communicating in an arena which has a potentially global scope, people's discourse is often very context-specific and comprised of a content and style which is replete with in-group reference points (Seargeant *et al.*, 2012). Furthermore, these interactions also generate their own shared culture: they produce new reference points for the community to orient to (for example, the development and spread of internet memes). These online communities are therefore not simply replicating offline ones, but are developing and expanding them (Jones, 2009).

One of the key features of SNSs, then, is how they facilitate different types of social organization – around shared interests, ambient affiliation and/or the extension of offline groups – and how particular patterns of group interaction develop as a result. As is evident from the above, these patterns often differ from or extend the types of social organization that are available offline due to the affordances of the technology and software, and the connective and communicative possibilities these make possible. In surveying and describing these different patterns of affiliation, the book seeks not to enter the debate as to whether online affiliations measure up to some pre-determined, often offline standard (Parks, 2011), but instead to explore the ways in which people come together through social media and how they themselves perceive, value and act on these connections (Fontaine, 2006), thus developing our understanding of what community in an increasingly internet-mediated world may entail.

4 The structure of the book

Based upon the research context outlined above, the chapters in this book are grouped into two sections, the first covering topics relating to the performance of identity on social media, and the second on the construction of community on social media. The first of these looks predominantly at how people use the linguistic and communicative resources available in social media to perform online identities, along with the ways that this differs from – but also draws upon – offline identity work. The second section looks at the forms and structures of connection with other people, the communities established and maintained via social media, and the language and communication strategies which facilitate this. As has been noted, the discipline of sociolinguistics is itself based very much around these two concerns: language in society operates as a marker of identity, and its use is influenced by – and instrumental in shaping – the social groups people form. Many of the other important issues that sociolinguistics engages with – most notably those to do with social politics – then stem from these two concerns. And social media is reshaping the landscape for both of these issues. In both cases language and communication play a crucial role, and the chapters in the book dissect elements of this role, and in doing so offer a detailed picture of the social dynamics of language use and communication on social media.

Part I considers the way in which identity online is constructed. It looks at the ways in which the online context facilitates forms of self-presentation due to the fact that it is disembodied, that it allows for anonymity and selectiveness, and that discourse operates as its key resource. In Chapter 1, Ana Deumert, drawing upon empirical studies in South Africa, considers the way that social media can act as a 'much-needed' ludic space for the performance of identity. She argues that the interactivity of social media along with its playfulness – encouraged not only by its current affordances but by the hacker culture of its past – creates a space where people can come to know themselves through light-hearted, unregulated, and sometimes transgressive play, as well as through the adoption of masks and nicks. The word play and multimodal creativity evident on social media are not characterized by Deumert as breaking with previous practices or offline identities, however, but rather as giving people a brief respite from the realities of the offline world. Social media in this sense serve as 'third spaces', she argues, replacing the traditional venues such as pubs and street corners.

In Chapter 2, Ruth Page examines the ways that the construction of identities on social media can lead to acts of 'impersonation', and looks at the diverse social effects that this can have. The acts of impersonation she examines (hacks on Twitter, and 'frape' on Facebook), and the discourse around them, indicate that identity work on SNSs is exactly that: one *works* to project and protect an identity within a particular framework provided by the technology and social setting. The chapter also highlights the importance of authenticity – the relationship between the persona and the projected identity – and shows how authenticity in this respect is a social product reliant on the way that the projected identity is viewed by interlocutors.

This notion of authenticity is a key theme for Chapter 3 as well. In this chapter, Camilla Vásquez looks at how the performance of certain types of identity can be purposefully and immediately relevant to the context in which they are enacted; in this case, identity cues are used as a strategy of persuasion by people leaving comments on the travel advice site TripAdvisor, and in doing so making claims to authority based on 'authentic' experience. Vásquez starts from the observation that identity is constructed not only in the 'profile' section of the site, but also in how one presents oneself when giving opinions, even in very brief posts asserting one's identity as a seasoned traveller or a reasonable customer.

Users are able to construct themselves in discourse because of the relative anonymity afforded by the site, but perceptions of authenticity – the ability to convince others that your experience and authority are genuine and based on real-life experiences – remain paramount.

Chapter 4, by Carmen Lee, similarly begins with the premise that the properties of identity are a product of interaction, and looks at how different social media (and the practices around them) lead to the presentation of different selves. Drawing on a study of young HongKongers, she argues that identity is not static, but is related to scenario, which is a mix of technology and its social use. In taking this approach, the chapter takes a step back from the previous three and, rather than focusing specifically on the discursive strategies and practices people use online and how these relate to their social positioning, it considers the language-related practices that people engage in, in relation to new technology and social media in general, and the role this plays in their lives. In other words, identity is not just a product of what people write and share, but of the way they are inducted into various social practices relating to technology.

The final chapter in Part I, by Sirpa Leppänen, Samu Kytölä, Saija Peuronen, Henna Jousmäki and Elina Westinen, begins more explicitly to make the link between the performance of identity and the related issue of community. The authors look at identity via 'acts and processes of identification and disidentification' and argue that semiotic resources and communicative practices on social media allow people – in their cases, Finns from a variety of backgrounds – to align (or disalign) themselves with groups, thus negotiating identities in relation to community – or as they put it in the chapter: 'identity performances were achieved by the participants in each social media setting by their self-selection as legitimate participants in the social media activities in question, and by demonstrating competence in responding to or crafting the discourse in appropriate ways'.

Part II of the book follows on from the ideas introduced in Chapter 5 to examine the different types of community that exist on social media. Chapter 6, by Michele Zappavigna, looks at how and why people interact in 'non-traditional' ways (ways which were previously not possible) on the micro-blogging site Twitter. She adopts a systemic functional linguistic (SFL) approach to look at the way in which people align around shared values, and the type of 'ambient community' this results in. As Knight says, in a quote cited in the chapter, 'we discursively negotiate our communal identities through bonds that we can share, and these bonds make up the value sets of our communities and culture, but they are not stable and fixed' (Knight, 2010, p. 43).

In Chapter 7, Caroline Tagg and Philip Seargeant consider the importance of audience design for the discursive construction of community
on social network sites. The chapter looks at the way people shape content and style as a projection of their understanding of the communities
they are engaging with. It looks closely at the ways in which people –
in this case, multilingual Europeans from various countries – work to
actively construct communities through their language choices in the
course of unfolding interactions on Facebook, and in this way negotiate
the collapsed context of their audience. As with the Twitter affiliations
discussed by Zappavigna, these 'communities' can cross geographical,
political, and social boundaries. However, unlike hashtag communities,
they tend not to orient around a shared topic of interest but around a
particular node (a mutual friend) in the network, and this gives rise to
distinct communicative patterns.

Chapter 8, by Toshie Takahashi, also examines how people negotiate different circles of affiliation on social media, focusing in this
case on the cultural practices of connectivity among young people in
Japan. Examining the topic from a communication studies perspective, Takahashi looks at how the affordances of different types of social
media allow for different forms of community maintenance. Based on
extensive ethnographic research, she shows how cultural values within
Japanese society, which stress community relations that are built upon
indirect communication, non-verbal cues and complex politeness patterns, do not translate readily to publicly 'open' media such as Twitter,
but are well-suited to a closed medium such as Line which allows people to manage their networked communication within small, bounded
groups. Analysing the consequences of this, she shows how the use
of social media and mobile technology in Japan is being adapted to
traditional community values, while also leading to a disruption and
reconfiguration of those values in some contexts.

Chapters 9 and 10 both examine communities which are connected
around issues and actions. In Chapter 9, Aoife Lenihan looks at how
translators for international versions of Facebook operate as a specific
community, and how this relates to wider concepts of community.
Using a case study of Irish language translators, she asks to what extent
Facebook gives a speech community a voice, and how the issue of language regulation relates to the participatory culture of social media. The
focus is predominantly on how language issues are regulated on SNSs –
and the respective roles that the users and the company have in this.
Her findings show that this is a dialectical process, and that the language policy for the translation of the site into Irish is a result of both

top-down (i.e. the company's regulations) and bottom-up (users' input) processes. As Lenihan explains, this has interesting implications for the extent to which social media are driven by a 'prosumer' culture and for the agency that users have in the creation of content.

In the final chapter in the book, Frank Monaghan presents a case study of football fan activism around a specific 'local' issue, in order to examine how online and offline technologies combine to facilitate the aims of a group. The use of social media by the Liverpool football club supporters' union to protest against the policies of the owners of the club facilitated the expansion of geographically bounded local action into a global network of people who shared a sense of affiliation to the club. This global 'community' could then be used in the local struggle against the owners. The chapter highlights the complex and diffuse interplay between online and offline interactions, and the way that social media (aided by traditional media) develop and extend the ways in which this community was able to communicate, protest, and publicize their actions.

Taken together, these ten studies present a detailed picture of the way that social media are offering enhanced means for people to communicate with each other today. They examine how performance of the self online exploits the semiotic resources and networked possibilities – especially in terms of the alignments one can make – that social media afford, and how people negotiate evaluations of authenticity so as to ground acts of communication and lend authority to the opinions and assertions expressed. The chapters reveal the possibilities that social media offer for issue-led social groupings, be these fleeting alignments around concepts and opinions on Twitter, or forms of social engagement and activism such as the Facebook translator community and Liverpool supporters' union. They explore the opportunities that social media offer for offline groups to maintain relationships, and how people adapt existing communicative practices to marry the new online affordances with offline norms and cultural values. And they show that it is in these complex and evolving ways that the social and linguistic practices that social media give rise to are having an impact on the way we relate to each other, on the communities we live within, and on the way we manage and present a sense of self in the twenty-first century.

Acknowledgements

Many thanks to Frank Monaghan and Esther Asprey for providing feedback on early drafts of this chapter.

Notes

1. Although the term 'six degrees of separation' originates with Karinthy, it became a popular notion in mainstream culture following John Guare's 1990 play, which adopted it as its title.
2. As boyd and Ellison (2008) point out, these various features also existed in earlier forms of social media. Member profiles, for example, are a key component of dating sites; directories of buddies or Friends are part of the architecture of instant messaging and other chat services; and linking oneself to existing, although often dormant, social networks was the purpose behind sites such as Classmates. com and Friends Reunited, both of which reactivated networks established at school and allowed people to search and navigate links in these networks.

References

Androutsopoulos, J. (2006a) 'Introduction: Sociolinguistics and computer-mediated communication', *Journal of Sociolinguistics*, 10(4): 419–38.

Androutsopoulos, J. (2006b) 'Multilingualism, diaspora, and the internet: Codes and identities on German-based diaspora websites', *Journal of Sociolinguistics*, 10(4): 520–47.

Androutsopoulos, J. (2010) 'Localising the global on the participatory web'. In N. Coupland (ed.) *The Handbook of Language and Globalisation* (Oxford: Blackwell Publishing), pp. 203–31.

Baron, N. (2008) *Always On: Language in an Online and Mobile World* (Oxford: Oxford University Press).

Barton, D. & Lee, C. (2012) 'Redefining vernacular literacies in the age of Web 2.0', *Applied Linguistics*, 33(3): 282–98.

Baym, N. (2000) *Tune In, Log On: Soaps, Fandom and Online Community* (Thousand Oaks, CA: Sage Publications).

Blommaert, J. (2010) *The Sociolinguistics of Globalization* (Cambridge: Cambridge University Press).

boyd, d. m. (2001) 'Taken Out of Context: American Teen Sociality in Networked Publics'. Ph.D thesis, University of California, Berkeley.

boyd, d. m. & Ellison, N. B. (2008) 'Social network sites: Definition, history, and scholarship', *Journal of Computer-Mediated Communication*, 13(1): article 11.

Bucholtz, M. & Hall, K. (2005) 'Identity and interaction: A sociocultural linguistic approach', *Discourse Studies*, 7(4-5): 5856–14.

Danet, B., Rudenberg-Wright, L. & Rosenbaum-Tamari, Y. (1997) '"Hmm... where's that smoke coming from?" Writing, play and performance on internet relay chat', *Journal of Computer-Mediated Communication*, 2(4). http://online library.wiley.com/doi/10.1111/j.1083-6101.1997.tb00195.x/full

Ellison, N. B., Steinfield, C. & Lampe, C. (2011) 'Connection strategies: Social capital implications of Facebook-enabled communication practices', *New Media & Society*, 13: 873–92.

Ensslin, A. (2012) *The Language of Gaming* (Basingstoke and New York: Palgrave Macmillan).

Fontaine, L. (2006) 'Where do we fit in? Linguistic inclusion and exclusion in a virtual community'. In K. Buhrig & J. D. ten Thije (eds.) *Beyond*

Misunderstanding: The Linguistic Reconstruction of Intercultural Communication (Amsterdam: John Benjamins), pp. 319–56.

Goffman, E.1990[1959] *The Presentation of Self in Everyday Life* (London: Penguin).

Grice, H. P. (1975) 'Logic and conversation'. In P. Cole & J. Morgan (eds.) *Syntax and Semantics, Volume 3*. (New York: Academic Press), pp. 41–58.

Herring, S. C. (2008) 'Virtual community'. In L. M. Given (ed.) *Encyclopedia of Qualitative Research Methods* (Thousand Oaks, CA: Sage).

Jones, R.H. (2011) 'C me Sk8: Discourse, technology, and "bodies without organs"'. In C. Thurlow & K. Mroczek (eds.) *Digital Discourse: Language in the New Media* (Oxford: Oxford University Press), pp. 321–39.

Jones, R. H. & Hafner, C. A. (2012) *Understanding Digital Literacies: A Practical Introduction* (Abingdon: Routledge).

Jones, S. (2009) 'Bilingual Identities in Two UK Communities: A Study of the Languages and Literacies of Welsh and British-Asian Girls'. PhD thesis, Univeristy of Nottingham.

Karinthy, F. (2007 [1929]) 'Chain-links (Láncszemek)' (translated by Adam Makkai). In M. E. J. Newman & D. Watts (eds.) *The Structure and Dynamics of Networks* (Princeton, NJ: Princeton University Press), pp. 21–6.

Katsuno, H. & Yano, C. (2007) '*Kaomoji* and expressivity in a Japanese house-wives' chat room'. In B. Danet & S. C. Herring (eds.) *The Multilingual Internet: Language, Culture, and Communication Online* (Oxford: Oxford University Press), pp. 278–300.

Kennedy, H. (2011) 'Beyond anonymity, or future directions for internet identity research', *New Media & Society*, 8(6): 859–76.

Kirkpatrick, D. (2010) *The Facebook Effect: The Real Inside Story of Mark Zuckerberg and the World's Fastest Growing Company* (London: Virgin Books).

Knight, N. (2010) 'Wrinkling complexity: Concepts of identity and affiliation in humour'. In M. Bednarek & J. R. Martin (eds.), *New Discourse on Language: Functional Perspectives on Multimodality, Identity, and Affiliation* (London: Continuum), pp. 35–58.

Lave, J. & Wenger, E. (1991) *Situated Learning: Legitimate Peripheral Participation* (Cambridge: Cambridge University Press).

Mandiberg, M. (2012) 'Introduction'. In M. Mandiberg (ed.) *The Social Media Reader* (New York: New York University Press), pp. 1–10.

Marwick, A. & boyd, d. m. (2011) 'I tweet honestly, I tweet passionately: Twitter users, context collapse and the imagined audience', *New Media & Society*, 13 (1): 114–33.

Meyerhoff, M. (2006) *Introducing Sociolinguistics* (Abingdon: Routledge).

Milroy, J.& Milroy, L. (1992) 'Social network and social class: Toward an inte-grated sociolinguistic model', *Language in Society*, 21: 1–26.

Myers, G. (2010) *The Discourse of Blogs and Wikis* (London: Continuum).

Newton, L. (2011) 'Multimodal creativity and identities of expertise in the digi-tal ecology of a *World of Warcraft* guild'. In C. Thurlow & K. Mroczek (eds.) *Digital Discourse: Language in the New Media* (Oxford: Oxford University Press), pp. 131–53.

O'Reilly, T. (2012 [2005]) in M. Mandiberg (ed.) *The Social Media Reader* (New York: New York University Press), pp. 32–52.

Page, R. (2012) *Stories and Social Media: Identities and Interaction Online* (Abingdon: Routledge).

Palfreyman, D. & Al Khalil, M. (2007) '"A funky language for teenzz to use": Representing Gulf Arabic in Instant Messaging'. In B. Danet & S. C. Herring (eds.) *The Multilingual Internet: Language, Culture, and Communication Online* (Oxford: Oxford University Press), pp. 43–63.

Parks, M. (2011) 'Social network sites as virtual communities'. In Z. Papacharissi (ed.) *A Networked Self: Identity, Community, and Culture on Social Network Sites* (Abingdon: Routledge), pp. 105–23.

Pentzold, C. (2010) 'Imagining the Wikipedia community: What do Wikipedia authors mean when they write about their "community"?', *New Media & Society*, 13(5): 704–21.

Pew Internet and American Life Project (2012) http://pewinternet.org/Commentary/2012/March/Pew-Internet-Social-Networking-full-detail.aspx (accessed 18 January 2013).

Reid, E. (1991) Electropolis: Communication and Community on Internet Relay Chat. Honours thesis, Dept of History, University of Melbourne.

Rheingold, H. (1994) *The Virtual Community: Finding Connection in a Computerised World* (London: Secker and Warburg).

Seargeant, P., Tagg, C. & Ngampramuan, W. (2012) 'Language choice and addressivity strategies in Thai-English social network interactions' *Journal of Sociolinguistics*, 16(4): 510–31.

Stommel, W. (2008) 'Conversation analysis and community of practice as approaches to studying online community', *Language@Internet*, 5: 1–22.

Su, H.-Y. (2007) 'The multilingual and multiorthographic Taiwan-based internet: Creative uses of writing systems on college-affiliated BBSs'. In B. Danet & S. C. Herring (eds.) *The Multilingual Internet: Language, Culture, and Communication Online* (Oxford: Oxford University Press), pp. 64–86.

Tagg, C. (2012) *The Discourse of Text Messaging: Analysis of SMS Communication* (London: Continuum).

Tagg, C. & Seargeant, P. (2012) 'Writing systems at play in Thai-English online interactions', *Writing Systems Research*, 4(2): 195–213.

Thurlow, C. & Jaworski, A. (2011) 'Banal globalisation? Embodied actions and mediated practices in tourists' online photo sharing'. In C. Thurlow & K. Mroczek (eds.) *Digital Discourse: Language in the New Media* (Oxford: Oxford University Press), pp. 220–50.

Tsiplakou, S. (2009) 'Doing (bi)lingualism: Language alternation as performative construction of online identities', *Pragmatics*, 19(3): 361–91.

Turkle, S. (1995) *Life on the Screen* (New York: Simon & Schuster).

Vaisman, C. (2011) 'Performing girlhood through typographic play in Hebrew blogs'. In C. Thurlow & K. Mroczek (eds.) *Digital Discourse: Language in the New Media* (Oxford: Oxford University Press), pp. 177–96.

Wenger, E. (1998) *Communities of Practice: Learning, Meaning and Identity.* (Cambridge: Cambridge University Press).

Wesch, M. (2008) Context collapse, http://mediatedcultures.net/projects/youtube/context-collapse.

Zappavigna, M. (2011) 'Ambient affiliation: A linguistic perspective on Twitter', *New Media Society*, 13: 788–806.

Part I
The Performance of Identity on Social Media

1

The performance of a ludic self on social network(ing) sites

Ana Deumert

> Cyberspace is often anarchic, playful and even carnivalesque.
>
> Brenda Danet, *Cyberpl@y* (2001, p. 8)

1 Introduction

This chapter explores contemporary social network(ing)[1] applications as a space for the performance of a ludic self and the carnivalesque. Although digital media are also used for serious, information-focused communication, many interactions appear to follow the broad conversational maxim of 'keep it light/fun', and as such these media have become a vehicle for what the philosopher Jos de Mul (2005) has called 'ludic self-construction', that is, they provide a space in which we relate to ourselves and others in a playful manner.

That there is a 'primacy of play' in digital communication was argued already more than ten years ago by Brenda Danet in her book *Cyberpl@y* (2001), and the concept of play has been productive in a range of publications (e.g. Rao, 2008; Chayko, 2009; McIntosh, 2010; an important early study is Baym, 1995). This playfulness is visible in the types of interactions people engage in online – they play games, joke, flirt, or just hang out with one another – as well as in the language and multimodal imagery they use.

The chapter is structured as follows: Section 2 describes de Mul's notion of ludic identity, and explores possible reasons for the pervasiveness of a play frame in digitally mediated interactions. Sections 3 and 4 discuss examples of playful performances in a range of social network(ing) applications: internet relay chat (IRC), Twitter, Facebook, and MXit, a South African mobile instant messaging service. The broad theoretical perspective which underlies the argument is based on the work of the Russian language philosopher Mikhail Bakhtin. Two of his theoretical concepts will be central to the discussion: heteroglossia and the carnivalesque.[2] The chapter concludes with a brief reflection on Roy Oldenberg's (1996/7) notion of a third space: are digital spaces the twenty-first century equivalent of the tavern, the café, the street corner?

The data presented come from ongoing work in South Africa, a strongly multilingual and multicultural 'new' democracy. Problems with digital infrastructure notwithstanding, growth of social network(ing) applications has been rapid across Africa. Facebook is among the top sites on the continent and mobile access is common (Deumert, forthcoming). The broad appeal of these applications is illustrated by a study which looked at internet usage in two remote villages in Southern Africa: Macha in Zambia, and Dwesa in South Africa. In both villages, a wireless network had been installed as part of a development project. Social network(ing) applications were the top sites accessed and more than two-thirds of (interviewed) villagers had accounts on Facebook (Johnson *et al.*, 2011). What is it that makes social network(ing) applications so attractive to people in Africa and across the world? I will argue that such applications allow people not only to stay in touch with one another (social connectedness), but also provide a much needed space to interact with one another in an informal, playful and enjoyable manner.

2   A ludic state of mind

Jos de Mul (2005) has drawn on Paul Ricoeur's (1992) theory of narrative self-construction to develop his idea of ludic self-construction in new media contexts. Ricoeur's work is based on the fundamental insight that we don't have access to our 'selves' through mere introspection, rather we come to know about us through mediation: we construct an image of who we are – for others and for ourselves – through the way we act, move and dress, the music we enjoy, the food we eat, the beliefs we hold, and the stories we tell. We might, for example, tell stories in which we overcome obstacles, and appear victorious and strong. And as we tell such stories we also project ourselves as a particular *persona*: we will not speak with a soft voice, huddled in the corner of an armchair, but we will be assertive in our demeanour, that is, our voice and body language (see also Wortham, 2000). Speaking about ourselves thus *makes* us into a particular person, and can transform the way we feel about ourselves. For Ricoeur, telling a story is a dramaturgical event, and the notion of a plot is central. That is, narrators try to establish a storyline, which brings together the varied and poly-interpretable elements of their past experiences into 'a series of mutually connected and motivated actions' (de Mul, 2005, p. 254).

De Mul, whose work focuses on computer games, is critical of Ricoeur's conception of narrativity and his emphasis on a cohesive, continuous, and ultimately concordant, plot. Linear and coherent narratives, typically characterized by a single authoritative voice, are certainly important building blocks for our identities. However, just as important for the formation of self are multilinear plots, lack of closure (i.e. the absence of a Freudian end-pleasure), and interactivity. De Mul calls identities based on the latter processes, ludic identities. Whereas narrative identities are oriented towards the past and coherence, ludic identities are oriented towards the future and the multiple possibilities of being.

> Whereas in the case of narrative identity the predominant tendency is toward an increase of closure and thus concordance [...] in the case of ludic identity the predominant tendency is an increase of openness. [...] A possible objection could be that life is no game, but we could formulate an analogue answer as Ricoeur did in reply to the critique that life is no story. Just because our life is no game, not always joyful and full of possibilities, we need games to oppose the continuous threat of closure. And just as in the case of narrative identity, ludic identity is a creation of our imagination that creates real life effects in our daily lives. (De Mul, 2005, pp. 260–1; see also Ibarra & Petriglieri, 2010).

The ability to make interactive choices – i.e. choices which lead to feedback from the computer program and/or those who are engaging with us via the program – is an important aspect of online engagement. Every time we log onto Facebook we experience the volitional dimension of who we are: we might receive a comment to which we respond in turn, play a game or fill in a quiz, open the chat window, approve a friend request, post a photo, comment on a photo in which someone we know has been tagged, and so forth. Interactivity in this sense is more than interaction. It simultaneously refers to:

> (a) our ability to change what is represented online, not merely to read or consume it (Cameron, 1995), and
> (b) the fact that we do so in a social context where we are always also responding to others and their representations.

The dual interactivity of online interaction facilitates a playful, experimental, yet social, state of mind, and the online space becomes 'a playing field that enables us to (re)configure all kinds of different worlds' through our actions and interactions (De Mul, 2005, p. 262). The shift from consumption to dialogic production is at the heart of Web 2.0, the participatory web, and the openness it creates is essential to the articulation of a ludic self.

However, playfulness is not solely a consequence of the medium and its affordances, that is, the vast array of actions it makes possible. It is also part of the history of the internet: the early days of the internet were not only characterized by the dominance of a particular language (i.e. English), but also by a particular cultural slant: the subculture of programmers. A central characteristic of this subculture is a broadly playful mood, with a particular focus on manipulating linguistic material for aesthetic and intellectual pleasure:

> Hackers,[3] as a rule, love wordplay and are very conscious and inventive in their use of language. These traits seem to be common in young children, but the conformity-enforcing machine we are pleased to call an educational system bludgeons them out of most of us before adolescence. Thus, linguistic invention in most subcultures of the modern West is a halting and largely unconscious process. Hackers, by contrast, regard slang formation and use as a game to be played for conscious pleasure. (*The Jargon File*, 2004; see also Danet, 2001, p. 26ff. for examples).

The hacker subculture, which shows important overlaps with the gaming community, has thus played a central role in establishing a general ludic mood in the digital world from its inception. This has resulted in a situation where certain types of action are favoured over others, thus contributing to the ritual construction of the internet as a place of enjoyable and playful interaction (Rao, 2008; Raessens, 2006).

Recent developments in computer gaming also need to be mentioned in this context. Play has often been seen as standing in opposition to the routine of everyday life, occurring only in specific spaces and at specific times. Following Johan Huizinga (1955), some game researchers have described this space using the metaphor of a 'magic circle', that is, a play area or playground, where the normal rules of behaviour are suspended. However, this 'magic circle' is not a separate space which is hermetically sealed off from everyday life: its boundaries are always porous, 'variously punctuated by the demands of "real" life' (Moore, 2011, p. 376). This permeability has become even more pronounced with the proliferation of mobile technologies and the convergence of social network(ing) and 'casual' – as opposed to 'hard-core' – gaming applications (Juul, 2010). These casual games have relatively simple rules, are flexible and do not require the long-term engagement typical of hard-core gaming: they can be played in-between meetings, on the bus, or while waiting at the doctor's surgery. Since 2008, social network(ing) sites such as Facebook have begun to provide a wide range of deeply social (i.e. interactive and multiplay) gaming applications (e.g. Farmville, developed in 2009) as well as props for social play (poking, quizzes). As a consequence, being on Facebook is becoming more and more 'like a game':

> On Facebook life is a game. Although participants can open chat windows or belong to special interest groups of a more serious nature, the daily drivers of Facebook exchanges are games and quizzes. As technology mediates more and more of our daily social exchanges, the forms of our interaction change. Gaming – light, breezy and fun interactions with friends near and far – keeps ties without being burdensome. (McClard & Anderson, 2008, p. 12).

As we engage in this playful mode, we mobilize (and desire) a particular type of self, as well as a particular set of social relations: light-hearted and creative, enjoyable and full of possibilities. That is, how we communicate (through text, sounds and images), conveys important information about who we are, how we want to be seen, and how we perceive the world. And we follow conversational maxims which are different from those at work in non-playful encounters: truth, relevance and clarity are no longer required for communicative cooperation (see Grice, 1975, for the original formulation of these maxims which define the canonical, proto-typical norm for successful social interactions). In much digital communication, obscurity and ambiguity are licensed, relevance a matter of choice, and truthfulness at times unnecessary. What matters is amusement, laughter and creative enjoyment, or in the words of web designer Jonathan Follett (2007), 'pure fun' and 'interactive silliness'. This is not to say that we do not use social network(ing) applications for more serious communication and that truthfulness never matters; it obviously does since many of our online friends are people with whom we also interact offline. However, there is a broad tendency towards the humorous (even when we discuss serious issues), and playful exaggeration (as in the following Facebook status update from an academic colleague: 'Suffering from flu and footnotes', 2012).

3 Playful performances: poetic, dramatic and heteroglossic

Internet relay chat, a popular protocol for real-time (synchronous) internet text-messaging, is one of the early genres of social network(ing). In October 2008, we conducted two chat experiments at the University of Cape Town: in each experiment, five speakers (in their early 20s, both male and female) were connected to a chat program (mIRC) which allowed them to interact with one another in a specifically created chat room.[4] One group was bilingual Afrikaans/English, the other isiXhosa/English. Some participants knew each other informally from lectures, others had never met, none were close friends. Both groups were free to speak about whatever they wanted, in whatever language they wanted, during the two-hour session. The only instruction they received was: 'log on and see what happens'. They were also free to engage with other online activities – such as sending emails or searching the web. Multitasking, a central feature of online language use (see Baron, 2008, pp. 36ff.), was thus permitted. Although the experimental set-up created a somewhat artificial situation initially, this was overcome quickly since participants were not asked to do something they never do, but instead were asked to engage in an everyday practice (albeit in a controlled setting).

What happened? What did the participants choose to do? They did indeed check their emails, read the news and even sent inquiries to prospective employers. Yet, they also talked, for two hours, non-stop, and some hardly wanted to leave when the time was up. In the words of two of the participants, young women in their early 20s:

> Loved it, absolutely loved it, oh my goodness, the best two hours I've had in the past four weeks! It was fun! I was so much like, chat is one of the best things for me, randomly fabulous, there we go! Everything was just fab by itself [...] the interaction was, wow, just the different personalities! [<umgqusho>]

> It was funny, it was funny, and ja, I think it, I think writing in a sense, just because we know each other, but just hiding behind the words [...] a sense of say whatever, there is much, there is more freedom. [<Ziya>]

There seems to be something deeply attractive and enjoyable about 'chatting', that is, communicating with others informally in a digital mode: it is *funny, fabulous*, there is *freedom*, and you can *say whatever*. The transcripts of the chat sessions are filled with ludic interactions.

'Serious' topics (politics, studies, looking for work) are few and far between and, when raised, quickly transformed into humour. The two examples discussed below illustrate salient aspects of ludic, online interaction: word-play and the dramatic. Both are examples of performances as discussed by Richard Bauman (1977), that is, sequences within an interaction where the act of speaking itself is on display and open to evaluation by an audience (also Bauman & Briggs, 1990).

Example (1) comes from the Afrikaans group: <james> tried to dominate the conversation, for example, by posting sequences of typographic symbols (...) or by simply listing, without any apparent motivation, names of African countries. <Nina> challenged him and the noun she used (*middelpunt*) then became part of a rap-like word-play sequence. It is an example of poetic language in the sense introduced by Roman Jakobson (1960) in that the focus is on form – the manipulation of linguistic material – not content, and repetition plays a central role in shaping the rhythm of the exchange. In terms of the above mentioned Gricean maxims, this exchange violates the maxim of manner: to be as clear and concise as possible, to avoid ambiguity and obscurity. Instead, playful replication, ambiguity and obscurity are used to amuse, impress and establish interactional rapport between participants.

Example (1)

	Participant	Chat	Translation
1	<james>	....	
2	<james>	..	
3	<james>	..	
4	<james>	NEE	NO
5	<Whispershout>	Ek stem saam	I agree
6	<james>	XIMBABWE	
7	<james>	ZIM	
8	<Nina>	james jy hou van om middelpunt te wees ne?	james you like to be at the centre, hey?
9	<james>	drc	('Democratic Republic of Congo')
10	<james>	mmmm	mmmm
11	<Nina>	jy praat lekker met jouself	you are speaking nicely with yourself
12	<james>	dalk	absolutely
13	<james>	nie	not

14	\<Whispershout\>	Middelpunt?	Centre?
15	\<james\>	middelpunt	centre
16	\<eevy\>	middelpunt van verlange	centre of desire
17	\<james\>	middelpunt van idiocy	centre of idiocy
18	\<Nina\>	is jy die middle kind?	are you the middle child?
19	\<james\>	'n middelsin	a middle sentence
20	\<james\>	sin – middel	sentence – middle
21	\<Nina\>	oh my hat!	

Example (2) comes from the isiXhosa group and shows a playful, flirtatious interaction between \<Ziya\> and two outsiders who joined the experimental chat room: \<engen\>, about whom we know very little as he/she had been rather quiet, and \<Bechari\>, an English-speaking Muslim woman from Durban. \<Ziya\> uses their presence in the chat room to stage a mini-drama, declaring her love and affection for \<engen\> (who, however, does not show much interest), and playing a teasing game of where-are-you-I-don't-want-you with \<Bechari\>.

Example (2)

	Participant	Chat	Translation
1	\<Ziya\>	Engen ndikuthanda ngoku Ndingekakwazi...	Engen I love you now even though I don't know you ....
2	\<Ziya\>	Engen kutheni ungandifuni	Engen why don't you want me
3	\<engen\>	am a petrol station, not human at al	
4	\<Ziya\>	Nam kaloku I'll be your petrol!	I too then
5	\<umgqusho\>	waze wa ADVANCE man!!!!! a ptrol station that can chat!!!!	you are so ADVANCED man!!!!!
6	\<Ziya\>	Bechari where r u?	

7	\<Bechari\>	Im here my darling	
8	\<Ziya\>	Andifuni wena thou, where is me petrol station	I don't want you though
9	\<Bechari\>	Wat	
10	\<Ziya\>	Undivile ANDIKUFUNI!	You heard me I DON'T WANT YOU!
11	\<umgqusho\>	Ziya n Bechari...ur love hate relationship is astounding...so entertaining it needs 2b on tv.	
12	\<Ziya\>	uPHI u my sweet and Darling Engen?	wHERE are you
13	\<Bechari\>	Ziya	
14	\<Bechari\>	Mwah	
15	\<Bechari\>	Wena funa meena	You want me
16	\<luvu\>	bechari control ur self	
17	\<Ziya\>	bECHARI KUDALA NDISITHI ANDIKUFUNI.. Let me try it in Chinese ChING, CHONG, CHU, CHU, CHU!	bECHARI I'VE BEEN SAYING FOR A WHILE THAT I DON'T WANT YOU..

Linguistically, this example is far removed from the monolingual standards characteristic of written language or formal registers: we see linguistic mixtures of isiXhosa and English, but also mock-isiXhosa as well as mock-Chinese. *Wena funa meena* (correct spelling would be *wena funa mina*) is reminiscent of the local pidgin variety Fanakalo. The expression shows analytic morphology where isiXhosa would have agglutination (the correct phrase would be *uyandifuna*). *ChHING, CHONG, CHU, CHU, CHU!* is a stereotypical representation of the perceived sound structure of Chinese languages. In addition, capitalization and punctuation are used to indicate tone and rhythm, as well as to express emotions of annoyance and admiration (as in 'Undivile ANDIKUFUNI' [You heard me I DON'T WANT YOU] and 'waze wa ADVANCE man!!!!!' [you are so ADVANCED man!!!!!] in turns 10 and 5 respectively).

Heteroglossia, a term which was introduced by the Russian language philosopher Mikhail Bakhtin (1981[1935]), is useful for understanding this mix of overlapping voices. The ontology of heteroglossia is quite unlike that of traditional Labovian sociolinguistics, which remains rooted in Saussurian structuralism and explains variation in terms of correlations between the linguistic system and seemingly well-defined aspects of the social world (age, sex, class, ethnicity). Heteroglossia, on the other hand, is not a feature of 'the system'. The diversity of language-in-use is actively created by speakers whose behaviour, although normative and habitual at times, is frequently unpredictable and innovative, often even artistic. To engage in communication always means to select from a multitude of pre-existing ways of speaking; creativity thus does not emerge *ex nihilo* but involves the appropriation and novel combination of existing linguistic forms and their meanings. These include:

> [S]ocial dialects, characteristic group behaviour, professional jargons, generic languages, languages of generations and age groups, tendentious languages, languages of the authorities, of various circles and passing fashions, languages that serve the specific socio-political purposes of the day, even of the hour (Bakhtin 1981[1935], p. 262).

Each of these different ways of speaking carries with it distinct motivations, intentions and implications. Each word, each expression 'has a taste', that is, prior to being spoken in the *here and now* it has existed in 'other people's mouths, in other people's contexts, serving other people's intentions' (Bakhtin, 1981[1935], pp. 293, 294).

<Bechari>'s *wena funa meena* in turn 15 is an example of the 'taste of words' Bakhtin writes about. The phrase is shot through with conflicting possible meanings: one could read it as a second language speaker's (inept) attempt to produce a basic isiXhosa utterance, and thus to signal respect to the interlocutor (<Ziya>), accommodating – however imperfectly – her preferred language use. However, the social history of such constructions brings with it different voices and meanings: namely those of the colonizers, who could never be bothered to learn the local language(s) properly, and thus relied on corrupted, simplified versions for basic communication. This moves us into a semantic domain which is diametrically opposed to ideas of respect and speech accommodation; rather we are looking at disrespect and confrontation, deeply rooted in the voices of the past (as indicated by <luvu>'s gentle admonishment, 'control yourself'). <Ziya> responds with a string of mock syllables. Her

language use is playful, respecting the mood of the overall interaction, but also meant to silence: the use of mock-Chinese constructs <Bechari> as the ultimate 'other', the one with whom meaningful communication is impossible. This dramatic performance – playful yet mindful of historical under-currents of political-racial tension – is greeted with an overtly aesthetic response by the audience: 'so entertaining it needs 2b on tv'.

Heteroglossia, in the view of Lachmann, Eshelman & Davis (1988, p. 144), allows for endless recombination of linguistic material according to a 'joyous grammar'. Heteroglossic practices occur in all genres, but are most pronounced in everyday, informal contexts where playful creativity is encouraged and the norms of the monolithic standard are relaxed, or even suspended (Carter, 2004). While pidgin-like utterances (as discussed above) carry with them meanings of de-civilization and primitivization of 'the other', mixed forms of languages can allow for the celebration and exploration of a hybrid, modern subject. Example (3) comes from Twitter and was posted in early 2012 by a male South African. The language, again, is playful, combining English, Afrikaans (bold) and Nguni-based urban slang (underlined).[5] Translations are in square brackets.

Example (3)
I was raised by Jay'z's music so <u>vele</u> **ek sal** <u>camtha</u> **oor sy kind**.
['I was raised by Jay'z's music of course I will talk about his child']

While the content is trivial – the author asserts his right to gossip as much as he wants to about the child of the US rapper Jay-Z – the language is deliberately artful, a stylized register which draws on elements of local urban slang, but combines them in unique ways. Example (3) represents just one of many styles that the writer puts on display in his tweets; Examples (4) to (6) articulate quite different voices.

Example (4)
Be ndithi ndiya sweleka.
['I thought I was dying']

Example (5)
German efficiency – Timing is everything. Practice, Power and Precision = Perfection. Deutschland uber alles!
['Germany above everything']

Example (6)
Ek <u>nyisa</u> **daai moegoe** *ka* **my** TWA **en hy di** GATAS **bel. Dom kop.** (Kofifi Taal on Twitter)

['I threatened the idiot with my gun, and he called the cops. Stupid person. (Kofifi language on Twitter)']

In Example (4), he uses a formal and monolingual style of isiXhosa; Example (5) is a linguistically playful ode to German efficiency which incorporates an overtly German voice; and finally, Example (6) is a linguistic enactment and stylization of a historically distant voice: *Kofifitaal*, the language used by gangs in the 1940s and 1950s in Sophiatown (known as *Kofifi*) in Johannesburg. Similar to the urban youth slang in (3), it is a multilingual variety, showing a mixture of Afrikaans (bold), Nguni (underlined), Sotho (italics) and gangster slang (small caps).

4 Digital carnivals: laughter, the grotesque and the theatre of me and you

From the heteroglossic performance, the playful engagement with multiple voices and styles for the entertainment of an audience ('the festival of heteroglossia', Hay, 1992, p. 771), it is just but a step to the 'carnival' as discussed by Bakhtin.

Mikhail Bakhtin's (1984[1965]) reflections on medieval carnivals provide the theoretical frame for the use of 'carnival' as an analytical category in the study of popular culture. Bakhtin's text emphasizes the importance of play and laughter as an integral element of the experience of freedom that is inherent in folk carnivals:

[Carnival] is life itself, but shaped according to a *pattern of play* [...] Carnival is not a spectacle seen by people; they live in it, and everyone participates because the very idea embraces all people [...] During carnival time life is subject only to its laws, that is, *the laws of its own freedom* [...] carnival is the *people's second life*, organized on the basis of laughter, *the entire world is seen in its droll aspect* (1984[1965]pp. 7, 11; my emphases)

To describe carnival as a 'second life' directly brings to mind a well-known social network(ing) application: Second Life (launched in 2003), a 3D virtual, parallel world. Facebook, Twitter and instant messaging applications, even though they have fewer technological bells and whistles, also provide digital social spaces in which the carnivalesque spirit flourishes. And just as during real carnivals, there can be loss of self and pure enjoyment: online users often experience a sense of flow and lose track of time as they become absorbed in the interaction (De Mul, 2005; Danet, 2001, pp. 24ff.).

Carnival is more than a safety-valve where the tensions and frustrations of everyday life are temporarily suspended; it reflects a deep quest for freedom from constraints, dogma and authority. Liberation is achieved through play and the transgression of the 'proper' order and values: carnival is 'free-time' and 'free-space' (Lachmann *et al.*, 1988). Heteroglossia, as discussed in the previous section, is an essential resource in this context: pre-existing voices and forms of speech are combined playfully, creating new voices and meanings which reflect a carnivalesque mood.

Digital spellings are a case in point. When I recently asked for advice from a much younger Facebook friend about how I should write online, she (in her early 20s) replied with a general tone of laughter (indicated by the repeated use of *lol*), and emphasized the fundamental freedom which underlies such spellings:

> lol all u do z replace letterz wit othr funky letters lol nun major 2 it (April 2012)

This is not to say that digital writing does not show emergent norms and conventions. It certainly does, such as the by now standard use of *u* for *you*, or *2* for *to(o)*. However, it does not have to stop there: I may, if I want, invent new 'funky' spellings at will. In other words, it is ultimately my choice as to whether to conform or to create. Creative orthographic forms, which we frequently see in interactive digital writing, are licensed misrule, they allow us to engage in 'linguistic clownery' (Bakhtin, 1984[1965], p. 472) and to present ourselves as 'funky', 'cool' people (Sebba, 2007, p. 40).

Table 1.1 summarizes the various spellings found in the *happy birthday* wishes posted to the Facebook page of a young South African woman in 2010. These variations are artful/creative re-inventions of a highly conventionalized and iterative phrase. They are meaningful on two different levels: wishing a friend *happy birthday* on Facebook is as much an

Table 1.1 Wishing *Happy Birthday* on Facebook: orthographic variations (2010)

happy (17 different spellings)	birthday (22 different spellings)
happy, hapy, hapi, hempie, hApPi, hapee, HAppY, H@PP¥, haaaaaaaaapppppy, haa, happi, hApPy,hppi, eppy, happ, hpy, HaPpi	Birthday, birthdae, bday, bdae, bdAy, born day, vday, brn dae, Be$dae, ß£§+D@¥, befday, befdae, b-day, bdaE, B-, bEef-dAy, best day, b.dae, b.day, burfday
HBD	

important social ritual as it is an opportunity to publicly display one's linguistic creativity and originality. This does not only involve words, but also images, such as the virtual birthday cake in Example (7).

Example (7) A textual/virtual birthday cake (2011)

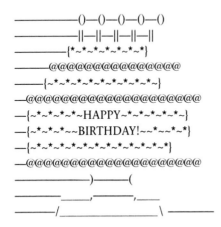

Laughter is central to the carnival spirit, and in digital writing it is epitomized in the use and invention of numerous laughing acronyms. These acronyms can function as interjections and are part and parcel of what Jakobson (1960, p. 354) has called the 'emotive' function of language (see also Deumert, 2006, for an analysis of laughing acronyms as discourse markers). Although bilingual users in South Africa make frequent use of English laughing acronyms, there exist local versions. In isiXhosa, GPY (*giligidi, phansi yintsini,* 'falling down laughing'), and its variant GBPY (*giligidi bhu phansi yintsini,* 'falling down laughing with a bang'),[6] imitate the structure of ROFL ('rolling on the floor laughing'). Examples (8) and (9) illustrate prolonged, multilingual laughter sequences on Facebook status updates.

Example (8)
Lol Nontlahla usile kodwa chomam damn, u realy made ma day! Gxada akazelanga apha kuwe. Lmao, Gpy, Lol, Ha ha ha ha ha ha (May 2012)

('Lol Nontlahla but you are naughty my friend damn, you really made my day! Gxada [name of one of her parents] has not given birth to you. Lmao, Gpy, Lol, Ha ha ha ha ha ha')

Example (9)
Lol, lolment, lmao, gpy, gbpy *efa insini* ('*dying with laughter*')

The English laughter acronym LMAO ('laughing my ass off') draws attention to another aspect of the carnivalesque: grotesque realism. Bakhtin (1984[1965], pp. 145ff.) calls this the language of the marketplace, and it includes profanities, abuse and indecent expressions. This form of language overtly challenges the prevailing norms of society where such topics tend to be taboo and improper. The social expectation for polite euphemisms is thus replaced by one for crude dysphemisms, that is, words, phrases or images which are intended to be offensive (Allan & Burridge, 2006, pp. 31ff.).

The Afrikaans versions of laughing acronyms reflect crude vulgarities similar to LMAO: LMIMP is an abbreviation of *lag my in my poes* ('laughing in my cunt') and LMJ stands for *lag my jas* ('laughing myself horny'). Like English LMAO, their inherent profanity does not restrict their use to topics marked as vulgar. Rather they pepper everyday digital interactions as a constant reminder of the exuberant and transgressive spirit of the medium. Examples (10) and (11) illustrate their use in context, and provide further examples of playful digital performances: there is linguistic play with rhymes (*excited/united*) as well as the playful enactment of a popular local insult using a mock-Somalian accent (which adds stressed vowels to all words ending in unstressed vowels and consonants, i.e. *ma's/ma se* becomes *masa*, *poes* becomes *poesa*, and *naiy* becomes *nayia*).

Example (10)
　　Lmimp.....Eks sooo excited......Ek support vir MAN UNITED....Lol
　　(May 2012)
　　('I am so excited, I support Manchester United')

Example (11)
　　Soemalien sak nogal vi my af "Jou masa poesa jou naiya" lmj funny
　　stuff (May 2012)
　　('A Somali actually said to me: "You fuck your mother's cunt" lmj
　　funny stuff')

Although transgressive and rebellious, the carnival mode remains light and playful: crude profanities are uttered, yet they are transformed into laughter, not taken as offence, since they are 'filled with the carnival spirit' (Bakhtin, 1984[1965], p. 17). Example (12) is a Facebook status update (2012), followed by four comments. The image of a 'horny chicken', initially intended as a rude insult towards someone who angered the writer, is dialogically transformed into laughter by exploring its literal, bodily, interpretation: what exactly would such a horny chicken look like?

Example (12)

	Text	Translation
Status update	damn u,acting lyk a horny chicken*veri angry*	
Comment 1	Lol...@horny chicken	
Comment 2	I wanda injani xa ihorny,lol	I wonder how it is when it is horny
Comment 3	Ndanomdla wokuyibona xa sele ikweloqondo	Now I am interested in seeing it [the chicken] when it is at that stage
Comment 4	Where do U get such a chicken?	

The multimodal nature of digital communication allows the grotesque to move beyond the *language* of the marketplace towards the visual depiction of grotesque *bodies* (Bakhtin, 1984[1965], pp. 315ff.). Images which circulate on Facebook, often photoshopped or otherwise modified, frequently foreground the body's carnality and corporeality: its biological profanity and excess (burping, farting, defecating, over-eating), its sexuality (copulating), decline and destruction. The exaggeration of bodily parts (noses, genitals, body mass) is a common feature of these images.

Example (13) is a status update which was posted on Mother's Day 2012. The wall post is accompanied, tongue-in-cheek, by a photo of an extremely overweight black woman with a colourful weave; the image is deeply corporeal, a body that is bulging outwards, protruding into the world (see also Stukator, 2001, on the spectacle of fat women in contemporary media culture). It is an image which has circulated widely on different 'funny pictures' websites under the file name 'ugly woman. jpg'.[7] It is used here to enact a parody of unconditional filial love: even a grotesquely ugly and overweight mother will be loved by her son.

Example (13)
  Mom I love u.....noma bengathini ('whatever they say').....u are my Mother...we can choose frnds but we can't choose parents....simple as that.. (Facebook, 2012)

Comments to the image engaged with the parody and complimented the writer, again tongue-in-cheek, on the likeness to his fictional mother: *Haw [name] cha niyafana*, 'Oh [name] really you look alike'.

Such globally circulating 'funny' images are sometimes also used as profile pictures, thus fashioning a carnivalesque form of self-presentation. One image shows a (white) child of about 2 years old holding a life-sized sex doll in such a way that it stands right between the doll's legs, as if about to engage in a sexual act.[8] This image was used as a Facebook profile picture by a black South African man in his mid-20s in 2012. The use of such images transforms the very meaning of 'profile picture' – this is not meant to represent a particular individual, but to communicate a generally humorous mood.

The importance of presenting a laughing, fun persona on applications such as Facebook was clearly indicated in interviews one of my students conducted in 2008: participants described their Facebook behaviour consistently as 'funny', 'joyful', 'light-hearted', 'happy go lucky', and 'bouncy' (Van Blerk, 2008). And indeed they stressed that they enacted a particular Facebook *persona* when online, a mask: 'You put on the face. You know what I mean?'

Masks are a popular part of carnival: they are intimately connected to the joys of change, of stepping out of the everyday, of being someone else, and even, avoiding taking responsibility for one's actions. As noted by Brenda Danet (2001, pp. 32ff.), in many digital environments typed text can provide the mask in the form of nicks, sometimes, but not always, accompanied by an image. Although it is generally possible to change one's nick, most people choose the name carefully and stick with it. In this sense, the nick comes to stand for a second, imagined self (Bechar-Israeli, 1995). Typically, the nick will highlight or foreground certain aspects of this imagined, second identity, and background others. Thus, like a performer who chooses a stage name, participants in digital exchanges perform themselves, not only through the act of writing, but also by constructing a specific persona through the choice of a nick. Wearing a virtual mask (a nick), does not necessarily mean anonymity: even in the chat rooms of the 1990s, those interacting frequently knew each other in 'real life'; yet online they interacted using names such as *Barbie12* or *Tulipomania*. The same is true for social network(ing) applications: although many people use their real names on Facebook (mainly so that friends can find them easily), other social network(ing) applications (such as instant messaging) continue to favour the use of nicks.

In 2011, we interviewed teenagers (aged 15–17) in a Cape Town high school about the nicks they use on the mobile instant messaging service

MXit. The school is located in a low-income, working-class neighbour-hood with a long history of gangsterism. Although local gangs are responsible for countless deaths, rapes and drug trafficking in the area, their lifestyle holds a certain allure. The danger and violence gangsters personify is simultaneously taboo and attractive, and stylizations of gangster identity are deeply embedded in popular culture (especially rap music).

Irrespective of gender, many of the nicks selected by the teenagers represent gangster *personae* and reflect a tough gang-related identity. Examples are given in (14) and (15); the Americans and British are two well-known gangs in the area.

Example (14)
   Male nicks: ..."MR:KONVICTED"...
                American Boy

Example (15)
   Female nicks: BR!T!§# B!TC#
                "@merican Girl"!!!
                MRS. MAIFA GAL

Frieda Coetzee (2012) has shown that for female teenagers such digital *personae* can be used to index complex identities which mix global and local imagery, and can evoke connotations of toughness as well as feminine vul-nerability. One of the participants in her study, a 14-year-old girl, uses the following nick: ◊Precious L!l D!aMoNd◊. This nick draws simultaneously on global popular culture (Lil Wayne, an American rapper), traditional images of femininity (precious, diamond), and the symbolism of local gangster culture: a hand sign signifying the shape of a diamond (◊) is used by a local gang to identify members and sympathizers.

The adoption of gang-related nicks does not indicate actual involve-ment with gangs, but is mainly done 'for fun': it reflects a deeply local identity (which is not easily decipherable to those unfamiliar with gang culture in the area), a tougher trial version of oneself, someone who does not get easily intimidated, someone who is in control. At the same time it is transgressive: an oppositional identity *vis à vis* the 'proper' world of, especially, the school. Stallybrass and White (1986) have argued that such transgressions of taboos, the symbolic subversion of cultural codes and norms, are salient and consistent features of the carnivalesque.

In addition to styling oneself and playing with alternative *personae*, the technological environment also allows users to assign stage *personae* to others. This is achieved via an application which allows one to group one's instant messaging friends. These groupings are private and not seen by one's friends (unless volunteered). Some examples are listed in Example (16); all spellings are as provided by the teenagers.

Example (16)

Own nick	Groupings of friends
Play gal	Play gals, Soulja boys, Bad Boys, Toy Boys
ZAKES as ZUKO as B.ROCK	Manskape, Sexe girls, Kak girls, neards
#KIÐ nExTÐooR®	Girls, Boys, hotties, grenades, school friends, Young Moneys
...;-) Jockey dropper :-) ;-)...	VIP-gals, Hot propaty, boys, jst gals
Errisisteble #□tty	Mad people, Hott girls, Hot boys, Freeks

The imagined stage is firmly located within popular culture: *Soulja Boy*, for example, is an American rapper; *Young Money* the record label which was established by *Lil Wayne* (see above) in 2005; and *B-Rock*, a member of the hip-hop group *B-Rock and the Bizz*. It is a playful, make-believe world, where one can be a gangster bride or a rapper, one's friends are hot and sexy, VIPs and part of one's crew (*manskape*, 'soldiers'). It is a world where those not liked or appreciated can be discarded, either by grouping them in an overtly negative group (*kak girls* 'shit girls'), or by simply deleting their contact details. These teenagers thus create their own personal and private theatre, a theatre which stands in deliberate opposition to the everyday world of school uniforms, classrooms and expected good behaviour. They become, within limits, directors of their own show, their own carnival.

5   Conclusion: a digital tavern?

The 'ludic state of mind' described in this chapter is best interpreted as a temporary role and interactional stance which reflects the writers' orientation towards the textual and visual utterances produced (Bucholtz & Hall, 2005). The guiding principle was formulated aptly by Bakhtin: 'the whole world is seen in its droll aspect' (1984[1965], p. 11). This is not to say that digital spaces cannot also be places for serious interactions, or that creative freedom prevails throughout. As noted by Tania Bosch (2011) in her discussion of young women's representations on

Facebook, there are also areas of strong normativity and even surveillance. Facebook stalking, creeping, bullying and malicious gossip (carried out on the semi-public walls) show the potentially dark side of such interactive applications (Jones, Schieffelin & Smith, 2011; and Page, this volume). Nevertheless, playfulness remains a pervasive feature of digital interaction. By engaging in a wide range of ludic practices – drawing on Bakhtinian heteroglossia, the grotesque and the theatre of masks – writers position themselves as a certain kind of person: not only as someone who is fun, playful and creative, but also as someone who is familiar with the genre and the potential freedoms such informal spaces can offer to the expression of the self.

The sociologist Ray Oldenburg (1996/1997) has lamented the disappearance of informal public gathering places – so-called 'third spaces' – in many contemporary societies. Third spaces – cafés, pubs, street corners – are neither home nor work. They are places full of *joie de vivre*, where one's only responsibility is to keep the conversation going: 'there is a festive spirit and laughter is frequent' (p. 19). It has been suggested that, perhaps, digital spaces – with their strongly playful mood – could be new digital versions of such 'third spaces' (e.g. Rao, 2008; Soukup, 2006). In other words, they are new public and semi-public spaces where even serious conversation is punctuated by laughter and the play element can break through any moment, allowing us a moment's respite from the daily responsibilities of work/ school and family: 'we need games to oppose the continuous threat of closure' (De Mul, 2005, p. 261).

Acknowledgements

The work reported in this chapter forms part of a larger project which investigates digital communication in multilingual African societies. It is funded by the *National Research Foundation* (South Africa), the *South African Netherlands Programme for Alternatives in Development* (SANPAD), and the University of Cape Town. I have profited greatly from debates with colleagues and graduate students. As always Nkululeko Mabandla deserves a special 'thank you' for helping with translations from isiXhosa and for patiently answering my questions about the sociolinguistic minutiae of language variation.

Notes

1. danah boyd and Nicole Ellison (2007) have argued that although Facebook and other applications can be used for 'networking', they are primarily used by people to 'articulate and make visible their [existing] social networks'. They consequently favour the term 'social network site' over 'social networking

site'. In this chapter I will use the combined term 'social network(ing) site' to indicate that participants use these applications for both network maintenance and network formation.

2. Bell (2007, pp. 94–5) provides an important caveat for the application of Bakhtinian language philosophy in sociolinguistics: the aim is not to contribute to scholarship about Bakhtin and his oeuvre, but to look from the perspective of sociolinguistics at Bakhtin's work; to 'view him through that lens'.

3. Note that the use of 'hacker' as a negative term to describe someone who breaks into a computer's security system differs from its use and positive connotation as a self-identifier for programmers and system designers.

4. I would like to thank my graduate students Yolandi Klein and Oscar Masinyana for their help in setting up this experiment.

5. Nguni refers to a group of closely related South African languages, including isiZulu, isiXhosa, isiNdebele and siSwati.

6. *Bhu* is an onomatopoeic expression imitating the sound of something bang-like (e.g., a gun shot, a solid object falling on the ground).

7. A copy of the image can be viewed at: http://corniche31i.skyrock.com/2830272342-chaba-bezaf-khmous-3lik-lol.html.

8. A copy of the image can be viewed at: http://www.flixya.com/photo/1964494/funny-kid-holding-plastic-sex-doll.

References

Allan, K. & Burridge, K. (2006) *Forbidden Words. Taboo and the Censoring of Language* (Cambridge: Cambridge University Press).

Bakhtin, M. (1981[1935]) *The Dialogic Imagination. Four Essays*, edited by M. Holmquist (Austin: University of Texas).

Bakhtin, M. (1984[1965]) *Rabelais and His World* (Bloomington: Indiana University Press).

Baron, N. (2008) *Always On: Language in an Online and Mobile World* (Oxford: Oxford University Press).

Bauman, R. (1977) *Verbal Art as Performance* (Rowley, MA: Newbury House).

Bauman, R. & Briggs, C. L. (1990) 'Poetics and performance as critical perspectives on language and social life', *Annual Review of Anthropology*, 19: 59–88.

Baym, N. K. (1995) 'The performance of humour in computer-mediated communication', *Journal of Computer-Mediated Communication*, 1. Available at: http://jcmc.indiana.edu/vol1/issue2/baym.html.

Becher-Israeli, H. (1995) 'From <bonehead> to <cLoNehEAd>: Nicknames, play, and identity on Internet Relay Chat', *Journal of Computer-Mediated Communication*, 1. Available at: http://jcmc.indiana.edu/vol1/issue2/bechar.html.

Bell, A. (2007) 'Style in dialogue: Bakhtin and sociolinguistic theory'. In R. Bayley & C. Lucas (eds.) *Sociolinguistic Variation: Theories, Methods and Applications* (Cambridge: Cambridge University Press).

Bosch, T. (2011) 'Young women and 'technologies of the self': Social networking and sexualities', *Agenda*, 15: 75–86.

boyd, d. m. & Ellison, N. B. (2007) 'Social network sites: Definition, history and scholarship', *Journal of Computer-Mediated Communication*, 13. Available at: http://jcmc.indiana.edu/vol13/issue1/boyd.ellison.html.

Bucholtz, M. & Hall, K. (2005) 'Identity and interaction: A sociocultural linguistic approach', *Discourse Studies*, 7: 585–614.

Cameron, A. (1995) 'Dissimulations: The illusion of interactivity', *Millenium Film Journal*, 28: 33–47.

Carter, R. (2004) *Language and Creativity: The Art of Common Talk* (London: Routledge).

Chayko, M. (2009) *Portable Communities. The Social Dynamics of Online and Mobile Connectedness* (Albany: State University of New York Press).

Coetzee, F. (2012) 'Local and Trans-local Literacies in an Urban 'Village'. A Sociolinguistic Study'. Unpublished MA Thesis, University of Cape Town.

Danet, B. (2001) *Cyberpl@y. Communicating Online* (Oxford/New York: Berg).

De Mul, J. (2005) 'The game of life: Narrative and ludic identity formation in computer games'. In J. Raessens & J. Goldstein (eds.) *Handbook of Computer Game Studies* (Cambridge, MA: MIT Press), pp. 251–66.

Deumert, A. (2006) 'Semantic change, the internet and text messaging'. In K. Brown *et al.* (eds.) *Encyclopedia of Language and Linguistics*, Second edition (Oxford: Elsevier), pp. 121–4.

Deumert, A. (forthcoming) *Sociolinguistics and Mobile Communication* (Edinburgh: Edinburgh University Press).

Follett, J. (2007) 'Engaging user creativity: The playful experience', *UXMatters*. Available at: http://www.uxmatters.com/mt/archives/2007/12/engaging-user-creativity-the-playful-experience.php.

Grice, H. P. (1975) 'Logic and conversation'. In P. Cole & J. Morgan (eds.) *Syntax and Semantics*, Volume 3 (New York: Academic Press), pp. 41–58.

Hay, M. (1992) 'Bakhtin and popular culture', *New Literary History*, 23: 765–82.

Huizinga, J. (1955) *Homo Ludens. A Study of the Play Element in Culture* (Boston: Beacon Press).

Ibarra, H. & Petriglieri, J. L. (2010) 'Identity work and play', *Journal of Organizational Change Management*, 23: 10–25.

Jakobson, R. (1960) 'Linguistics and poetics'. In T. A. Sebeok (ed.) *Style in Language* (Cambridge, MA: MIT Press), pp. 350–77.

Johnson, D., Pejovic, V., Belding, E. & Van Stam, G. (2011) 'Traffic characterization and internet usage in rural Africa'. 20th International World Wide Web Conference (WWW11), Hyderabad, India, 28 March–1 April 2011.

Jones, G. M., Schieffelin, B. B. & Smith, R. E. (2011) 'When friends who talk together stalk together: Online gossip as metacommunication'. In C. Thurlow & K. Mroczek (eds.) *Digital Discourse. Language in the New Media* (Oxford: Oxford University Press), pp. 26–47.

Juul, J. (2010) *A Casual Revolution. Reinventing Videogames and their Players* (Cambridge, MA: MIT Press).

Lachmann, R., Eshelman, R. & Davis, M. (1988) 'Bakhtin and carnival: Culture as counter-culture', *Cultural Critique*, 11: 115–52.

McClard, A. & Anderson, K. (2008) 'Focus on Facebook: Who are we anyway?', *Anthropology News*, 49: 10–12.

McIntosh, J. (2010) 'Mobile phones and Mipoho's Prophecy: The powers and dangers of flying language', *American Ethnologist*, 37: 337–53.

Moore, C. (2011) 'The magic circle and the mobility of play', *Convergence*, 17: 373–87.

Oldenburg, R. (1996/1997) 'Our vanishing "Third Places"', *Planning Commissioners Journal*, 25: 6–10.

Raessens, J. (2006) 'Playful identities, or the ludification of culture', *Games and Culture*, 1: 52–7.

Rao, V. (2008) 'Facebook applications and playful mood: The construction of Facebook as a "Third Place"', MindTrek 2008, Proceedings of the 12th International Conference on Entertainment and Media in the Ubiquitous Era (New York: ACM Publisher), pp. 8–12.

Ricoeur, P. (1992) *Oneself as Another* (Chicago: University of Chicago Press).

Sebba, M. (2007) *Spelling and Society* (Cambridge: Cambridge University Press).

Soukup, C. (2006) 'Computer-mediated communication as a virtual third place: Building Oldenburg's Great Good Places on the World-Wide Web', *New Media & Society*, 8: 421–40.

Stallybrass, P. & White, A. (1986) *The Politics and Poetics of Transgression* (Ithaca, NY: Cornell University Press).

Stukator, A. (2001) '"It is not over till the fat lady sings": Comedy, the Carnivalesque and body politics'. In J. E. Braziel & K. LeBesco (eds.) *Bodies out of Bounds: Fatness and Transgression* (Berkeley/Los Angeles: University of California Press), pp. 197–213.

The Jargon File (2004) version 4.4.8., http://www.catb.org/~esr/jargon/.

Van Blerk, L. J. (2008) 'Identity Work and Community Work through Sociolinguistic Rituals on Facebook. Unpublished Honours Research Project, University of Cape Town.

Wortham, S. (2000) 'Interactional positioning and narrative self-construction', *Narrative Enquiry*, 10: 157–84.

2

Hoaxes, hacking and humour: analysing impersonated identity on social network sites

Ruth Page

1 Introduction

This chapter explores the relationship between identity, impersonation and authenticity in the context of two contrasting social network sites: Twitter and Facebook. I draw on sociolinguistic concepts of authenticity (Coupland, 2003) as a contextualized process in which members of the audience (addressees, auditors and overhearers (Bell, 1984)) draw on offline and online resources in order to detect impersonations with greater or lesser success. The effects of impersonation on the relational work (Locher, 2006) between the impersonated member and the different subgroups of the audience can vary. The difference in the types of relational work (fostering or reducing trust; building or undermining solidarity) are related to a number of factors, including the privacy settings which predominate in particular social network sites, the relationship between members (symmetrical or asymmetrical), and the communities of practice which form the basis of the two case studies (a group of academic professionals who use Twitter, and university students who use Facebook). The chapter begins with an overview of the relationship between identity and impersonation in computer-mediated contexts, then moves on to each case study in detail.

2 Identity and impersonation

Research in computer-mediated discourse analysis does not conceptualize identity as a stable attribute maintained by individual participants. Instead, identity is understood as constructed through interaction, fluid and open to revision. Computer-mediated contexts bring to the fore the centrality of language in performing identity, where the typed words on a screen (sometimes in conjunction with other modes such as image and sound) become primary resources for identity work. As a result, early work in computer-mediated communication made significant claims for the plasticity of online identity where anonymous or pseudonymous representation was often regarded as a 'mask' which could be adopted or discarded at will (Turkle, 1995). The metaphor of the mask implies playful performativity (see Deumert, this volume), where there need be no assumed correlation between the online and offline identities constructed by an individual. But the lack of authenticity implied by such performativity is by no means the whole picture.

The ambiguity associated with online representation of the self sits within a wider complex of debates about the nature of authenticity, trust and reputation that are crucial to the discussion of impersonation in online contexts. On the one hand, all online representation is treated with distrust: no individual's identity is taken to 'be what it seems' and all internet sources are deemed in need of verification (Degroot, 2011). On the other hand, the reliance on text alone in online (as opposed to face-to-face) interaction has led to increased self-disclosure and affective connections (including trust) (Henderson & Gilding, 2004). As social media genres have evolved from the mid 1990s into the twenty-first century, the use of multimodal formats and close interweaving of online and offline interactions means that a simplistic correlation between 'authenticity' and mode is hard to sustain. It is not that online representation is inherently inauthentic as compared with offline representation. Indeed, many studies in recent years have pointed out that individuals do not 'give up' their notions of authenticity when they interact with others online (Rak, 2005). Online impersonations are not then regarded as harmless pranks but can result in serious repercussions with 'devastating effects' (Jordan, 2005). The question of how impersonation operates in more recent social media genres, such as social network sites, requires careful consideration.

Hoaxes and impersonations are by no means limited to online contexts. Examples date back over the centuries, including literary and non-literary hoaxes. In computer-mediated contexts, linguistic analysis has been made of email hoaxes (Heyd, 2008), Nigerian scam letters (Gill, 2011), and hoax blog authors, such as Debbie Swenson's creation, Kaycee Nicole, who purported to be an American teenager diagnosed with leukaemia (Jordan, 2005) or Tom Macmaster's authorship of the blog 'Gay Girl in Damascus' in which he posed as a lesbian, Arabic girl (Afroz, Brennan & Greenstadt, 2012), and video-bloggers such as Lonelygirl15 who claimed to be a homeschooled teenage girl but turned out to be a fictional creation played by a New Zealand actress (Walker Rettberg, 2008; Page, 2012). The impersonations examined in this chapter are similar to these earlier examples in that a third party authors a deceptive text with the intent of passing off the text as if it had been written by someone else. Inauthenticity occurs and is more or less successfully detected by members of the text's audience. But the qualities of a social network site in general, and the particular characteristics of the two sites chosen for analysis (Facebook and Twitter) illustrate how the construction and interpretation of inauthenticity in these sites can vary from that performed in other computer-mediated genres.

Social network sites have been described as 'networked publics', that is, the spaces and communities which are created through networked (usually internet-enabled) connections (boyd, 2010; boyd & Marwick, 2011). Like other networked publics, boyd points out that sites like Facebook and Twitter are characterized by 'collapsed contexts'. Collapsed contexts occur when segments of an individual's audience which are normally kept separate in offline contexts are conflated into a single group in an online context. For example, the audience who chooses to receive updates from my Twitter account (in Twitter's nomenclature, my follower list), includes work colleagues, acquaintances met at conferences, friends from the church I attend, my husband and a number of people whom I have never met in face-to-face interactions. These groups do not usually overlap in offline contexts, but online they all receive the same updates from my account. Managing collapsed contexts poses a communicative challenge for participants because they have to simultaneously address various groups towards whom they may act very differently in offline situations. Recent studies have suggested that participants adopt creative strategies in order to re-create boundaries between different segments of the audience (boyd & Marwick, 2011; Tagg & Seargeant, this volume). Yet the possibility of miscommunication or unwanted disclosure of information between the site member who maintains their profile (which for convenience I call here the updater) and their aggregated audience remains an ongoing risk. The outcomes of impersonation may be similarly various and understood differently by contrasting segments of the collapsed audience of a Friend or follower list.

The audiences constructed in Facebook and Twitter blur the distinction between online and offline contexts, where the interactions online influence the identities and interactions that spill over into offline contexts. Impersonation in these public, or semi-public interactions thus carries considerable potency as the means by which the online reputation and relationships of the impersonated participant are put at risk. The relative visibility of the impersonated participant (for example, as indicated through the size of the known audience articulated as Facebook Friends or Twitter followers) and the nature of the relationship between updater and their audience may influence the scale and nature of the risk to the impersonated participant's reputation. A Twitter member with a public account and a sizeable follower list may need to preserve their professional reputation. A Facebook updater may lose social capital if their account security is compromised and unwanted messages are sent by a third party to Friends on their list. The value of interaction within social network sites, the nature of collapsed contexts and the blurred boundaries between online and offline interactions mean that the practices, construction and effects of impersonation on sites like Twitter and Facebook are underpinned by perceptions of authenticity. Given the discursive nature of identity, judgements of a text's authenticity are tightly bound up with judgements of a site member's identity. The complex, intersubjective nature of perceiving authenticity is discussed next.

3 Definitions and dimensions of authenticity

Authenticity has been a key concept in both sociolinguistics and computer-mediated discourse analysis. Despite its centrality, defining authenticity is far from easy, and it is not an absolute quality which a person, text or object may or may not exhibit (Coupland, 2003). Instead, authenticity is better conceptualized as an intersubjective process of authentication that takes place between participants. The process of authentication thus depends on the cues supplied by the textual sender, and the judgements made by the text's audience(s): in Coupland's (2003) terms, the 'expert authenticators' who reach a consensus about an item or person's value.

Judgements of authenticity are often measured against textual and contextual conditions, which include the need for consistency. Gill (2011) describes consistency as the 'over-riding requirement' for an authenticity effect to be successful. Consistency entails both text-internal features, where unexpected stylistic shifts prompt suspicions of inauthenticity, and the correlation between the participant's assumed identity and their linguistic behaviour: linguistic and non-linguistic signals are required to match, even when imagined in various ways by members of the audience brought together in the collapsed contexts of the Friend or follower list. The expectation of consistency – as a fixed match between the user and their online representation – is formulated as terms and conditions on specific sites. For example, Facebook's terms and conditions (as of March 2010) state:

> You will not provide any false personal information on Facebook, or create an account for anyone other than yourself without permission.

Deception through impersonation is also forbidden by Twitter, whose terms and conditions at the time of writing in 2012 explain:

> Twitter accounts pretending to be another person or entity in order to confuse or deceive can be permanently suspended under the Twitter Impersonation Policy.

The interpretation of authenticity is highly contextual. As Coupland (2003) points out, authenticity is governed by 'systemic coherence', that is, the value that a text is attributed with by its wider social context. Thus what might be deemed authentic in one context might not be deemed as such in another. The ability to detect authenticity (and its counterpart, inauthenticity) has important contextual outcomes for both updater and audience as a form of heightened social value. As Austin (1962) points out, speech acts have effects on their listeners: there are perlocutionary effects to impersonation. These effects extend to impact on the participants' face needs (Goffman, 1959). Impersonation threatens the reputation and status of the impersonated updater (especially if the impersonated information added to an account is defamatory in some respect), and may undermine the solidarity between updater and their audience if trust can no longer be maintained. The ability to identify impersonation may impact the social status or reputation of the audience, as a signal of their digital literacy (Heyd, 2008) and of their being a member of the knowing 'in-group' who avoid falling for the hoax. Of course, the converse is also true, and failure to detect inauthenticity can be face-threatening for audience members who do not 'get the joke' (Page, 2012, p. 170) or worse still, are fooled into compromising their accounts if taken in by deceptive strategies.

The following discussion falls into two parts. I will compare and contrast the textual and contextual characteristics of two somewhat different forms of impersonation found in dominant, mainstream social network sites: a phishing scam which operated in Twitter and the impersonations on Facebook which have become prevalent among young Facebook users in the last few years. The two case studies highlight the importance, to social media relationships, of authenticity – the idea that someone's projected identity should match who they 'really' are – but they also show that what counts as authentic is discursively constructed and that perceptions of authenticity can vary among the different parts of a social media audience.

4   Data and methodology

Collecting examples of impersonation from social network sites is no easy task. Examples of inauthentic updates or messages are often deleted rapidly by the person who has been impersonated. In terms of ethics, accessing impersonated examples of updates is difficult as it is not always possible to identify who the original author of the material is in order to seek consent to observe or archive material. The content of the impersonated material may in some cases prove distressing, and admitting to carrying out impersonation may be regarded as a moral breach. These factors may inhibit discussion of impersonation by impersonators, victims and audiences. Given that the processes of authentication are highly contextualized, the investigation of impersonation needs to go beyond the analysis of text alone, and draw on the ethnographic methods increasingly adopted in sociolinguistic analysis of computer-mediated discourse (Androutsopoulos, 2008). To that end, the data collected for this analysis includes textual examples of impersonation, and interviews with participants involved in the impersonation, all of which were elicited with informant consent and have been anonymized in the discussion that follows. Specifically, I draw on examples taken from my own Twitter account which was hacked by a spambot in October 2011, and six interviews with members of my Twitter follower list. The data from Facebook includes examples of Facebook impersonation observed by 29 university students, a survey and three hours of focus group discussion with those students gathered in March 2012. The students were all between 18 and 20 years of age, and from a mixture of ethnic groups.

In order to explore the contextual dynamics of impersonation I combine discourse analysis with concepts from pragmatics. Austin's model of speech acts separates the textual and contextual elements of communication under the following headings:

the *locutionary act*: the literal meaning of the utterance
the *illocutionary act*: the act which is performed by making the utterance (such as welcoming, promising, identifying)
the *perlocutionary act*: the effect of the speech act on a listener (being warned, amused, offended).

I am particularly interested in the ways in which the perlocutionary force of an impersonated speech act operates within the audiences found in social network sites. In order to describe these effects, I use Locher's (2004, 2006) model of relational work. Locher's (2006) model usefully points out that politeness is only one dimension of the face management carried out in communication. Politeness is part of a broader spectrum which also includes unmarked appropriate and inappropriate forms, along with impoliteness (see also Culpeper, 1996). Locher makes a general distinction between the activities which generate involvement and solidarity between participants and those which relate to the speaker's independence and relative status within the group. Based on the contrast between involvement and independence, she sets out three broad categories of relational work (Locher, 2006, p. 114):

> *Face-enhancing work* which aims to increase the involvement between participants, or their self image.
> *Face-threatening work* which disrupts the co-operative communication or social order between participants.
> *Face-saving work* which might mitigate the effects of face-threatening behaviour.

As we will see in the discussion that follows, the perlocutionary effects of impersonation can range from face-threatening loss of trust and reputation to face-enhancing banter and in-jokes, while an impersonated victim may need to carry out face-saving work to remediate the effects of impersonation in a social network site. The difference in these outcomes varies in part due to the nature of the social network in question, but also to the position that an audience member occupies within the collapsed contexts of Facebook Friend and Twitter follower lists.

5   Twitter: hacked by a spambot

Twitter is a micro-blogging site, sometimes also described as a social network site. Originally launched in 2005, the uptake of Twitter increased exponentially in 2009 so that it is now considered a mainstream platform for internet use. Like many other social network sites, Twitter enables its members to create an account and then communicate with other members of the site via short updates (known as 'tweets'), or through private messages (known as 'Direct Messages'). Twitter is distinct from many other contemporary social network sites in two ways. First, the default for Twitter communication is public. It is estimated that only

7 per cent of Twitter accounts apply privacy settings (Page, 2012, p. 79). Although you must be a member of Twitter to post content via the site, anyone with access to the internet can view the content which is made available in Twitter's public timeline. Second, the relationship between a Twitter updater and their followers is non-reciprocal. In other words, if member A chooses to follow member B, there is no guarantee that member B will follow member A in return. Kwak, Park and Moon (2010) point out that this distinguishes Twitter from most other human networks, where the relationship between members is usually reciprocal (Twitter is discussed in greater detail by Zappavigna, this volume).

Both the public and non-reciprocal nature of Twitter influence the risks of impersonation on this site. If a public Twitter account is compromised, impersonated information (which might be false or defamatory) can be viewed by both the follower list for that account and the general public. The threat to reputation and status is significant. The non-reciprocal nature of the updater's relationship with their follower list means that, if impersonation occurs, the potential damage to others can be hard to remediate: it is not easy to carry out face-saving work when you do not know who all the members of your audience are. The opportunity to damage the reputation of a Twitter member has resulted in impersonations which have been reported in the mainstream news. High-profile celebrities with follower lists consisting of millions of fans have been targets, such as Lady Gaga's account which was hacked in December 2011, sending false messages to her 23 million followers in an attempt to dupe them into a phishing scam. Other high profile impersonations appear to be motivated politically. For example, the activist hacker group 'Anonymous' was accused of posting material on Senator Chuck Grassley's Twitter account in December 2011 in order to contest particular policies. The material that is discussed in the following analysis is a much smaller-scale example of impersonation, which occurred when my own Twitter account was compromised in October 2011.

The deceptive Twitter messages which compromised my account operated in the following way. I received a Direct Message, apparently from a fellow Twitter member who I follow and who I have met in real life. The member is a well-established writer, with academic credentials and a significant Twitter following. By chance I had seen the member in person the afternoon before I received the fake message, while I had been visiting a local museum with my children. The message said 'What were you looking at in this photo?' and was followed by a link. Once the link was clicked, a fake error message appeared, asking for Twitter password details. The result of falling for the hoax message was that

Direct Messages of a similar nature were then sent from my account to everyone on my follower list, stating, 'I saw a real bad blog about you, you seen this? http://t.co/sgTbTcr'. If followers clicked on the link, the action perpetrated a similar chain of disruption.

By the following morning, my Twitter account and personal email account were flooded with messages from contacts warning me that my Twitter account had been hacked. It was straightforward to remedy the compromise to my Twitter account: changing my password sufficed. It was less easy to remedy the damage to my online reputation and relationship to my follower list. Although I repeatedly apologized for the inconvenience caused via updates in my public timeline, there was no way I could contact everyone who might have received a fake message from me. Some contacts reported me to Twitter, and still do not trust messages from me which contain links. I updated my Twitter account recently with a link to a genuine and reputable site I was using for a fundraising charity event, but a colleague replied on Twitter saying, 'I've made it a rule never to click on links you send me ☺'.

The locutionary contents of the two fake Twitter Direct Messages were more or less plausible statements, followed by a question. But the perlocutionary force of the messages was a request, enticing the addressee to carry out an action which would benefit the impersonating software (by allowing them access to sensitive information such as password and account details) but damage the impersonated victim, as well as those who fell for the victim's impersonated message. Given that spam messages are both suspect and prolific, it is worth questioning what factors caused addressees to detect the inauthenticity of these impersonations, and conversely what made the messages appear authentic.

The fake messages appeared at least partially plausible because of their content. In the case of the fake message I received, it was possible that the sender had indeed taken a photograph of me that afternoon and was building solidarity between us by sharing the photograph with me. Given the ease with which photos taken from smartphones can be shared on sites like Twitter (as opposed to being sent via email), this action would have some measure of credibility. In the case of the fake message that impersonated me, it is possible that I might have read an untoward blog post and wanted to warn the recipient of the content so that they could address the matter. Both messages shared a common incentive to review some other implied source of social media (either a photo sharing site or a blog) where material about the addressee had apparently been published. As such, both messages appealed to the addressee's need to monitor their online reputation: a common concern for social network site members. As one member of my follower list put it:

> To my knowledge, none of my social media accounts have ever been hacked (knock on wood) but the prospect of it happening is certainly terrifying. Building an online presence is a lot of work, and a lot of that work involves being consistent and trustworthy.

Similarly, the possibility that their online reputation had been compromised by a blog post left another follower 'really rattled' as the fake message 'got to one of my real fears in having people write bad things about me in blogs and putting it out there'.

The plausibility of the fake messages was also judged in relation to the addressees' contextual knowledge. This included the relative expectation of interaction with the sender based on the addressee's position within the collapsed context of a Twitter follower list. Unlike tweets which are publicly or semi-publicly sent as broadcasts to an entire follower list (and also viewable by a wider, overhearing audience of the general public), Direct Messages are dyadic exchanges which can only take place between members of Twitter who follow each other. In this respect, the reciprocity between sender and addressee is higher than general updates between a sender and the multi-levelled audience of a follower list which also includes groups which Bell (1984) describes as 'auditors' and 'overhearers'. Bell's description of these speaker roles are based on conversational and broadcast spoken data, and reflect the relative distance between the speaker and the member of the audience. Auditors are described as known and ratified interlocutors, while overhearers may not be known to the speaker, nor be part of the ratified group. While the extent to which these categories can be unequivocally transferred to computer-mediated environments is an issue (see Tagg & Seargeant, this volume), there are parallels in the case of Twitter between auditors as members of the follower list who the updater does not follow in return and overhearers (the general public). The expectations of interaction and anticipated modes of engagement for each of the audience's subgroups will vary. While auditors might not expect to receive a Direct Message, and the overhearers of the general public would not be in a position to receive such a message, addressees may well assume the proximal social distance sufficient to entail interaction with the updater via the private, dyadic mode of Direct Messages.

The recipients of the impersonated Direct Messages juxtaposed their actual positions (as addressees of a Direct Message) with their self-perceived position within the collapsed audience of a given follower list. Those who did not deem themselves 'first order contacts' or familiar enough with the sender, interpreted the receipt of a Direct Message from me to be out of character and so implausible. One follower explained their suspicion, 'Twitter gets hit with such hacking events so immediately wary of a DM from someone who's never DM'd me before'. Another follower wrote, 'I wasn't expecting a DM from you (a public tweet would be more likely)'. However, the collapsed contexts of follower lists make distinguishing between the roles of an auditor and addressee difficult in some cases. For example, one follower said that they gave the message passing credibility because they had 'Not [...] communicated with you enough to be absolutely sure it wasn't you'. My own faulty judgement of the fake Direct Message I received was similarly complicated by the changing contexts in which I positioned myself relative to the assumed sender of the message. In normal circumstances I would not have expected a Direct Message from the sender in question. We were passing acquaintances, not colleagues who worked closely enough to warrant the private, dyadic communication of a Direct Message. However, having seen the sender in person within the hours immediately prior to receiving the message, my perception of myself as an addressee rather than an auditor shifted such that I misjudged the authenticity of the message.

Other recipients based their judgements of inauthenticity on the lack of consistency between the text and contextual knowledge of the sender. For example, one recipient of the impersonated message said that the timestamp of the message made it unlikely to be genuinely sent from me, saying that they 'clicked it would have been ~4am in UK and you really should sleep more!' Many other recipients interpreted a dissonance between the grammatical style of the fake message and the writing style that they usually observed in my updates, or judged appropriate for me based on my position as an academic. One recipient tweeted,

> Nearly fell for a spam/phishing DM but luckily robots use bad grammar and the DM came from a senior lecturer in linguistics.

Others said, 'I'm familiar enough with your presence on Twitter that I trust you would be capable of constructing a properly worded message – the poor grammar an immediate red flag'. Another follower pointed out that the style was not in keeping with British English, 'the use of the terms "real bad blog" and "you seen this?" are not only grammatically poor, they instantly made me think they were American in nature (source of a great deal of spam) or even from (with respect) a very young person who did not have a good command of the English language'. It would seem that standards of authenticity are increasingly founded on 'consistency rather than absolute certainty' (Jordan, 2005, p. 204). If a text appears to be stylistically at odds with expectations generated from contextual knowledge, then inauthenticity may be suspected.

The wider effects of this kind of impersonation in Twitter are clearly face-threatening. One Twitter member described the loss of reputation in the following way:

> It can be a cause of embarrassment and concern that a person's reputation could in some way be damaged. Reputation is representative of our core values and is harder to rectify than damage.

The face-threatening effect of impersonation also affects the social order of communities in social network sites through an increased sense of distrust more generally. As one member put it:

> ... it reminds us we have to be cautious of tweets even from people we trust. It reminds us that it is a public forum.

Others suggested that the loss of trust and increase of suspicion might escalate and so inhibit the growth of connections which enable social networks to operate successfully.

> I don't think it has hit any epidemic proportions yet but will cause angst if it gets to that stage. Saw Usenet killed by spam. Would cause a corralling of the wagons and networks would patrol their borders, be less open to unknown people joining or following back.

These comments suggest that the playful performativity of online identity conceptualized as a 'mask' has been replaced by the need to achieve and maintain an online reputation that engenders trust, at least within the professional community of practice on Twitter in which this example of impersonation occurred. But the effects of impersonation can vary considerably. Processes of authentication can operate differently in other contexts and communities, as the following discussion of impersonation in Facebook demonstrates.

6   Impersonation amongst Friends: Facebook 'rape'[1]

Facebook 'rape' (also known as 'frape') occurs when a third party gains access to and then alters the content of another member's account, for example if the victim leaves their Facebook account logged in but is absent from the device used to access the site. 'Frape' is a multi-voiced speech act which involves at least two participants: the victim (the authentic Facebook member) and the perpetrator, who impersonates the victim by publishing false information on the victim's Facebook profile without their consent or knowledge. Examples of 'frape' can vary enormously from relatively harmless pranks (such as changing the details of a victim's birth date so that they receive greetings posted on their wall on the wrong date) to posting seemingly offensive updates or engaging in inappropriate online chat with members of a Friend list. Often (although not always) the 'frape' can be embarrassing or offensive for the victim. Examples of 'frape' updates observed by the participants in this study (a group of 29 university students based in the UK) exemplify the vulgar subject matter frequently associated with the practice.

I'm such a filthy girl when I've had a drink.

I have just done the worst fart in the world. A bit of my hair fell out and my left bum cheek fell off. What an evening I am having.

I am a lesbian with my sister.

But 'frapes' can also be more subtle impersonations that are not so obviously at odds with the victim's 'genuine' identity in other ways. In my focus group discussions with students, they described alteration to profile information such as changing relationship status to 'engaged' (particularly if a couple had been in a long-standing relationship), posting sonograms as profile pictures, or changing profile details to a cartoon character who was judged to be similar in appearance to the victim.

The processes of (in)authentication that operate around 'frape' contrast with those typical of the Twitter spam hacking in various ways. In terms of plausibility, the 'frape' impersonations are not intended to pass as the victim. Instead, there is always a gap between the 'frape' and the victim's usual identity or behaviour. Unlike impersonations which aim to minimize inconsistency for their success, 'frapes' depend upon their audience being able to spot inconsistency to work effectively. The scale of this inconsistency can vary a great deal, from content which is stylistically incongruent with other profile information (such as the insertion of humiliating or sexually explicit details in an update when the norms for appropriate update content are considered to be either low-key or upbeat in tone), to 'frapes' which are more plausible (such as changing a relationship status).

The effects of the 'fraped' impersonations are also different to the Twitter spam hacking. The perlocutionary effects of 'frapes' are not requests which might entail members of the audience compromising their security or putting their resources at risk. Instead, the wider effects of 'frapes' reflect the value of social capital as the currency within Facebook. That is, the negative effects of 'frape' are directed at the victim's relationships with others. On one level, this is evidenced through the content of the 'frapes', which often misrepresent the victim's relational identity with others, such as the aforementioned examples of altering a relationship status, or listing friends as family members. Another student described changing his gay housemate's interests to 'women'. Yet another student explained that other recent iterations of 'frape' involve posting offensive content in a Facebook group, such as 'You are all massive geeks and no one likes you' on a university society group page.

The face-threatening nature of such impersonations is clear. 'Frapes' of this kind are seldom left undeleted, and are usually contested by the victim. One student described seeing the aftermath of a fake sonogram inserted into a Friend's profile with the victim's exasperated comment, 'I want to sort out once and for all I am not fucking pregnant'. Students in the focus groups described their own and other victim's reactions to 'frape' in various terms, but at least some included annoyance and anger. Repeated 'frapes' can be reported to Facebook, who can authorize penalties against perpetrators. However, not all responses to 'frape' appear to frame the effects as face-threatening. As I have documented elsewhere (Page, 2012), 'frape' can also be interpreted as non-serious impoliteness: a form of banter.

The potential for 'frape' to function as a face-enhancing form of solidarity in the form of banter exposes the different reactions of addressees and auditors within the collapsed contexts of a Facebook Friend list. In the context of an impersonation, addressees (in line with Bell's 1984 framework) can be thought of as the intended audience who can be relied upon to detect the inconsistency in the 'frape', interpret the intention behind it as non-serious, and recognize the impersonation as a playful joke. Auditors are those members of the Friend list who may receive the update or see the change in profile information, but may not be imagined by the impersonators to be part of the victim's audience. Having described a 'frape' that a number of students had participated in (altering a fellow student's profile to a cartoon character), the students clearly equated the intended audience of the prank with the victim's friends in the offline world, saying, 'If they had been his friends they would have known it wasn't him'.

Often the perpetrators are within the close circle of friends who participate in creating such in-jokes. Although it is not true in every case, often perpetrators of 'frape' are those close enough to be trusted with a device like a laptop or a smartphone that has been left logged on, or those trusted with information like a Facebook password. The implicit trust in such friends or family members was expressed by one student who (perhaps naively) pointed out that 'frapes' are 'genuinely only done by people you trust enough to leave your account logged in with in the first place'. As boyd and Marwick (2011) point out, exhibiting trust by sharing this kind of information is one means by which social connection between participants can be enhanced. In a paradoxical sense, although 'frapes' are on the surface an abuse of such trust (as they publish usually embarrassing or, at the very least, untrue information about the victim), they also display the shared offline context of apparent trust between the participants (close proximity to the victim's valued goods, or knowledge of their password) to the rest of the Friend list.

The close interweaving of offline and online interactions also goes toward explaining the face-enhancing effects of solidarity brought about by banter. Earlier research has indicated the combative but face-enhancing role of insulting sequences in playful talk between young girls (Ardington, 2006). In a similar way, the teasing and sometimes insulting nature of 'frape' can provoke similar patterns of retaliation, which students described in the focus groups as 'frape wars'. For example, the student whose profile had been turned into a cartoon character then altered the update of the original perpetrator, posting the lyrics of a song that the original perpetrator particularly disliked. In this way, teasing in-jokes circulate within a closed group of Friends who understand the points of reference, and use this to strengthen their social bonds. As another student in this circle of friends put it 'They loved it, so it's fine'.

Unlike addressees, auditors are often outside the social circle which interprets 'frape' as non-serious banter. Auditors might make the mistake of taking the locutionary content of the 'frape' at its face value, and judge it to be sincere. This kind of miscommunication is problematic. One student described the negative effects of 'frape', saying:

> I think it depends on how everyone around you reacts because even the most explicit frape is considered a joke but if people believe it and take it seriously, that's when it gets very annoying.

The inability to detect a 'frape' as inauthentic is particularly troublesome when the impersonation is plausible, and when the nature of the 'frape' invites a response. Explicit 'frapes' which are rude or derogatory might be ignored on the auditor's need to exercise civil inattention, that is to avoid interaction that is deemed inappropriate on the grounds of social intimacy (Goffman, 1959).

However, events such as a forthcoming family wedding or an announcement of a pregnancy might be expected to prompt congratulatory expressions. The face damage of falling for 'frapes' such as these operates on multiple levels which cross between online and offline interactions. One student's story illustrates the damage to face and relational work. She explained that her (now) ex-boyfriend had altered her Facebook profile status to indicate that she was engaged to him, and altered his own profile to also say that he was engaged to her, posted a photograph of a ring and then tagged her in it. Because she was travelling abroad immediately after the 'frape' had taken place, she was unable to delete the information and the false information remained on her account for a week. Both sets of parents saw the information and were 'very cross', and the student had to go to considerable pains to convince friends and family members that the 'fraped' information was not authentic.

In the focus group discussions with students, the auditors who bore the most face damage from 'frapes' (both in terms of their own loss of face through being unable to spot the joke and in terms of their threatened loss of solidarity with the victim) were family members of the victims. One student described how she took great pains to segregate the collapsed contexts of her Friend list by blocking her family members from seeing her updates, so that they could only use Facebook as an online chat tool. Another student commented that 'frapes' which were unacceptable were those which were likely to be misinterpreted by family members.

> It affects how you are perceived by people in the real world then you are definitely crossing the line yeah one of my friends has a really strict like religious family and one of his friends posted a coming out statement on his Facebook and he had a lot of explaining to do.

boyd and Marwick's (2011) work on teenagers' perceptions of privacy on Facebook describe the strategies that some teenagers use to demarcate Facebook as a 'space for friends' (p. 17), and to limit what is seen by parents. The ability (or lack thereof) to detect inauthenticity in 'fraped' impersonations appears to be another means by which distinctions between addressees (the students' peers) and auditors (family members) become apparent. Fellow peers are assumed to 'get the joke' and recognize the non-serious nature of the 'frape' while family members do not, thus exposing a boundary which is particularly salient for the teenagers and young adults as they mediate a transition between living independently as college students and maintaining contact with family members.

7   Concluding remarks

The perceptions of authenticity within the communities that evolve in social network sites like Facebook and Twitter vary according to the position that audience members adopt within the collapsed contexts of Friend and follower lists. In particular, the ability to detect the inauthentic interactions of impersonated identities may depend on whether the audience member is an addressee (and so believes that they are the intended audience for a message), or an auditor (who overhears the message, but may not feel that they are the intended recipient). This distinction occurs because of an assumed relational difference in these two groups. Addressees are assumed to be first order contacts, or to have obtained sufficient social proximity to be able to judge the consistency of an impersonated message correctly and interpret it as a hoax. Auditors may not hold this level of contextual knowledge, and therefore fail to detect inconsistency, interpreting the locutionary content of impersonated messages at surface level. The relational work that results from impersonation in social network sites also varies for addressees and auditors. When auditors fail to detect inauthenticity they may lose face, in terms of a loss of reputation if they were to fall for a phishing scam in Twitter, or to be positioned as an out-group excluded from a joke in a Facebook Friend list.

The relational work which results from impersonation also points to differences between the social network sites considered in this chapter. Many different kinds of communities of practice operate within Twitter and within Facebook. Nonetheless, the public nature of Twitter is well suited to the professional community of practice which was put at risk through the phishing scam I have described. In this context, impersonation threatened the reputation of the victim, and undermined trust between academic colleagues and contacts. The semi-public environment of Facebook, where relationships between an updater and their Friends closely mirror, if not match, offline relationships, are somewhat different. In this context, while the playful impersonations of Facebook 'rape' are still at least superficially face-threatening, they may also function as a form of face-enhancing banter which results from trust between Friends who share potential access to a Facebook account, and so increase solidarity between Friends who share an in-group joke. Given the complex forms of impersonation that are emerging on social network sites, and the multiple pragmatic effects which result, these case studies should only be considered as first steps towards a fuller understanding of how impersonation will continue to be reconfigured in social media contexts. More work is needed in a variety of localized contexts in order to explore how impoliteness, sarcasm and humour operate in social network sites. It is only as this wider picture emerges that we will be able to observe more general patterns of impersonation and its effects. These case studies suggest that far from abandoning authenticity, participants retain a strong need to establish and maintain their reputation and trust with others in social network sites, although this can vary considerably depending on the communities within which they are participating.

Note

1. The term 'Facebook rape' is highly contentious. By using the term, I do not wish to imply that the impersonations in Facebook which are referred to by this name are synonymous with acts of rape. However, because the term is used by the participants in this study about their practices, I will retain its use in this chapter.

References

Afroz, S., Brennan, M. & Greenstadt, R. (2012) 'Detecting hoaxes, frauds, and deception in writing style online'. Paper presented at the IEEE Symposium on Security & Privacy, May 2012.

Androutsopoulos, J. (2008) 'Discourse-centred online ethnography'. In J. Androutsopoulos & M. Beißwenger (eds.), *Data and Methods in Computer-Mediated Discourse Analysis*. Special Issue, *Language@Internet* 5. Available at http://www.languageatinternet.de/articles/2008 (accessed 5 April 2011).

Ardington, A. (2006) 'Playfully negotiated activity in girls' talk', *Journal of Pragmatics*, 38(1): 73–95.

Austin, J. L. (1962) *How to do Things with Words* (Cambridge, MA: Harvard University Press).

Bell, A. (1984) 'Language style as audience design', *Language in Society*, 13(2): 145–204.

Bourdieu, P. (1977) 'The economics of linguistic exchanges', *Social Science Information*, 16(6): 645–68.

boyd, d. (2010) 'Social network sites as networked publics: Affordances, dynamics, and implications'. In Z. Papacharissi (ed.) *A Networked Self: Identity, Community, and Culture on Social Network Sites* (Abingdon: Routledge), pp. 39–58.

boyd, d. & Marwick, A. (2011) 'Social privacy in networked publics: Teens' attitudes, practices and strategies'. Paper presented at the Oxford Internet Institute's 'A Decade in Internet Time: Symposium on the Dynamics of the Internet and Society', 22 September 2011.

Coupland, N. (2003) 'Sociolinguistic authenticities', *Journal of Sociolinguistics*, 7(3): 417–31.

Culpeper, J. (1996) 'An anatomy of impoliteness', *Journal of Pragmatics*, 25: 349–67.

Degroot, J. (2011) 'Truth in urban legends? Using Snopes.com to teach source evaluation', *Communication Teacher*, 25(2): 86–9.

Gill, M. (2011) 'Establishing authenticity in computer-mediated communication: The case of Nigerian letter fraud'. Paper presented at the Georgetown Roundtable of Linguistics, 11 March 2011.

Goffman, E. (1959) *The Presentation of the Self in Everyday Life* (New York: Anchor Books).

Henderson, S. & Gilding, M. (2004) '"I've never clicked this much with anyone in my life": Trust and hyperpersonal communication in online friendships', *New Media and Society*, 6(4): 487–506.

Heyd, T. (2008) *Email Hoaxes* (Amsterdam: John Benjamins).

Jordan, J. W. (2005) 'A virtual death and a real dilemma: Identity, trust, and community in cyberspace', *Southern Communication Journal*, 70(3): 200–18.

Kwak, H., Lee, C., Park, H. & Moon, S. (2010) 'What is Twitter, a social network or a news media?' Paper presented at the World Wide Web Conference 2010, April 26–30, Raleigh, North Carolina, USA.

Locher, M. (2004) *Power and Politeness in Action: Disagreements in Oral Communication* (Berlin: Mouton de Gruyter).

Locher, M. (2006) 'Polite behavior within relational work: The discursive approach to politeness', *Multilingua*, 25: 249–67.

Page, R. (2012) *Stories and Social Media: Identities and Interaction* (Abingdon: Routledge).

Rak, J. (2005) 'The digital queer: Weblogs and internet identity', *Biography*, 28(1): 166–82.

Turkle, S. (1995) *Life on the Screen: Identity in the Age of the Internet* (New York: Simon Schuster).

Turkle, S. (2011) *Alone Together: Why We Expect More From Technology and Less from Each Other* (New York: Basic Books).

Walker Rettberg, J. (2008) *Blogging* (Cambridge: Polity Press).

3
'Usually not one to complain but…': constructing identities in user-generated online reviews

Camilla Vásquez

1 Introduction

This chapter focuses on identity in TripAdvisor, a user-generated online consumer review site. Online consumer reviews are a genre of social media which is referred to by the international marketing community as 'eWOM,' or electronic word-of-mouth (Hennig-Thurau *et al.*, 2004). eWOM is a relatively new genre, which has no exact analogue in the offline world (Pollach, 2006). Before eWOM, consumers had basically two options for gathering information to guide their decision-making. They could rely on the opinions of a handful of experts, such as professional reviewers or critics, who published their reviews in traditional print formats (e.g., magazines or guidebooks). Or they could rely on traditional forms of word-of-mouth: assessments of individuals personally known to the consumer, such as family members, friends, or acquaintances. In either case, the scope of goods and services covered was restricted either to what could be experienced by a handful of individuals whose job it was to review them (experts), or to what could be experienced by the individuals in one's immediate social network. However, online social media have radically enlarged the scope of first-hand information about goods and services available for consumers' consideration. There are now millions of user-generated reviews available online about every imaginable product. Indeed, 'user-generated content' is one of the defining characteristics of social media, and it means that today, anyone with internet access can provide their opinions about any of their consumer experiences. In addition to the broadened scope and sheer amount of consumer information available, this also means that now – more than ever before – we are relying on vast quantities of information provided by complete strangers to guide our decision-making. Previously, the individuals whose reviews we read in traditional print formats typically established their expertise via their professional credentials – or by virtue of being published authors. Alternatively, because of our close personal connections to traditional word-of-mouth information, we knew those sources of information personally, and thus could more easily assess the validity of their claims. However, with eWOM, expertise has become distributed, geographically dispersed, and interpersonally removed. Consequently, establishing the credibility of reviewers – as well as the authenticity of reviews – has become a significant issue for users of this form of social media.

eWOM is a quintessentially 'late modern' form of interaction (Benwell & Stokoe, 2006) in that it centres around practices of consumption and it takes place in a technologically mediated form, between an author and a potentially vast audience, both of whom are, and will most likely remain, unknown to one another in the offline world. Yet reciprocal anonymity does not render reviewers' identities irrelevant in this form of social media. On the contrary, some researchers (Sen & Lerman, 2007; Vermeulen & Seeger, 2009) argue that reviewers' identities are very much of interest and of use to readers of online reviews. In their studies, they found that users are sensitive to reviewers' expertise as well as their possible motivations for posting a review – related, for example, to issues of a review's authenticity. This means that a more thorough understanding of the types of identities that reviewers construct – as well as the particular linguistic resources they recruit for this purpose – is a matter which merits closer investigation.

In order to situate the topic, this chapter begins with a brief discussion of the central role of discourse in the construction and performance of online identities. This discussion is followed by a focused survey of interdisciplinary research on the phenomenon of online reviews. Specific information about the dataset in the study (a corpus of 100 travel reviews), as well as about the general approach used to analyse features of identity in this social media genre, is presented next. Finally, I consider various types of explicit and implicit identity claims made by reviewers, as well as their use of other types of discursive devices (i.e., humour, cultural references, intertextuality) which contribute to the identities that they construct online.

2   Identity online

In contrast to traditional notions of identity as fixed, essential, or biologically determined, contemporary social scientific understandings of identity highlight the performative, dynamic, socially constructed and socially situated aspects of identity (e.g. De Fina, Schiffrin & Bamberg, 2006). Although this more recent understanding of identity as an interactional achievement – and one that is discursively formed – has much broader relevance, it is especially resonant with scholars studying identity in online contexts. Because of the potential for anonymity online, individuals can portray themselves in potentially more varied ways than they can in their offline realities, where their presentation of self is often more constrained by their physical appearance. Recognizing the online/offline dimension of identity as a continuum rather than a polarity, Page (2012, p. 18) draws on Zimmerman (1998) to offer a useful distinction between 'transportable identities' ('attributes or characteristics that a participant carries across multiple discourse situations') as opposed to 'discourse and situated identities' ('locally occasioned roles adopted in relation to a particular speech situation'). She explains further that 'transportable identities can be inscribed (explicitly stated in the text) or invoked (indexed through stylistic choices)'. As will be illustrated in the examples below, both transportable and situated aspects of reviewers' identities appear in online texts – and these identities are sometimes inscribed and, at other times, invoked.

One limitation of early research on identity in social media (e.g. Ellison, Steinfield & Lampe, 2007; Joinson, 2001; Gibbs, Ellison & Heino, 2006; Gonzales & Hancock, 2008; Lampe, Ellison & Steinfield, 2007) was that it often restricted its focus to include information from only the profile[1] section of the respective social media application. This analytic over-emphasis on the user profile is problematic, as pointed out several years ago by Marwick (2005), because the range of resources for constructing the self is restricted by the platform designers' decisions about relevant information categories, as opposed to the user's own notions of what is relevant. Individuals posting online clearly have a much wider range of discursive resources at their disposal to perform identity, which inevitably extend beyond the boundaries suggested by a particular platform's profile structure. Accordingly, more recent research has begun to attend to identity in social media beyond merely the categories found in the user profile. For example, Ziao, Grasmuck and Martin's (2008) study of the identities of 63 Facebook users focused primarily on the personal profile pages, but also took into consideration information found in participants' photos. Similarly, Bolander and Locher's (2010) pilot study of ten Facebook users, in addition to profile information, also included textual data found in users' status updates.

In order to expand the understanding of online identity construction, this chapter similarly moves the analysis of identity away from the profile to include other sections of online text. Rather than focusing on users' profiles, I instead examine how aspects of reviewer identities are constructed and interwoven within the textual fabric of the actual online reviews themselves. This chapter also shifts emphasis from online identities in social network sites, to online identities in another form of social media: consumer reviews. Unlike social network sites, where members typically share an offline connection as well as an online one, consumer reviews represent a form of social media where members most likely do *not* have offline connections with one another. Consequently, there is a greater need for reviewers to provide information about their identities, especially with respect to establishing credibility, and to give readers reasons for trusting the information offered in a review. This includes showing – and not just telling – 'who one is' as a reviewer.

Internet scholar Sherry Turkle's (1999, p. 643) observation that online 'self-presentation is written in text' remains as true today as it was over a decade ago. However, what has changed since Turkle's pioneering adventures in cyberspace, is an expanded conceptualization of online 'texts,' which includes the increasing options for multimodal forms of self-presentation that are now available to internet users. Nevertheless, words, language, and discourse continue to serve as key resources in the presentation of self online and in the construction of identities in social media. As communication researchers Wood and Smith (2005) explain, 'both what people say about themselves and how they behave with others contribute to the perception of personal identity online. The use of language is consequently of immense importance in cyberspace, for *it is through the use of language that people construct their identities*' (p. 60, emphasis mine). Within the fields of sociolinguistics and discourse analysis, there is widespread recognition that language is central to creating, performing, and negotiating one's identities (e.g. Benwell & Stokoe, 2006; Bucholz & Hall, 2005); however, studies examining the linguistic construction of identity in social media remain quite rare. As an increasingly popular – and global – form of social media, user-generated online reviews, offer fertile ground for considering issues of identity online. Therefore, this chapter offers an examination of how context-specific identities are constructed in a set of consumer reviews from the popular travel website, TripAdvisor.

2.1 Research on online reviews

Sites such as TripAdvisor have clearly changed the way that consumers make travel decisions (Tancer, 2008). The growing impact of consumer reviews on consumer decision-making is already well-documented in marketing and tourism research (Briggs, Sutherland & Drummond, 2007; O'Connor, 2008; Yoo & Gretzel, 2009). Tourism researchers Zehrer, Crotts and Magnini (2011) explain the factors underlying the immense popularity of travel review sites:

> The tourism product is an experience good, which, by its nature, is hard to assess prior to purchase. [...] To explore or reduce the risk of unfamiliar product experimentation, tourists seek information. [...] Available advice from other consumers who have already experienced the tourism product will emerge as not only the preferred source of pre-purchase information, but also the most influential in travel decision-making mainly because it influences consumers' images and expectations (p. 108)

In other words, in order to reduce uncertainty and to access first-hand information about a hotel – information which previously would have been more restricted, and available through either a guidebook or one's personal contacts – consumers today have at their disposal millions of reviews about virtually any travel destination. And, to put it simply, prior to travelling, consumers want to know what the experience will be like – ideally, from someone who has personally been there.

The influence of internet-based consumer reviews is powerful and far-reaching, and a clear relationship has been found between online reviews and consumer purchasing. Interestingly, this extends beyond information about the product itself. For example, Forman, Ghose and Wiesenfeld (2008) found that when reading online reviews, consumers simultaneously process information about the reviewer as well as information about the product. Moreover, they found a positive and significant relationship between reviewer self-disclosure (e.g. information about a reviewer's geographical region or hobbies) and consumer purchases on the Amazon website. This means that online audiences are not only sensitive, but also responsive, to identity cues provided by authors of reviews, even when those reviewers remain anonymous. In a more recent work, Kuehn (2011) argues that self-disclosure in online reviews serves a number of functions, not the least of which is the provision of information that can be used to determine how 'alike' a reviewer is to a reader:

> ... writing one's lifestyle, tastes and preferences into a review enables other readers to evaluate businesses and services on these terms. The

goal here, of course, is that readers are more likely to take the opinions of those with whom they identify or whose status they might seek to emulate... (p. 164)

Besides determining what they have in common with a reviewer, when reading online reviews, readers must also make decisions about whether or not a reviewer is 'credible'. Mackiewicz (2010b) explains that credibility is a two-part construct which subsumes both trustworthiness (sincerity and honesty) as well as expertise (accuracy and authority). When considering the context of online consumer reviews, Mackiewicz (2008, 2010a, 2010b) identifies several ways that reviewers can communicate their credibility. Some are determined by the review platform (i.e., what she calls 'preconfigurations of credibility') and include badges that are conferred by the website and which designate, for example, reviewers' 'elite status' or their 'real name.' However, other markers of credibility include textual properties of the review itself (such as spelling, and careful editing for grammatical correctness) – as well as rhetorical or discourse features in the review text that are related to reviewers' identities (e.g., claims of expertise, mention of relevant occupational status). To arrive at a deeper understanding about the discursive construction of identity in social media, this final category is the focus of this chapter. In user-generated content, reviewers must work to establish their expertise and credibility – and language is the primary resource they have to rely upon, since their personal ties to readers are normally 'loose' rather than 'strong'. Therefore, as will be shown, discursive identity work – which is often anonymized yet able to index a considerable amount of information for the purpose of lending authority to opinions – is particularly salient in this form of social media.

3　Methodology

Social media are characterized by distributed, user-generated participation, and online reviews are no exception. Review forums enable anyone with an internet connection to post an opinion – and allow innumerable others to access those user-generated opinions via the internet from anywhere else in the world. The data for this study consist of a sample of 100 negative reviews from TripAdvisor. TripAdvisor, the most prominent online travel review platform (Zehrer *et al.*, 2011), aims at providing 'unbiased'[2] user-generated recommendations for travel destinations and accommodation. As such, it represents an ideal and unexplored medium for investigating the discursive construction of identity in online reviews.

Rather than restricting the analysis to only one specific city or region (as TripAdvisor research in the field of tourism studies has tended to do – for example, Au, Buhalis & Law, 2009, on Hong Kong hotels; or Briggs *et al.*, 2007, on Scottish hotels), an alternative sampling procedure was used in order to yield a broader range of review writers and travel destinations. Each week on its homepage, TripAdvisor showcases approximately five of 'The Worst' and the same number of 'The Best' hotel reviews: this section is labelled 'Rants and Raves'.[3] Over a six-month period (November 2008–April 2009), once per week, the website's featured 'Rants' were downloaded and saved, until a corpus of 100 hotel reviews was created. The focus of this analysis is on negative reviews because, according to prior research (Ricci & Wietsma, 2006; Sen & Lerman, 2007), online audiences pay more attention to negative than to positive reviews.

This study was guided by the following research question: 'What are some of the rhetorical strategies and linguistic resources used by reviewers to construct identities as particular types of individuals in this online context?' In the following analysis, I draw on insights from social psychology (Davies & Harré, 1990) and systemic functional linguistics (especially work that focuses on the interpersonal dimension of language use, such as Martin & White, 2005), as well as discursive approaches to understanding identity (Benwell & Stokoe, 2006; Bucholz & Hall, 2005; Gee, 1999, 2000). In particular, Gee (2000) writes that 'discourse identities' emerge and are recognized in discourse and dialogue. In other words, identity is always a bidirectional accomplishment: i.e. it is constructed by an individual, yet it must also be recognized as such by an audience. Moreover, Gee writes that discourse identities '...can be placed on a continuum in terms of how active or passive one is in "recruiting" them, that is, in terms of how much such identities can be viewed as merely ascribed to a person versus an active achievement or accomplishment of that person' (p. 104). Consequently, it is important to bear in mind that while some of the identity information that reviewers include is deliberate and strategic, other types of information may be 'given off' in a less conscious fashion. For example, a reviewer may deliberately choose to include (or not) particular information in an online profile; and yet this same reviewer may transmit – with varying levels of self-awareness or intentionality – information about him/herself within the actual review text. The identity categories (both 'inscribed' and 'invoked') discussed in the analysis below emerged from multiple readings of the corpus of reviews, followed by several rounds of coding.[4]

4   Analysis

The analysis begins with 'genre-specific' types of identity claims, which position reviewers as certain types of travellers. This is followed by a discussion of how discourse features such as humour, cultural references and intertextuality function to construct reviewers' identities. Finally, I conclude with an explanation of how these discursive resources work together to bolster a reviewer's expertise and credibility in this relatively anonymous computer-mediated environment, and what it all means for an audience reading the reviews.

4.1   Construction of identities within the review text

In this corpus of reviews, only about half of the reviewers chose to populate the fields of their user profiles. Similar to other consumer review websites, TripAdvisor includes a section within the profile called 'About Me', where reviewers can share various types of personal information. In this corpus of 100 reviews, only one reviewer opted to use this feature.[5] For researchers who consider identity by focusing exclusively on the user profile, it would appear that TripAdvisor reviewers generally choose not to reveal very much personal information. However, when looking closely at the review texts, a different picture emerges. Nearly all of the reviewers represented in the corpus include some type of personal information in their review texts. For example, the excerpt below illustrates how, in just a short segment of text, a reviewer can construct for readers a very specific identity. In it, the reviewer mentions the following characteristics: her marital status, her spouse's occupational affiliation, general information about the family's income level, as well as their reason for travel.

Example 1
I booked this hotel with the intention of taking my husband to a "fancy" hotel in which we usually cannot afford. At $266 per night I THOUGHT that's what we would be getting.[...] My husband is a soldier in the US Army, and I wanted to take him out for a nice weekend on one of his ONLY weekends off. We ended up spending over $600 on this place and now we are in debt. $30 a night for parking really took a toll on us. <73>

In this brief segment of the review text, the reviewer is able to project an identity of a married woman (*my husband*), with a military spouse

(*My husband is a soldier in the US Army*), and a limited family income (*a "fancy" hotel in which we usually cannot afford*). Whether or not it is the reviewer's intention to reveal all of these details about herself, Example 1 illustrates how much information about one's identity can appear within just a brief stretch of a review. (It also illustrates how much could be missed by looking only at the reviewer's profile to learn about her identity!) This type of identity work can be viewed as a claim to credibility – in this excerpt, the reviewer establishes that she is a 'real' person, with economic constraints as well as legitimate consumer expectations. It is likely that readers will take this identity information into account (though again, with varying degrees of awareness) as they interpret her comments throughout the rest of the hotel review.

4.2 Experience and expertise

Whereas some of the identity categories illustrated in the previous example might be relevant in reviews of other products or services as well, other aspects of identities that were foregrounded in this dataset are clearly more restricted to the genre of travel reviews. By this I mean any information that a reviewer included in order to position him/herself specifically as *a certain type of traveller*. This can relate to prior travel experience, or to various ways of constructing an identity of a traveller who has reasonable expectations.

There are many ways in which reviewers can construct their prior travel experience. For example, some reviewers refer to how long they have been travelling, in terms of kilometres or miles (2a), while others quantify how long they have been travelling, in terms of months or years (2b).

Example 2a
This is the worst [name of motel chain] *I have stayed at in my 9,000 miles of travel!* <9>

Example 2b
In my 25 years of business travel, I have never experienced such a consistently, depressingly mediocre property. <4>

As can be seen in Example 2b, another means by which reviewers construct their expertise has to do with employment-related travel. Reviewers such as those in 2b above, and in 3a and b below, explicitly refer to their occupational categories (e.g. *business travel[ler], experienced businessman,* or *professional traveller*), which are highly relevant to this genre, since presumably business travel is equivalent to frequent travel, and therefore means exposure to more hotels. In Example 3a, the author's explicit warning to readers is prefaced by a strong claim to authority, as she explicitly positions herself as a professional traveller.

Example 3a
I am a <u>professional traveller</u> so please take heed. <24>

Example 3b
I sprung into action as only an <u>experienced businessman</u> in fear of missing his flight and having to spend another night at the [name of hotel] *would react.* <8>

Example 3c
I am a <u>very experienced</u> <u>international</u> traveler who <u>stays at all categories</u> <u>of hotels</u> in <u>my job as an international events manager</u>. I have never experienced anything like this, and in particular, the complete lack of customer service. <21>

The author of 3c includes a great deal of relevant identity information which serves to construct him as a credible source. He describes his degree of travel experience (*very experienced*); he indicates the scope of his travel experience (*international*); he mentions the range of his hotel experiences (*all categories of hotels*); and he includes his occupational category (*international events manager*). Example 3c comes from a negative review of a famous 5-star hotel in Las Vegas and it is likely that the amount of identity work found in this example is considered necessary by the reviewer to contextually situate his negative comments about what is normally considered to be a superior hotel.

Rather than referring more generally to international travel (such as reviewer 3c and reviewer 4a), other reviewers were much more specific about where they had travelled. For example, the reviewer in 4b restricts the scope of his claim. By limiting his travel history to a very specific geographic region (i.e., the lower half of Ireland), he positions himself not only as an expert, but also one with highly specialized knowledge of a relatively narrow domain.

Example 4a
<u>I have stayed in many small, basic hotels around the world</u> and have learnt that the difference between a good one and a bad one is the love, care and attention given by its owners. This place has none of this. <27>

Example 4b
*I can honestly say that it was the worst hotel I have ever stayed in and
I have stayed in nearly every hotel in the lower half of ireland.* <67>

Other reviewers use multiple appeals to credibility, and combine both
the duration of their experience in travelling, as well as the destinations
to which they have travelled. This can be seen in the three examples
below.

Example 5a
*In 20 years of travel in Russia the room I paid $216 for one awful night
was among the worst rooms I have encountered, not easy to do given the
generally low standard of abusive hotels encountered in the Soviet era.* <8>

Example 5b
*We have traveled extensively within Europe and Worldwide for the last
20 years, this must rank as one of the most mediocre experiences we have
ever had.* <28>

Example 5c
*We have been traveling for the past three and a half months, and have
stayed in hostels in many different countries... This was our WORST
experience by far.* <79>

Once again, some reviewers are very specific in describing the destinations of their past travel (5a), whereas others (5b, 5c) are much more
vague. However, in each of the three examples the reviewers quantify,
in rather precise terms, either their past travel history (5a, 5b), or the
amount of time travelling on a current trip (5c). In this way, they restrict
their scope of expertise, assert the limits of their qualifications, and
thereby provide readers with information about their trustworthiness.

In the majority of the preceding examples (2–5), the strategies which
highlight reviewers' claims of expertise co-occur – very often in the
same sentence – with either some type of extreme case formulation
(*none, never, complete lack of*) or with a superlative (e.g. the *worst hotel/
room/experience*). Therefore, reviewers' claims of expertise and experience, in a sense help to ground these hyperbolic claims, which intensify
the overall negative assessment of the hotel. Previous research has suggested that extreme case formulations, or ECFs (Pomerantz, 1986), are
not common in complaints occurring in face-to-face contexts (Edwards,
2005, as cited in Vásquez, 2011). In contrast, it is noteworthy that ECFs

do occur with some frequency in these online complaints – perhaps making them more characteristic of communicative genres where there is some degree of anonymity or social distance between participants. In addition, when they occur, it is typically in close co-textual proximity to reviewers' claims of authority or expertise.

Another discourse strategy used by reviewers to establish their authority on the subject consists of referencing multiple prior visits to the same hotel, as seen below in Examples 6a and b. In 6b, the reviewer's opening metadiscourse (*Let me begin by saying that...*) helps to emphasize – by drawing the reader's attention to – that which follows: his claim of loyalty as a consumer. By underscoring their familiarity with a specific hotel property, mentions of prior visits help position reviewers as qualified to make claims about consistency of quality with respect to a given hotel.

Example 6a
I have stayed with my friends many times at this hotel BEFORE it became the [hotel name]. <10>

Example 6b
Let me begin by saying that we have been very loyal to the [hotel name] *for our 15 years of traveling there and have recommended the* [hotel name] *to many friends and family.* <85>

Table 3.1 provides a summary of the frequency of strategies used by reviewers to claim expertise through experience. The information in the table suggests that nearly one-half of the reviewers in this dataset (42%) used at least one of these strategy types to indicate their context-specific expertise. The most common type of expertise invoked was other destinations that the reviewer had visited in the past (often in various parts of the world), followed by experience with a wide range of hotel types.

Table 3.1 Frequency of discourse strategies associated with reviewers' construction of expertise

Type of strategy used	Number of tokens
Past destinations visited	15
Range of property types experienced	9
Number of months/years of travel, or miles travelled	7
Business/professional traveller	6
Multiple stays in same hotel and/or chain	5
TOTAL	42

Explicit quantification of the amount of prior travel, one's professional status as a business traveller, or mentions of prior experience with the same property were also common, although less so than the first two categories.

It is reasonable to assume that readers of reviews take this information into account when determining whether the reviewer is a knowledgeable and reliable source, as opposed to someone who is a less experienced, or inexperienced, traveller. Indeed, travel industry research (e.g., Vermeulen & Seeger, 2009) suggests that sophisticated users of reviews *do* take into account a reviewer's expertise when making consumer decisions based on social media reviews. In this context, providing information about one's past travel experiences can help readers make judgements about the expertise of the reviewer.[6] Furthermore, these types of claims are often linked with emphatic, categorical statements about low quality, or with warnings or advice. Consequently, the identity claims serve to provide additional context for readers' interpretation of those strong and forceful statements, and enable them to assess the reviewer's credibility, even though the reviewer may remain anonymous to them.

4.3 'Non-complainers' and reasonable expectations

With respect to the construction of a particular type of traveller identity, another common strategy used by reviewers is to highlight their fair, reasonable, or realistic expectations. This appeal to reasonableness takes various forms in negative reviews. A number of reviewers construct identities as 'non-complainers,' by mentioning *never complaining*, or not being *a fussy person*. By making these types of oppositional identity claims (7a–d), reviewers position the negative review as an exceptional case, thereby constructing an identity as someone who is not impossible to satisfy.

Example 7a
Usually not one to complain but the service is just terrible. <89>

Example 7b
I have never had cause to complain but felt compelled! Fantastically marketed! I feel so misled. <71>

Example 7c
The most important thing for us when we travel is cleanliness. We are not picky travelers. <55>

In the above examples (7a–c), the 'non-complainers' highlight one specific dimension of the overall negative experience (e.g. service, cleanliness, being misled), thereby restricting the scope of the complaint. The reviewer in 7d uses a different strategy: rather than restricting the scope of his complaint to a single issue, he uses multiple discursive resources to position himself a 'non-complainer'. This repetition serves to underscore the highly uncharacteristic nature of his complaint. Once again (and similar to the reviewer in 6b) the reviewer in 7d begins with metadiscourse (*Please let me make it clear…*), which emphasizes and draws readers' attention to his self-description of his moral character.

Example 7d
Please let me make it clear that I am NOT a fussy person at all. I am not the complaining type and just take things on the chin with my mouth shut. So it is a big deal for me to be writing this review. [...] As I said before, I don't complain about much in life. So these complaints I've made have had to be pretty severe. <86>

Closely related to the discursive construction of being a 'non-complainer' is the representation of having realistic expectations – especially given the hotel's cost or star category. Referring to these factors, the reviewers below are explicit about the standards of quality they were expecting prior to their visit. For example, the reviewer in 8b compares her actual hotel visit with other well-known hotel chains in the same price range. According to Zehrer *et al.* (2011), the expectancy-disconfirmation paradigm in tourism research posits that consumers tend to compare actual outcomes against their pre-travel expectations, in order to make a judgement about their satisfaction or dissatisfaction with their experience. Therefore, it is not surprising that a number of reviewers, such as those in the examples below, make explicit reference to their expectations in their complaints (see also Vásquez, 2011).

Example 8a
I was not expecting the Hilton but I was expecting something clean and comfortable. <88>

Example 8b
I was expecting the accommodation to be on a par with a Four Seasons or Ritz Carlton (as you are paying a similar price) but sadly its a shabby run down castle without the amenities that one would expect in a 5 star property. <96>

Example 8c
I love to travel and usually stay at 3 to 5 stars hotels. <u>My expectations</u> are <u>very fair</u>. I <u>don't really have high standards or by any means high main-</u><u>tenance</u>. As long as these hotels and rooms are somewhat similar to the pictures I see in their websites and providing decent level of service then I'm satisfied. <46>

The reviewer in 8c combines approaches by immediately following her claim of having *very fair* expectations with another claim underscoring her identity as reasonable person (e.g. *I don't really have high standards or by any means high maintenance*).

In a similar fashion, the next two reviewers (8d, 8e) establish that they are well aware of the existence of several classes of hotels, and that they are not treating all hotels as belonging to the same category. Rather, they specify that their hotel experience was exceptionally negative in terms of what could be reasonably expected at the type of property they selected. In doing so, they demonstrate their ability to discern, discriminate, and to apply their standards selectively to the various properties they have encountered. Example 8d begins with another instance of metadiscourse (*I want to emphasize…*), which, in this instance, draws readers' attention to the more narrowly restricted scope of the reviewer's evaluation.

Example 8d
I want to emphasize <u>I am not slamming Russian hotels in general</u>. The [hotel name] *(a completely different chain) at the other main Moscow airport, Sheremetyevo, is a fine hotel, albeit at higher cost, as are many other Russian hotels at which I have stayed.* <8>

Example 8e
<u>I've stayed in [hotel name]'s before, so won't say that all [hotel name]'s are</u> <u>bad</u>, JUST STAY AWAY FROM THIS HOTEL! <57>

The reviewer in 8e uses orthographic emphasis in the formulation of a warning to other travellers: a warning which serves as the closing move in this review. Orthographic emphasis is a conventionalized means for expressing intensification in online writing, often serving as a resource analogous to effects that might be achieved by shifts in stress, intonation, or other contextualization cues used in face-to-face communication. Orthographic emphasis is not unusual is this genre, as can be seen in examples 1, 5c, 6a, 7d, 8f, and 10a. In addition to drawing attention to a final warning (as in example 8e), emphasized words also tend to include extreme case formulations (lexical items such as *ONLY, NEVER*) or superlatives such as *WORST*.

In the final example of this category, 8f, the reviewer uses multiple discursive resources within the same review: references to reasonable expectations, mention of past travel experience, and listing of prior experience with multiple types of well-known hotel chains. This combination of resources works together to construct an identity of a traveller who is reasonable, knowledgeable, and experienced – and who is therefore a credible source of information.

Example 8f
I know $125 is not a great deal of money these days. I was not expecting a heck of a lot. However, I was expecting basic clean and comfortable accommodations. I have traveled quite a bit and I have stayed in everything from Marriott Resort Hotels and Hyatt Resorts to Days Inns, Hampton Inns, Best Westerns, Residence Inns, La Quintas, and various Mom and Pop Motels to name a few. I have NEVER felt this ripped off. My stays have not always been perfect but I have always felt like I got what I paid for. <81>

The opening sentence of example 8f consists of a 'concede + counter' pairing, a type of evaluative move which, according to Martin and White (2005, p. 156), functions to 'construct writer and reader as sharing certain assumptions about what is "normal"'. In addition, the hyperbolic uses of ECFs such as *always* and *NEVER* in this excerpt are used to convey the reviewer's strong investment in the proposition, as opposed to conveying a more literal meaning (Martin & White, 2005).

Table 3.2 provides a quantification of the strategies associated with the construction of the self as a traveller with reasonable expectations. Nearly a quarter of reviewers in this dataset (22%) used at least one of these strategies, and references to having reasonable expectations were more than three times as common compared to descriptions of the self as 'non-complainer'.

Table 3.2 Frequency of discourse strategies associated with the construction of a reasonable self

Type of strategies used	Number of tokens
Reasonable expectations	17
Non-complainers	5
TOTAL	22

In positioning themselves as frequent, business, professional, experienced or international travellers, reviewers provide their readers with an additional perspective for interpreting the information found in the review. Similarly, the use of various discursive means to construct oneself as a person who seldom complains, as a traveller with reasonable expectations, or as a traveller familiar with various classes of accommodations, signals to readers that they should not immediately dismiss the review as the work of someone who is naive when it comes to travel, or of someone who is generally impossible to satisfy. These types of strategies appear to be quite useful in establishing a reviewer's credibility – especially when the reviewer also makes emphatic, categorical, or extreme assessments of quality in his/her review.

4.4 Cultural references and humour

Several reviewers incorporated popular culture references and/or humour in their reviews. The use of popular culture references indexes a reviewer's consumption of, and taste in, particular forms of mass media. The performance of taste can be an important aspect in constructing an online identity, and internet scholars have noted that online communities and interactions often come about as a result of shared interests or tastes (Kozinets, 2010). References to particular forms of popular culture and mass media, when shared, can contribute to a sense of affinity or co-membership. Therefore, this type of reference could be interpreted as a bid for sociability. In addition, popular culture references in this genre serve a metaphorical function: comparing a unique, subjective experience to something larger that is shared by many. In this dataset, several reviewers referred to the classic British situation comedy, *Fawlty Towers*, as in the next example.

Example 9a
I was appalled and totally mortified when we were shown our room. It was like something out of <u>Fawlty towers</u>. <15>

The relative frequency of references to *Fawlty Towers* (five instances in 100 reviews) is perhaps unsurprising, given these data come from negative reviews of hotels – and the setting of the comedy is a hotel where things continually go wrong.

Other references to popular culture were also found. In Example 9b, the reviewer's reference to an American movie review programme invokes the larger genre of the review more generally. And in another excerpt

(9c), the reviewer uses the cinematic reference to *Trainspotting* – in combination with hyperbole (*make your eyes bleed*) – for dramatic effect.

Example 9b
In the words of <u>Siskel and Ebert</u>, we give this hotel two thumbs down!! <19>

Example 9c
It consisted of a double bed that could only have been from a second hand shop, a colour scheme that would make your eyes bleed and a bathroom that would give the one in <u>Trainspotting</u> a run for its money. <49>

In 9d, another reviewer makes reference to the character of Felix Unger (a compulsive neat freak) portrayed in the classic American film and situation comedy, *The Odd Couple*.

Example 9d
First of all, it is dirty and shabby. Look, <u>Felix Unger</u>, I am not. For me to notice the dirt is saying something. <4>

By evoking a character from a popular culture source, and then claiming to be the opposite of 'Felix Unger,' the author uses this mass media reference metaphorically to position himself as not having excessively high standards for order and cleanliness. This example illustrates how a reference to a popular culture character can function as a means for constructing the self as having reasonable travel expectations. Of course the success of such a strategy depends on the extent to which readers are familiar with the particular form(s) of popular culture being invoked.

Benwell and Stokoe (2006), among others, have observed that the use of humour can contribute to an individual's online ethos, or the type of identity they wish to project in computer-mediated communication (CMC) contexts. Humour in online contexts is often realized by means of word-play (St. Amant, 2002). In this dataset, a few reviewers engaged in word-play, as can be seen in the following examples.

Example 10a
My wife and I discovered by being woken up in the middle of the night, that we were being eaten alive by BED BUGS, giving a whole new meaning to Bed and Breakfast!! <70>

Example 10b
…and as for the so called continental breakfast I would love to know which continent eats what was given to us? <34>

Regardless of the larger discourse context in which it occurs, humour can, of course, be multifunctional. By using humour within the context of a negative review, it may be argued that these reviewers are positioning themselves as individuals who do not take themselves too seriously. Humour serves as a discursive resource that some authors choose to draw on in constructing identities as eminently reasonable people, who can thus be assumed to have normal expectations when they travel.

4.5 Intertextuality

Intertextuality has also been described as a characteristic feature of computer-mediated communication. As Benwell and Stokoe (2006) point out, users of CMC often comment metadiscursively on connections between messages. In this corpus, several reviewers referred to other TripAdvisor reviews they had read, as in the examples below.

Example 11a
How can a hotel with such nice rooms, a dynamite location, and such wonderful remarks on TripAdvisor.com now be on my "I will never stay there again list?" <36>

Example 11b
As we had read on trip advisor that the "a-la-cart" meals were better, we tried to make reservations for some. <45>

Example 11c
...and the restaurant some of you had complained about was no longer operating. <10>

While 11a and b refer to the TripAdvisor website by name, in 11c, the reviewer uses the second person pronoun *you* to address directly the community of TripAdvisor reviewers. In comments such as these, which exhibit varying degrees of intertextuality, authors position themselves as members of this online community who participate in dual roles: as both readers and writers.[7] Humour, references to popular culture, and referring to other reviews on the website can be seen as resources which are used by reviewers to 'write their readers into their texts' and to construct solidarity, alignment, and a shared viewpoint with their audience (Martin & White, 2005, p. 95).

Table 3.3 indicates that nearly 20 per cent of reviews in the dataset included instances of intertextuality, and another 20 per cent included either humour or popular culture references. Taken together, these

Table 3.3 Frequency of discourse strategies associated with humour, popular culture, and intertextuality

Type of features	Number of tokens
Intertextuality (reference to other online reviews)	18
References to popular culture	11
Use of humour (word-play)	7
TOTAL	36

proportions indicate that authors draw on these discursive resources with considerable frequency when writing reviews.

Interestingly, among the intertextual references, a subset of reviewers mention having read previous reviews, but ultimately disregarding or ignoring the warnings given in them. By including these references, and then following those mentions with accounts of their own personally unsatisfactory experiences, these reviewers strengthen the existing claims made about the hotels.

> Example 11e
> *I ignored the prior warnings on this and similar sites about this hotel – please believe it is as bad as we all say.* <42>

> Example 11f
> *We had read the reviews and knew what we were getting into. That being said, it was worse then what we expected.* <55>

However these examples also raise the following question: Why would users such as these bother reading reviews, especially if later they admit to having ignored those reviews? Certain forms of intertextuality found in reviews such as 11g may actually provide us with an answer to this question, as well as with insight into how consumers process and use such information when making decisions.

> Example 11g
> *My boyfriend and I read every single review for hotels in Dublin and decided that this hotel sounded fine, and that the noise could not possibly be as bad as people said it was, after all, we are in our early 20s and want to go out at night...* <69>

The reviewer in 11g provides a considerable amount of personal information within a short excerpt: about her travel companion, their ages, as well as their lifestyle choices. More importantly, she also sheds light on how readers may make use of the reviews they encounter online. After weighing others' remarks about the hotel against her own identity and values – and implicitly questioning other reviewers' reactions to the hotel – the author decided that previous reviewers' remarks were not applicable to her. It is likely that other readers consulting reviews engage in similar processes of filtering and evaluating the textual information they encounter online in order to assess its relevance to them. As they make decisions about where to stay or what to purchase, consumers inevitably compare their own desires and expectations against what they have read.

Marketing researchers (Forman *et al.*, 2008; Ghose & Ipeirotis, in press) argue that in reading online reviews, consumers take into account not only product information, but also reviewer information. There is no doubt that reviewers' linguistically constructed online identities become an indispensible source of information, as consumers engage in decision-making. Moreover, as suggested by example 11g (and by Kuehn, 2011), consumers may also assess the extent to which they themselves are similar to, or different from, the authors of reviews. In doing so, consumers inevitably consider, react, and respond to, the online identities produced by reviewers – as they extract the most relevant information from each review, given their own unique needs, experiences, and expectations. Marketing research has indicated that 'similarity between the reviewer and the consumer (e.g. in social class or gender)' plays a major role in influencing readers' perceptions of credibility (Mackiewicz, 2008, p. 257). Indeed, the relative success of a review may lie in the extent to which reviewers can establish solidarity with other consumers. This may also explain why users choose to more subtly interweave claims for credibility into reviews, as well as why they often downplay their complaints and set themselves up as 'reasonable' people.

5 Conclusions

Although many reviewers opt out of providing personal information in the website's user profile, often these very same reviewers do share personal information and construct various types of identities within the review text itself. Yet most research on identity in social media has focused almost exclusively on identity information included in the user's profile, which means that these researchers are likely only seeing a small part of the picture. When investigating identity performances in social media, there is a wealth of identity information presented in other areas found on websites, and it is necessary to look beyond the profile in order to examine them.

User-generated online consumer reviews represent an under-researched genre within sociolinguistics as well as within studies of social media. The present study has attempted to address this gap, and has found that reviewers use a range of discursive resources to construct various context-relevant identities. Moving beyond the basic demographic categories found in online profiles (identity information such as gender, location, family/relationship status, etc.), the review text allows individuals to construct other genre-specific types of identities, related to their travel expertise. Reviewers may construct these identities in relatively explicit terms ('inscribed' identities), or they may draw on more creative linguistic resources – such as the use of humour or cultural references – to perform ('invoked') identities as certain types of people, and to tell and/or show us who they are ... or, perhaps, who they would have us believe they are. Because just as Page (2012) notes that 'there are no guarantees of authenticity for the demographic information offered in profile slots' (p. 19), the same caveat applies to authenticity in the review texts themselves.

Another finding of the present study is related to the subcategory of intertextual references which lends support to claims that readers *do* read entire reviews, and do not simply rely on summarized information, such as star ratings (Ghose & Ipeirotis, in press). Perhaps even more interesting is the discovery that negative reviews do not necessarily lead others to avoid a particular product or service. Rather, if a reviewer provides consumers with enough information in a review – even if it is mostly negative – consumers are likely to extract out the relevant details, weigh them against their individual knowledge of the world, and go on to make subjective decisions based on those (and perhaps other) sources of information. Both the information about the goods/services as well as information about the reviewers are taken into account during the decision-making process. Writing specifically about social media reviews, Ghose and Ipeirotis (in press) take this point one step further: 'While review valence is likely to influence consumers, there is reason to believe that social information about reviewers themselves (rather than the product or vendor) is likely to be an important predictor of consumers' buying decisions' (p. 6). This information about reviewers' social identities is, by and large, linguistic and text-based in nature – and is interwoven into the review text. Furthermore, as consumers read user-generated reviews, they appear to be engaged in not only determining whether the reviewer is someone who is credible and whose advice should be followed, but also in discerning whether the reviewer's needs, expectations and experiences are similar enough to their own. This seems a plausible explanation for the observed intertextual phenomenon of 'reading but not heeding' the negative reviews of others.

Finally, one of the greatest ethical issues related to forms of CMC in general – and to eWOM more specifically – has to do with authenticity of authorship (Tancer, 2008). Zehrer *et al.* (2011) and others in the tourism industry indicate that there is growing concern over the authenticity of online reviews. And for good reason: it has been observed that some companies pay individuals to fabricate reviews in order to either boost their own reputation, or to undermine competing businesses (Scott, 2009). In such an environment, it can be expected that consumers may wonder about the offline identities of reviewers. Recent work in computing has explored the detection of deception online: one group of researchers (Ott, Cardie & Hancock, 2011) has even created an automated process to identify fake hotel reviews. Responding to this issue of authenticity and deception (sometimes called 'opinion spam'), online review sites are currently engaged in creating multiple ways of authenticating reviewer identities, as well as different ways of linking individuals' online identities to their offline identities.[8] As social media continue to evolve and develop, review websites will certainly discover new ways of validating their contributors' identities. None of these anticipated developments, however, will eliminate the need for online reviewers' discursive constructions of identity. In order to establish the relevance and credibility of their comments, reviewers will need to continue using a variety of linguistic resources in constructing an identity of one who is a knowledgeable, trustworthy, and convincing source of information.

Notes

1. Most social media applications include a profile section, where contributors can post pre-determined categories of personal information, such as age, relationship status, hobbies, etc.
2. However, Scott (2009) provides a useful critique of this claim of 'unbiased' reviews, as well as further insights into the shifting construction of knowledge, evaluation, and expertise in an era of user-generated consumer reviews.
3. In order to obtain information about how TripAdvisor selects which reviews to showcase on this section of their website, the company was contacted on numerous occasions, yet chose not to respond to the author's requests for information.
4. In the following section, numbers found in angle brackets following each example correspond to the unique number assigned to each review in the

corpus. This information is included to provide a sense of the representative-ness of excerpts included here. Also, the specific feature under examination has been underlined in the excerpts, in order to draw attention to the item being discussed. In addition, all reviews are presented exactly the way that they appear online, including non-standard forms, typographical errors, etc.

5. This is considerably lower than that which others have found in other online genres – yet, at the same time, somewhat consistent with previous findings. For example, Zhao *et al.* (2008) found that 67 per cent of their 63 Facebook users populated their 'About Me' sections with some content, although it was generally quite minimal. Similarly, Bolander and Locher (2010) found that only 3/10 of their Facebook users included any information in that section, and that these items were vague.

6. Far less frequently reviewers refer to their travel *in*experience, e.g.,

   Before heading off on our first trip to Italy and Cinqua Terra, our travel agent told us that we HAD to stay at [hotel name] *<95>*

7. In contrast, Pollach (2006) found that intertextuality was quite rare (3%) in her dataset: reviews of digital cameras. The precise nature of the product or service being reviewed (search good vs. experience good) – as well as the culture of the website – is likely related to degree of intertextuality that occurs in various types of online reviews. (Recently, I observed that, on TripAdvisor, this phenomenon also occurs in languages other than English: *Grazie a TripAdvisor, ci siamo trovati bene…*).

8. Since the time that these data were collected, TripAdvisor now allows users to log in through their Facebook account and to communicate with reviewers directly. This is known as an API (or application programming interface) and allows users to login to one site, and through that single login, be logged into other sites visited – serving to further reduce anonymity. (Of course, other sites use additional means to authenticate a reviewer's offline identity, such as *Amazon*'s 'Realname' or 'Verified Purchase' badges, or Yelp's 'Check in' function.)

References

Au, N., Buhalis, D. & Law, R. (2009) 'Complaints on the online environment – the case of Hong Kong hotels'. In W. Hopken, U. Gretzel & R. Law (eds.) *Information and Communication Technologies in Tourism, 2009* (Vienna: Springer), pp. 73–85.

Benwell, B. & Stokoe, E. (2006) *Discourse and Identity* (Edinburgh: Edinburgh University Press).

Bolander, B. & Locher, M. (2010) 'Constructing identity on Facebook: Report on a pilot study', *SPELL: Swiss Papers in English Language and Literature*, 24: 165–87.

Briggs, S., Sutherland, J. & Drummond, S. (2007) 'Are hotels serving quality? An exploratory study of service quality in the Scottish hotel sector', *Tourism Management*, 28: 1006–19.

Bucholz, M. & Hall, K. (2005) 'Identity and interaction: A sociocultural linguistic approach', *Discourse Studies*, 7: 584–614.

Davies, B. & Harré, R. (1990) 'Positioning: The social construction of self', *Journal of the Theory of Social Behavior*, 20(1): 43–63.

De Fina, A., Schiffrin, D. & Bamberg, M. (eds.) (2006) *Discourse and Identity* (Cambridge: Cambridge University Press).

Edwards, D. (2005) 'Moaning, whinging and laughing: The subjective side of complaints', *Discourse Studies*, 7(1): 5–29.

Ellison, N., Steinfield, C. & Lampe, C. (2007) 'The benefits of Facebook "friends": Social capital and college students' use of online social network sites', *Journal of Computer Mediated Communication*, 4, http://jcmc.indiana.edu/vol12/issue4/ellison.html

Forman, C., Ghose, A. & Wiesenfeld, B. (2008) 'Examining the relationship between reviews and sales: The role of reviewer identity disclosure in electronic markets', *Information Systems Research*, 19: 291–313.

Gee, J. P. (1999) *An Introduction to Discourse Analysis: Theory and Method* (New York: Routledge).

Gee, J. P. (2000) 'Identity as an analytic lens for research in education', *Review of Research in Education*, 25: 99–125.

Ghose, A. & Ipeirotis, P. (in press) 'Estimating the helpfulness and economic impact of product reviews: Mining text and reviewer characteristics', *IEEE Transactions on Knowledge and Data Engineering* (available online at: http://pages.stern.nyu.edu/~aghose/reviewstext.pdf)

Gibbs, J., Ellison, N. & Heino, R. (2006) 'Self-presentation in online personals: The role of anticipated future interaction, self-disclosure, and perceived success in internet dating', *Communication Research*, 33: 152–77.

Gonzales, A. & Hancock, J. (2008) 'Identity shift in computer-mediated environments', *Media Psychology*, 11: 167–85.

Hennig-Thurau, T., Gwinner, K., Walsh, G. & Gremler, D. (2004) 'Electronic word-of-mouth via consumer opinion platforms: What motivates consumers to articulate themselves on the internet?', *Journal of Interactive Marketing*, 18: 38–52.

Joinson, A. (2001) 'Knowing me, knowing you: Reciprocal self-disclosure in internet-based surveys', *CyberPsychology and Behavior*, 4: 587–91.

Kozinets, R. (2010) *Netnography* (London: Sage).

Kuehn, K. (2011) Prosumer-citizenship and the Local: A Critical Case Study of Consumer Reviewing on Yelp. Unpublished dissertation. Pennsylvania State University.

Lampe, C., Ellison, N. & Steinfield, C. (2007) 'A familiar Face(book): Profile elements as signals in an online social network'. In *Proceedings of Conference on Human Factors in Computing Systems* (New York: ACM Press), pp. 435–44.

Mackiewicz, J. (2008) 'Reviewer motivations, bias, and credibility in online reviews'. In S. Kelsey & K. St. Amant (eds.) *Handbook of Research on Computer Mediated Communication* (Hershey, PA: The Idea Group Publishers), pp. 252–66.

Mackiewicz, J. (2010a) 'Assertions of expertise in online product reviews', *Journal of Business and Technical Communication*, 24(1): 3–28.

Mackiewicz, J. (2010b) 'The co-construction of credibility in online product reviews', *Technical Communication Quarterly*, 19(4): 403–26.

Martin, J. R. & White, P. R. R. (2005) *The Language of Evaluation: Appraisal in English* (Basingstoke and New York: Palgrave Macmillan).

Marwick, A. (2005) '"I'm a Lot More Interesting than a Friendster Profile": Identity presentation, authenticity, and power in social networking services'.

Paper presented at Internet Research 6.0, Chicago, IL. Available at www.tiara. org/papers/marwick_friendster_authenticity_power.doc.

O'Connor, P. (2008) 'User-generated content and travel: A case-study on Tripadvisor.com'. In P. O'Connor, W. Höpken & U. Gretzel (eds.) *Information and Communication Technologies in Tourism: Proceedings of the International Conference in Innsbruck, Austria, 2008* (Vienna: Springer), pp. 47–58.

Ott, M., Choi, Y., Cardie, C. & Hancock, J. (2011) 'Finding deceptive opinion spam by any stretch of the imagination'. In *Proceedings of the 49th Annual Meeting of the Association for Computational Linguistics* (Portland, OR), pp. 309–19.

Page, R. (2012) *Stories and Social Media* (Abingdon: Routledge).

Pollach, I. (2006) 'Electronic word of mouth: A genre analysis of product reviews on consumer opinion web sites'. In *Proceedings of the 39th Hawaii International Conference on System Sciences*. IEEE Computer Society.

Pomerantz, A. (1986). Extreme case formulations: A way of legitimizing claims. *Human Studies*, 9(2-3): 219–29.

Ricci, F. & Wietsma, R. (2006) 'Product reviews in travel decision-making'. In M. Hitz, M. Sigala & J. Murphy (eds.) *Information and Communication Technologies in Tourism, 2006* (Vienna: Springer), pp. 296–307.

Scott, S. (2009) 'Social media through the lens of agential realism'. Paper presented at *Developing Theoretical Innovation: A Workshop on the Issues Surrounding Sociomateriality*. London School of Economics, Information Systems and Innovations Group, Department of Management, June 15–16.

Sen, S. & Lerman, D. (2007) 'Why are you telling me this? An examination into negative consumer reviews on the web', *Journal of Interactive Marketing*, 21: 76–94.

St. Amant, K. (2002) 'When cultures and computers collide: Rethinking computer mediated communication according to international and intercultural communication expectations' *Journal of Business and Technical Communication*, 16(2): 196–214.

Tancer, B. (2008) *Click: What Millions of People are Doing Online and Why it Matters* (New York: Hyperion).

Turkle, S. (1999) 'Cyberspace and identity', *Contemporary Sociology*, 28: 643–8.

Vásquez, C. (2011) 'Complaints online: The case of TripAdvisor', *Journal of Pragmatics*, 43: 1707–17.

Vermeulen, I. & Seeger, D. (2009) 'Tried and tested: The impact of online hotel reviews and consumer considerations', *Tourism Management*, 30: 123–7.

Wood, A. & Smith, M. (2005) *Online Communication: Linking Technology, Identity, Culture* (Mahwah, NJ: Erlbaum).

Yoo, K.-H. & Gretzel, U. (2009) 'Comparison of deceptive and truthful travel reviews'. In W. Hopken, U. Gretzel & R. Law (eds.) *Information and Communication Technologies in Tourism, 2009* (Vienna: Springer), pp. 37–47.

Zehrer, A., Crotts, J. C. & Magnini, V. P. (2011) 'The perceived usefulness of blog postings: An extension of the expectancy-disconfirmation paragdigm', *Tourism Management*, 32(1): 106–13.

Zhao, S., Grasmuck, S. & Martin, J. (2008) 'Identity construction on Facebook: Digital empowerment in anchored relations', *Computers in Human Behavior*, 24: 1816–36.

Zimmerman, D. H. (1998) 'Identity, context and interaction. Identities in talk'. In C. Antaki & S. Widdicombe (eds.) *Identities in Talk* (London: Sage), pp. 87–106.

4

Language choice and self-presentation in social media: the case of university students in Hong Kong

Carmen Lee

1 Introduction

> *When I leave a comment on my colleague's Facebook page, I know that some of his students may be able to see it...so I pretend to sound serious and formal...so that our students would think that we are talking about something constructive... I take time to polish and edit [my comments].*
>
> (Tony, 3rd year undergraduate student and a pre-service English teacher in Hong Kong)

This chapter focuses on the relationship between identity performance and language choice in social media, and how such choice may be shaped by existing practices in more traditional media. Identity is a fluid concept. Some aspects of identity are relatively static and not easy to change, such as age, gender, and nationality. Other aspects are defined by social domains (e.g. work, family, and education) and relationships (e.g. friends, colleagues, and family). Some forms of identity can change from time to time, such as hobbies, interests and social networks. The plural form *identities* thus seems a more appropriate term to use in the context of this chapter. What this understanding of identity also highlights is that these properties are not pre-determined and fixed, but are open to transformation and changes. These changes may be a result of different contexts of interaction, or the ways interlocutors interpret the identities being projected. In any given context of interaction, there may be one or more aspects of identity that people may or may not want to express or reveal. Identities, as Goffman (1990[1959]) puts it, are like masks that can be worn and taken off in different contexts of social interaction.

Paying attention to different forms of self-presentation is evident in new social media such as Facebook. The quote at the beginning of the chapter describes how a pre-service teacher, Tony, deliberately puts on a 'serious and formal' persona by carefully editing his comments on his colleague's Facebook wall. In a more casual context of Facebook use, he may assert a more playful identity through a different language and writing style. To explore such dynamics, this chapter first provides an overview of spaces for identity construction in social media. I then introduce a techno-biographic approach to researching identities online, using data from a study of Hong Kong undergraduate students' writing activities on Web 2.0. This method allows me to understand the participants' current linguistic practices in social media against the backdrop of their everyday experiences as well as their life-long relationship with technologies. Using a detailed discussion of Tony's case, I illustrate how his deployment of languages in two Facebook accounts is related to his existing linguistic practices in traditional forms of computer-mediated platforms (e.g. email and online forums), and to the changing roles in his life as he moves from being a student to a teacher. I conclude the chapter by discussing the significance of situating one's current linguistic practices online within one's life history of technology use.

2   Self-presentation in social media

Seeing identity as a multifaceted concept allows for a better understanding of the dynamics of self-presentation online. As many forms of computer-mediated interaction are largely text-based and support limited physical contextual cues, there is room for people to perform different features of identities, primarily through linguistic means. Identity management through language is evident in all forms of computer-mediated discourse, from Internet Relay Chat (IRC), a real-time chat platform, to newer social media. For example, in IRC, playful and carefully designed nicknames are an important means to catch other participants' attention so as to initiate a new conversation. This is because associative meaning is usually embedded in a nickname to signal aspects of one's identity (e.g. *Blondie* suggesting the user's hair colour). Of course, using nicknames is just a starting point to self-presentation. Other features of identity online may be less explicitly asserted, for example, through creative forms of spelling (Androutsopoulos, 2007) or style-shifting (Warschauer, Said & Zohry, 2007; Tagg & Seargeant, 2012).

The different forms of participation and senses of audience in social media seem to have changed the way people think about themselves and thus their ways of constructing self-identities online. An important feature of social media is *sharing* moments of life with large groups of people who may be close friends or complete strangers. Blogging and frequent updating of status messages on social network sites are examples of such social sharing. People may share their lives in a 'publicly private' manner (Lange, 2007), that is, where the identity of the content poster is revealed but access to the content posted is relatively controlled. An example of such publicly private behaviour is the use of real names on Facebook while not making posts available to the public. Others may do the opposite through 'privately public' behaviour, posting publicly available content without letting others know who the poster is. Posting a public comment on YouTube under a nickname is one example of this. On Flickr, identifying oneself with a screen name is a common practice. But compared to nickname use in IRC, it seems that people on Flickr are more willing to give themselves screen names that signal all or part of their real names (e.g. *Dave_George, Carolink*) (Lee & Barton, 2012).

The new technological affordances of social media provide opportunities for users to draw upon a wider range of multimodal resources in the expression of their identities. Not only can social media users present themselves through the written word, but also through a 'spectacle' page (Androutsopoulos, 2010), which is a self-presentation space that combines images, videos, written and spoken language, etc. Video blogs on YouTube are often accompanied by written information, including titles and tags. These resources combine to form a spectacle through which audiences can extract information about the video posters' identities. Flickr is another site where users can make use of profile pages alongside their photo streams to construct their identities. One interesting phenomenon on Flickr is how users often upload a self-portrait or a birthday cake, with the caption 'Happy birthday to me!'. What is perhaps unusual about this example is how these photos draw attention to the self and are then shared publicly. This is what Crandall (2007) refers to as 'presentational' culture, where people constantly pay attention to self. Here, the 'self' refers to one's image or aspects of identity to be projected to a wide range of audiences.

In impression management in social media there is often tension between the different kinds of self that people want to project (DiMicco & Millen, 2007). Sometimes the 'actual self' (aspects of identity that one possesses) is revealed. At other times people may want to project their 'ideal self' (what one wants to possess) and their 'ought self' (what one should possess) (Higgins, 1987). In view of this, identities in social media are not just about *who we are*, but also *who we want to be to others*, and *how others see us* or expect us to be. When participating in social media, people do not behave as just a single, self-contained identity, but as networked individuals (Wellman, 2001). As I will show in the data presented in this chapter, social media participants constantly present different aspects of identity through careful choice of language according to their audience and the technological affordances of different platforms. This also implies that identity management online is always situated in, and must be interpreted with reference to, a particular context. It is thus crucial to observe authentic interactional contexts as well as the participants' lived experiences in relation to their online participation.

3 A techno-biographic approach to language and identity

A meaningful way of studying the situated nature of language and identity online is via a techno-biographic approach. A *techno-biography* is, in short, a life story in relation to technologies. The notion itself is inspired by the traditional narrative approach to interviews, where an interviewee tells a story about certain significant events in life (Linde, 1987; Rosenwald & Ochberg, 1992). This storytelling process not only allows interviewees to recount facts, but also to make sense of their own experiences. The application of this approach to people's experiences with technology is motivated by the fact that using technologies now means something more than just skills – for one thing, most technologies have been domesticated (Berker *et al.*, 2005; Silverstone & Haddon, 1996), meaning that they are embedded in our day-to-day activities and the environments in which we use them. With smartphones and other mobile devices, we are 'always on' and this blurs the boundaries between our so-called online and offline lives, and between our public and private personae.

In her major work on women's technology-related lives, Kennedy (2003) defines techno-biographies as participants' accounts of everyday relationships with technology. Ching and Vigdor's work further refines the notion and considers techno-biographies as participants' encounters with technology 'at various times and in various locations throughout their histories' (Ching & Vigdor, 2005, p. 4). In a techno-biographic interview, questions for the participants may range from their past experiences with technology, to their current uses of technology and anticipated future technology use. Techno-biographic interviews are also highly reflexive in nature. How people feel about what they do with technologies is crucial in understanding possible changes in their practices.

Studies in different countries have demonstrated the significance of focusing on how technology is experienced by internet users throughout their lives – from childhood through to adulthood. For example, Selfe and Hawisher (2004) study what they call literacies of technology in the United States through the literacy histories of 20 informants. These literacies are defined as social practices embedded in people's larger cultural ecology, which in turn is shaped by a number of interrelated factors which affect different ways of using and experiencing technology. Ching and Vigdor (2005, p. 3) add that 'technology experiences are... imbued with meaning by the motivations, social interactions, and contexts surrounding technology tools and practices'.

A life history approach also implies that technologies are not just about 'kids' or 'teenagers' as many previous studies have focused on. After years of experiences with technologies, many adults possess their own histories of technology use, in which phases and changes are noted. In an innovative study of the 'digital histories' of a group of teachers in the UK, Graham (2008) looks into the relationship between how the teachers first learned about technologies and the ways in which they incorporate them into their teaching practices now.

This body of work has provided solid foundations for understanding how language use online relates to people's everyday experiences with technologies. It also provides strong evidence for the heterogeneous nature of technology use. However, the major problem with this limited body of research on techno-biography is that studies have relied solely on interviews as the only source of techno-biographic data. Despite its methodological merits, this traditional techno-biographic approach seems largely mono-dimensional, and often overly reliant on participants' own recounts. Researchers remain rather passive and uninformed when it comes to the participants' situated instances of technology use. The study reported in this chapter thus extends the scope of techno-biography and involves a wider range of research instruments and data sources (see next section for details), as well as paying closer attention to language-related issues in techno-biographies.

4   The study

The research reported upon in this chapter grew out of a broader study that looked into the ways in which a group of bilingual undergraduate students in Hong Kong deployed their multiple linguistic resources on Web 2.0 sites. These resources include not only the various spoken and written languages available to them, but also the text-making strategies they adopt in online communication. The methods of data collection in the study generally adopted an ethnographic style (Greene & Bloome, 1997; Barton & Hamilton, 1998). That is, instead of the full immersion in a culture involved in 'doing an ethnography', the present study has the narrower and more focused aim of drawing on concepts in ethnographic studies such as paying attention to details in people's lives (Barton, 2011). This involves observing participants' language use online and having close contact with the participants in the form of techno-biographic interviews. These interviews focused largely on participants' online writing activities. Two phases of data collection were involved and multiple methods were adopted: the first phase aimed to elicit demographic information about the students and to identify case participants through an initial online questionnaire survey with around 170 undergraduate students at a university in Hong Kong. This was followed by continuous observation of the Web 2.0 sites most frequented by the participants. The links to these sites were provided by the participants in the survey. The questionnaire also included questions about the participants' linguistic habits in different online and offline domains, such as the language(s) they would use when writing an email to a professor, or when they looked up information for their homework on the web, and so on. This first phase of the study then served as a basis for designing the interview protocol in phase two.

The core data came from the detailed techno-biographic style interviews carried out in phase two with 20 participants, all of whom agreed to further participate in the research as case participants. These student participants also share a similar linguistic repertoire: they speak Cantonese as their primary language in everyday life, while having knowledge of 'standard written Chinese' (a standard written variety taught in school and used in institutional contexts), written Cantonese (a non-standard local variety of writing, which may also be used for informal purposes), and English. English is one of the official languages in Hong Kong where it is taught as a second language. For these university students, English is mainly used as an academic language and perhaps the language of entertainment and pop culture. Mixing Chinese (both standard Chinese and Cantonese) and English in utterances has become a prevalent linguistic practice among educated Hong Kong people.

Each interview started with a screen recording session, where the participant was asked to go online for about 30 minutes with their screen activities recorded using Camtasia. This was followed by a 30–50 minute face-to-face interview, in which the screen-recording was played back and the participant went through what they had done with the researcher.

The questions in the interview centred around pre-determined themes as well as new topics that emerged during the conversation. Follow-up interviews were carried out via the private message function on Facebook (as all participants reported to be active Facebook users). Key areas and questions that were covered in the techno-biographic interviews included the participants' current practices of technology use, their ways of participation, their daily routine of internet use, their history of technology use in different phases of life, ways of using technology in different domains of life, and cross-generational comparisons.

Both within-case and across-case analyses were carried out. For each participant, a profile was first created according to the information obtained from field notes and the various stages of data collection described above. All of the transcripts were coded using ATLAS.ti. in order to look for emerging patterns across the data. Initially, most participants reported to be frequent users of Facebook, blogs, and MSN Messenger (now Windows Live Messenger). As discussed earlier, these social media provide new affordances and ways for online users to write about themselves, thus allowing them to create and constantly update their own autobiographies. In particular, such sites provide writing spaces for users to re-tell their life stories through textual means (Page, 2012), including the creation of profiles, continuous status updating, and visual representation of identities. Below I outline how these three textual means give rise to self-presentation on the participants' most frequented social media.

4.1   Creating an online profile

Many popular social media spaces are profile-driven. A profile is a sketch of basic information about someone. For example, on a Facebook user profile, information can range from demographic details such as name, location, date of birth and education to personal philosophy and interests (or in Facebook's terms, 'likes'). These are optional items and not all of my participants disclose all of these aspects of information about themselves. These profiles are not only an entry point to social networking, but also a key writing space to tell others who they are and how they want to be seen in their various social networks. In late 2011, Facebook launched a new profile layout called Timeline with the slogan: 'Tell your life story with a new kind of profile' which illustrates the auto-biographical affordances of profiles on social network sites. Many other older forms of media such as IM (instant messaging), which was first intended for instant messaging only, now also support social media features, allowing users to create their own profiles and even connect to other social media sites such as Facebook. However, my participants do not seem to be interested in developing profiles in IM, which they mainly use for message exchange.

4.2   Continuous status updating

Another form of self-representation online is posting short updates about your life. These short messages are written from a first person perspective, in the form of small stories (Georgakopoulou, 2007; Page, 2012) serving a wide range of discourse functions from sharing emotions to initiating discussion (Lee, 2011). An interesting example that is often found among my participants' status updates on Facebook is counting the number of words written for an assignment (e.g. 80/2000; 1500/2000). These short updates are evident not only on Facebook, but also in IM. In Windows Live Messenger (WLM), for instance, the status message appears in a text box on the top of the contact list. Documenting life through short messages is even evident in traditional blogging. For example, one participant recorded his day by way of a sequence of time-stamped short messages in one single blog post.

4.3   Visual representation

In addition to the written word, another important form of representation of techno-biography that is especially prevalent in social media is *visual images*, especially photographs. On Facebook, photos can be organized into albums. The names given by my participants to their Facebook albums can serve as a way of telling others about their lives, including their favourites ('the places I love the most') and important events in life ('graduation photos'). Photos uploaded can be annotated with meaningful captions. (See Mendelson & Papacharissi, 2011, on Facebook photo sharing among college students.)

5   An overview of the participants' techno-linguistic lives

Having outlined the various forms that a techno-biography may take in the realm of social media, in this section I present the themes which emerged from the across-case analysis of the 20 techno-biographies. In particular, I focus on the participants' language practices in relation to their technology-related life stories, or what I call their *techno-linguistic biography*.

5.1   Key phases of technology use

The first phase of my participants' technology experiences began when they were very young, at the age of about 9 or 10. Technology mentors, people who first introduced the participants to technologies, played a crucial role in this early stage. Their early experiences with the computer already involved a great deal of reading and writing, such as trying to understand how a piece of game software is installed by reading instructions on the screen, or writing their first email and text message. An important theme that emerged from this phase is the participants' school-based experience with online communication. This experience was relatively controlled, meaning that it involved the teacher asking them to write and send their first email to someone (who was likely to be the teacher as well); how the email should be structured was also prescribed by the teacher. One participant told me that although she writes most of her emails in English now, her very first email was written in standard Chinese because her Chinese language teacher told her to do it this way. Interestingly, when online interaction was taken out of the classroom context, the participants would take control over their language choice:

> *I wrote my first email to my Economics teacher when I was in Secondary 4 [around the age of 15]. One day I chatted with her on icq [an instant messaging service]. We talked about songs. I promised her to send her some great songs that I had heard. So I got her email address and attached a few songs in the mail that I sent her. It was a very rough email with not much editing done in terms of content and language because at that time I didn't mean to share words with her but merely songs. I enjoyed writing to her afterwards and I started bombarding her email account with lots of informal letters. I just loved writing to her. (Yan)*

This early experience clearly demonstrates the situated nature of language use online. When an email took the form of a piece of homework, the participants would take a longer time to proofread and polish their language; when online communication is taken to a more interpersonal level, such as Yan's private interaction with her teacher, 'not much editing' was needed. At this early stage, the participants already learned to deploy their languages and styles of writing according to the purposes of communication and their intended audiences. This attitude to language online seems to be evident in their current writing practices in social media such as Facebook, as I will show later.

Following this first experience with technology is the phase in life where the internet was regularly used for entertainment and socializing with school friends. This was also the time when the participants further developed their online linguistic practices according to their needs and purposes. For most of the university students I have studied (who were born in the late 1980s or early 90s), this exploration phase started in their early secondary school years, between the ages of 11 and 13. They spent a great deal of time on IM (instant messaging), first on ICQ (internet chat query) and later MSN, for interpersonal chat with friends. Language choice varied at this stage. Some started to write in English only because they were yet to learn how to type in Chinese, while others would write messages in Chinese with the help of software and hardware that recognize Chinese handwriting.

The third main phase is concerned with the participants' current practices online and their imagined future internet-related life. In this phase, technologies are perceived as indispensable and are indeed taken for granted. Social media such as Facebook, blogs, and YouTube play an essential role in the participants' lives. Crucially, to these university students, Facebook is where they connect with their friends from university. Some started blogging several years ago but have gradually moved away from blogging to regularly writing Notes (a blogging feature) or longer status updates on Facebook. Linguistically, most participants were able to clearly articulate what different languages meant to them in different domains of online interaction. For example, a few participants said they would use standard Chinese for more 'serious' posts such as status updates that express their emotions and opinions towards certain events in their lives. Cantonese or a mixture of Cantonese and English is reserved for more 'mundane' activity updates.

5.2   Interaction between online and offline language uses

The second theme arising from the 20 techno-biographies is the close relationship between the participants' language choice online and their linguistic repertoire in offline communication. For example, Yan, a second year History major, is also a Hakka speaker as she had lived in mainland China before she moved to Hong Kong at an early age. Even though she uses much Cantonese in her daily life, Hakka (a variety spoken in southern China) is still the dialect she uses when talking to her family. Her Hakka background then immediately broadens the resources she can draw upon in digital discourse. Now she still writes text messages using some stylized Hakka when interacting with her family and old friends in China.

Many participants also made a connection between a particular language and a role that they played in different areas of their lives, such as being a student of a certain subject area, a friend, a family member, a speaker of a certain language, and so on. On different internet platforms, the same language may allow participants to reveal (or hide) different roles they play in life. In the following excerpt, Mark explains how English has different meanings on Facebook and in public discussion forums:

> *I would leave Facebook comments in English because most of my Facebook friends are also English majors like me...because we are used to communicating in English. But at the same time, it is also because I am an English major that I want to avoid using English in public forums...People may judge me if I make mistakes...* (Mark)

Mark's different code preferences for Facebook and online forums demonstrate his ambivalent feelings towards his identity as an English major. When among his fellow English majors, he is happy to foreground his English major identity by maintaining the use of English where occasional errors are tolerated; at other times, he recognizes his possibly insufficient English knowledge may not fit in well with his 'ideal self' as a competent university English major. Mark's perception about his English can be situated within the larger context of public moral panics about university students' falling linguistic standards in Hong Kong and beyond (Bolton, 2002; Thurlow, 2007). He reported that he decided to avoid using English altogether when participating in public online forums because he felt that the public seems to be very judgmental of young people's English skills. Overall, Mark's decisions illustrate how the participants manage their identities through alternating between languages when interacting with different audiences.

5.3   Attitudes towards language online

Decisions such as Mark's also reveal the participants' attitudes towards certain linguistic resources online. In explaining whether or not to write in a particular language online, participants other than Mark explicitly evaluated their own knowledge of the language. Helen, for example, juxtaposed her lack of English skills and limited use of English in blogging with her secondary school life:

> *I never write an entire blog entry in English, as my English isn't good... I came from a Chinese-medium school, you know....* (Helen)

Helen's reference to her limited exposure to English before university shows how past experience is crucial in understanding current practices. Many participants, like Helen, made self-deprecatory comments about the languages they know ('my English isn't good') when talking about their language choice online. It appears that self-evaluations of language are equally prevalent in the texts produced by users of public social media such as Flickr and YouTube. Elsewhere, I have shown how the use of self-deprecatory comments about languages not only allows Flickr users to declare their linguistic identity online, it also seems to be a way of establishing solidarity among members of the Flickr community (Lee, 2013). For example, it is found that a seemingly negative comment about one's own English ability (e.g. 'Sorry about my poor English') tends to attract supportive and encouraging comments from other users. As a language-focused discussion develops on a Flickr page, users also begin to create an informal language learning community.

Others implicitly expressed their linguistic attitudes by aligning themselves with certain groups of speakers. For example, when Mark talked about his participation in mainland Chinese-based online forums, he identified himself as a Chinese person who was expected to write in Chinese, while being aware that in other contexts such as Golden Forum, a local Hong Kong discussion forum, he would have used some English if presenting himself as a Hongkonger. Such conscious positioning and repositioning are helpful in revealing a participant's stance towards different languages.

6   Tony's case: juggling between student and teacher identities on Facebook

Although I have outlined above some shared stages and characteristics of my participants' techno-linguistic biographies, a closer look at individual participants' lives can reveal how language use online is embedded in their lived experiences, and that everyone has a unique relationship with technologies at different stages of life. In this section, I present a case study of Tony, a quote from whom was introduced at the beginning of this chapter. Through a more detailed analysis of Tony's case, I demonstrate how his current linguistic practices on Facebook are shaped partly by his practices in more traditional online media and his perceptions of his identities in different contexts, as well as his relationship to his interlocutors.

At the time of interview, Tony was a third-year undergraduate student majoring in English Language Education at a university in Hong Kong. He was then half-way through his teaching practice in a secondary school. He reported to have started using the computer when he was about 10 years old. It was his elder brother who introduced him to the world of the internet, mainly through playing games online with strangers from other parts of the world. He recalled that the instructions and interfaces of the games he used to play were written in English only. English at that time was 'too complicated' for him, but he could work out how the games were played by 'trial and error'. There were no social media of the sort there are now back then in the 1990s. Tony nonetheless was able to develop his social network with his fellow gamers on international gaming sites such as MSN Games Zone (now MSN Games) using simple English phrases such as 'good' or 'good game'. Although at present Tony seldom uses English as a language of socializing (e.g. on Facebook with friends), it remains his primary language in online gaming.

Tony's early online relationship with English in gaming did not seem to carry over to IM, the platform that he regularly used to chat with school friends when he was a teenager. Although occasionally chatting in English, he viewed Chinese as his primary language in IM. He explained in the interview:

> *I can think faster in Chinese so I can form a sentence easily…If I write in English (online) I have to check my grammar.*
> [...]
> *When chatting in MSN, I used Chinese most of the time…Most of my friends speak Cantonese…We know each other very well…Communicating in Cantonese with them was more accurate than in English…I could say what I wanted to say in Cantonese…and there are many slang words in Cantonese that can't be captured in English…*

Tony's preference for Cantonese is in line with my findings in early studies of IM among Hong Kong university students (Lee, 2007). The various linguistic resources available to the Hong Kong participants, including Cantonese and English, are perceived to have different affordances for different communicative contexts. In particular, written Cantonese is often treated as the most expressive language by local Hong Kong students. In Tony's techno-biography, Cantonese was frequently mentioned as the language that allowed him to 'think faster' while chatting with friends informally online, as it was the primary spoken language that he used in everyday talk with friends. This 'perceived affordance' of Cantonese in IM seemed to have influenced Tony's current language practices on Facebook. On Facebook, especially when commenting on a friend's post, he writes primarily in Cantonese. Facebook commenting, to Tony, resembles a private chat exchange in IM, where close-to-real-time exchanges of comments with the same interlocutor may develop into a long conversation. Although Cantonese seems to be his primary language in social media, Tony does regularly insert English words and expressions into his Cantonese-based messages on IM and Facebook. His code-mixing practice will be discussed later.

A key factor that shapes Tony's language choice online is his self-image. Various instances of self-positioning are observed in Tony's techno-biography. First of all, his Hong Kong identity was frequently asserted when he explained his choice between English and Chinese. Tony regularly visits mainland China-based online discussion forums on which most participants interact in Mandarin Chinese only. When asked whether he would mix Chinese with English in these China-based forums as he would do in IM or Facebook, he rejected the idea. He implied that mainland Chinese online users possess a rather different linguistic repertoire from Hong Kong users. He added:

> *I am a Chinese too...Chinese is my mother tongue...[...] When I partici-*
> *pate in Chinese-based forums, most people use Chinese...If you switch to*
> *English, that shows you are a Hong Kong person...I am not saying that*
> *I am special...but using English may offend the mainland Chinese forum*
> *participants.*

In this comment, Tony first explicitly asserts his Chineseness as a way of aligning himself to other Chinese forum users. Chinese is seen as the language that validates his Chinese identity, thus legitimizing his use of it online. At the same time he is well aware of his identity as a Hongkonger, with a rather unique historical and political background, and thus a different range of linguistic resources. Tony's awareness of 'we' and 'they' codes (Sebba & Wooton, 1998) seems to be implicitly revealed here. That is, English is an immediate index of Tony's 'Hongkonger' identity ('we') which mainland Chinese people ('they') do not possess. His perceived national identity online is only one of the many aspects of identity that he performs through his constant negotiation of language choice.

Alongside his ethnic/national identities, Tony frequently made connections to his student-self and his teacher-self when justifying his language choices on Facebook. Currently he has signed up for two Facebook accounts – one as a student to communicate with his 'real' friends and the other, in his role as a teacher, for his students and colleagues only. In the interview, Tony seemed to have mixed feelings towards his 'English student' identity (cf. the comments of Mark mentioned earlier). He said he did not want to post in English only in his student Facebook account because his English was 'not good enough'. This resonates with Helen's and Mark's comments mentioned earlier, where language choice online is partly determined by the participants' self-conception of their English proficiency level. And in this case, avoiding posting in English only is a way of preventing his Facebook friends from judging his English knowledge in relation to his English major identity. This, however, does not mean that Tony avoids English altogether. He frequently inserts English words in his Chinese posts, as shown in two of his status updates:

收到了Jim Scrivener 2010的新作<<Teaching English Grammar>>, 如果我TP之前就買左就好lah......
(Translation: Just received Jim Scrivener's new work in 2010 *Teaching English Grammar*. I wish I had bought this before my teaching practice.)

薯片佬,今次我十卜你la!
(Translation: Pringles man, I support you this time!)
[followed by a link to a piece of local Hong Kong news online.]

The first example is a Cantonese-based post with insertion of English expressions such as 'TP' (teaching practice); 'lah' is a creative romanized spelling of the Cantonese discourse particle 喇. The use of ellipsis dots (......) at the end of the post has been recognized as a common feature in online writing (Crystal, 2001). The second example contains a case of phonetic borrowing – the Cantonese pronunciation of '十卜' resembles that of the English word 'support'; 'la' is again a romanized discourse particle in Cantonese. Both phonetic borrowing and writing discourse particles in the roman script have been documented in earlier studies of IM in Hong Kong (James, 2001; Lee, 2002). Ng's (2012) recent research on Facebook status updates among Hong Kong university students has also confirmed that Hong Kong students' bilingual interactions on Facebook preserve some linguistic features from their earlier practices on IM or even in email. Herring (2013) refers to such direct transfer of discursive practices from an older medium to Web 2.0 sites as 'familiar' practices. Mixing English in his Cantonese-based sentences is not an entirely new practice in Tony's history of technology use. Before Facebook, Tony had already been used to code-mixing in other forms of computer-mediated texts, especially IM, for about ten years. According to Tony's techno-biographic account of his previous language use online, mixed-code chat resembles an everyday conversation with friends. This hope for a conversation-like environment extends to his current Facebook use. Transferring an existing practice to a new platform also enables Tony and his friends to maintain their affinity space which is defined by their shared practice of code-mixing.

Tony's awareness of different audiences is another major reason why he switches between Cantonese, Standard Chinese, and English in different contexts of Facebook use. Referring to his second status update cited above, what is also interesting is that he is addressing the financial secretary of the Hong Kong government, the main subject of the news article shared underneath his words ('Pringles man' is the nickname given to the financial secretary who has a moustache resembling that of the man in the logo of Pringles crisps). Writing a personalized post and sharing external links at the same time on Facebook allows Tony to speak to multiple audiences – while his post seems to be addressing someone who may never read his Facebook site, it was shared to a wider group of Facebook friends who might also have a view after reading the news article shared by Tony.

Tony, as a pre-service English teacher, also keeps in touch with the students in his teaching practice school in his second Facebook account where he calls himself *Teaching Tony*. This nickname, which he has never used in other online spaces, immediately indexes his perception of who he should be in this other Facebook account. He said:

> *I started this teacher Facebook account towards the end of my teaching practice. I was worried that if my students discovered my 'real' Facebook account, I had to reshape my identity for them.*

Tony did make an effort to 'reshape' his identity on this teacher Facebook page. Compared to his student Facebook account, where he never friends his students and colleagues, he posts less regularly on this teacher site. He also takes on a more academic discourse style and only shares posts that he feels are of interest to his students, such as links to an online English dictionary and posts about the progress of his teaching and grading work. In terms of language choice, he writes almost all the posts in English. He said it would have been 'inappropriate' to use Chinese there because, as an English teacher, he had to stick to this medium of instruction in order to encourage students to write to him in English too. The following two status updates are indicative of his language choice and the communicative functions of his posts in his teacher Facebook:

> Dear 4R students,
> I have put copies of three sets of reading practice paper in my cabinet outside staff room. Please come and get it yourself if you need them.

Time to back to school again! Good luck for your homework and the coming tests!

Both messages are primarily directed to his students (and perhaps his colleagues who have access to his Facebook wall). From the content of the other status updates on his teacher Facebook wall, it is clear that Tony is using Facebook not just as a social network site to connect with his students, but also as a teaching and learning tool where he can make class-related announcements and share English learning links and videos and so on with his students.

Doing his best to maintain his image as a teacher, Tony was also very conscious of privacy issues and his level of self-exposure when posting on Facebook as *Teaching Tony*. As mentioned at the beginning of the chapter, although posting on his colleague's wall, Tony was well aware of the fact that his posts immediately became 'publically performed conversations' (Jones, 2012, p. 108), which are constantly read by people who might not be directly involved in the conversations at all (see also Tagg & Seargeant, this volume). This sense of audience is quite different from that on IM, where interlocutors are more clearly defined. Thus, while a high level of self-disclosure is evident on Facebook and many social media, it is still necessary for Tony to carefully negotiate his ways of writing in order to manage his social relationships with different kinds of audience.

To sum up, Tony's language use in different social media, and especially on Facebook, is shaped by a combination of identity-related factors. On the one hand, his decisions as to whether to mix languages or not are strongly determined by his various self-conceptions. On the other hand, his language practices and writing style vary when facing different audience groups in his two Facebook accounts. His language choice perhaps also reveals some tension between his different senses of self, or in Higgin's (1987) terms, his *actual self* as a Hongkonger, a student and friend; his *ideal self* as an English major who speaks and writes good English; as well as his *ought self* as an English teacher who interacts with his students in English only.

7 Conclusion

Writing online is writing oneself 'into being' (boyd, 2008, p.120). This chapter has shown how a group of 20 university students in Hong Kong 'write' their lives by taking up the new affordances or possibilities of social media, especially IM, blogs and Facebook. The practices of self-presentation on these sites are far more dynamic and complex than those in older media, from creating user profiles to regularly updating short messages and using multimodal resources to accompany their verbal posts. The 20 techno-biographic interviews also reveal how these new writing spaces allow participants to project or extend existing aspects of identity, such as being someone from a certain culture or country, or being a student of a particular subject.

Tony's case demonstrates various factors that shape language choice in social media. These include his previous linguistic practices online, his self-image and how he wants others to see him. His attitude towards mixing Chinese and English online is a familiar one, as he was used to doing so in IM, a platform that he frequented when he was a teenager. Tony's juggling between his student-self and teacher-self on two Facebook sites provides a telling case of his identity management when facing different audience groups. What Tony was doing was extending his offline identities as both a student and as a teacher, as well as his offline relationships with others. Switching between languages on two Facebook accounts allows him to maintain these personae and relationships. Certainly, these insider perspectives would not have been elicited by observing the texts on Facebook alone. The techno-biographic approach taken in the study pays closer attention to the situated nature of social media, tracing changes in language use at different stages of language users' technology-related lives. A focus on past experience reveals how older practices may shape newer ones.

More broadly, although the 20 techno-biographies reveal some shared activities online, individual participants' linguistic practices, their attitudes towards these media in relation to language choice and their sense of self-identity and audience vary to some extent. Every individual has a unique technology-related life, revealing how different aspects of identity are developed over time. The case study of Tony illustrates how his language use varies according to his particular sense of audience and context, and the different purposes for which he uses social media. As a result, the participants cannot be seen as part of a homogeneous *digital natives* generation (Prensky, 2001), a group of young people that has been over-generalized in mass media and public discourse (see Takahashi, this volume, for a similar critique). In fact, the idea of digital natives seems to overlook the variety of knowledge and experience in young people (Hargittai, 2010; Bennett, Maton & Kervin, 2008). As social media present new affordances and converge with other media in the digital world, it is predicted that newer social media will only give rise to even greater diversity of both technology users and linguistic practices.

Acknowledgements

The author would like to thank the editors Philip Seargeant and Caroline Tagg for their insightful comments and editorial support throughout the writing of the chapter. The project reported in this chapter was funded by the General Research Fund of the Hong Kong Research Grants Council (Ref: 446309).

References

Androutsopoulos, J. (2007) 'Style online: Doing hip-hop on the German-speaking Web'. In P. Auer (ed.) *Style and Social Identities: Alternative Approaches to Linguistic Heterogeneity* (Berlin: de Gruyter), pp. 279–317.

Androutsopoulos, J. (2010) 'Localizing the global on the participatory web'. In N. Coupland (ed.) *The Handbook of Language and Globalization* (Oxford; Wiley-Blackwell), pp. 203–31.

Barton, D. (2011). 'Ethnographic approaches to literacy research'. In *Encyclopedia of Applied Linguistics* (Oxford: Wiley-Blackwell).

Barton, D. & Hamilton, M. (1998). *Local Literacies* (London: Routledge).

Bennett, S., Maton, K. & Kervin, L. (2008) 'The "digital natives" debate: A critical review of the evidence', *British Journal of Educational Technology*, 39(5): 775–86.

Berker, T., Hartmann, M., Punie, Y. & Ward, K. (eds.) (2005). *Domestication of Media and Technologies* (Maidenhead: Open University Press).

Bolton, K. (2002) 'The sociolinguistics of Hong Kong and the space for Hong Kong English'. In K. Bolton (ed.) *Hong Kong English: Autonomy and Creativity* (Hong Kong: Hong Kong University Press), pp. 29–56.

boyd, d. (2008) 'Why youth (heart) social network sites: The role of networked publics in teenage social life'. In D. Buckingham (ed.) *Youth, Identity, and Digital Media* (Cambridge, MA: MIT Press), pp. 119–42.

Ching, C. C. & Vigdor, L. (2005) Technobiographies: Perspectives from Education and the Arts. Paper presented at the First International Congress of Qualitative Inquiry, Champaign, IL.

Crandall, J. (2007) Showing, http://jordancrandall.com/showing/index.html (accessed: 1 May 2012).

Crystal, D. (2001) *Language and the Internet* (Cambridge: Cambridge University Press).

DiMicco, J. M. & Millen, D. R. (2007) 'Identity management: Multiple presentations of self in Facebook'. In *Proceedings of the 2007 International ACM Conference on Supporting Group Work*, pp. 383–6.

Georgakopoulou, A. (2007) *Small Stories, Interaction, and Identities* (Amsterdam/Philadelphia: John Benjamins).

Goffman, E. (1990[1959]). *The Presentation of Self in Everyday Life* (London: Penguin).

Graham, L. (2008) 'Teachers are digikids too: The digital histories and digital lives of young teachers in English primary schools', *Literacy*, 42(1): 10–18.

Greene, J. & Bloome, D. (1997) 'Ethnography and ethnographers of and in education: A situated perspective'. In J. Flood, S. B. Heath & D. Lapp (eds.) *Handbook of Research in Teaching Literacy through the Communicative and Visual Arts* (New York: Simon Schuster, Macmillan).

Hargittai, E. (2010) 'Digital na(t)ives? Variation in Internet skills and uses among members of the "Net Generation"', *Sociological Enquiry*, 80: 92–113.

Herring, S. C. (2013) 'Discourse in Web 2.0: Familiar, reconfigured, and emergent'. In D. Tannen & A. M. Tester (eds.) *Discourse 2.0: Language and New Media* (Washington, DC: Georgetown University Press).

Higgins, E. T. (1987) 'Self-discrepancy: A theory relating self and affect', *Psychological Review*, 94(3): 319–40.

James, G. (2001) 'Cantonese particles in Hong Kong students' English emails', *English Today*, 17: 9–16.

Jones, R. (2012) *Discourse Analysis* (Abingdon: Routledge).

Kennedy, H. (2003) 'Technobiography: Researching lives, online and off', *Biography*, 26(1): 120–39.

Lange, P. (2007) 'Publicly private and privately public: Social networking on YouTube', *Journal of Computer-Mediated Communication*, 13(1). www.cs.uwaterloo.ca/~apidduck/CS432/Assignments/YouTube.pdf (accessed 1 May 2012).

Lee, C. (2002) 'Literacy practices of computer-mediated communication in Hong Kong'. Special Issue of *Reading Matrix: Literacy and the Web*, 2(2). www.readingmatrix.com/articles/lee/article.pdf (accessed: 1 May 2012).

Lee, C. (2007) 'Affordances and text-making practices in online instant messaging', *Written Communication*, 24(3): 223–49.

Lee, C. (2011) 'Texts and practices of micro-blogging: Status updates on Facebook'. In C. Thurlow & K. Mroczek (eds.) *Digital Discourse: Language in New Media* (Oxford: Oxford University Press), pp. 110–30.

Lee, C. (2013) 'My English is so poor...so I take photos'. Meta-linguistic discourse of English online'. In D. Tannen & A. M. Tester (eds.) *Discourse 2.0: Language and New Media* (Washington, DC: Georgetown University Press).

Lee, C. & Barton, D. (2012) 'Researching the texts and practices in an online photo-sharing site'. In M. Sebba, S. Mahootian & C. Jonsson (eds.) *Language Mixing and Code-Switching in Writing: Approaches to Mixed-Language Written Discourse* (Abingdon: Routledge), pp. 128–45.

Linde, C. (1987) 'Explanatory systems in oral life stories'. In D. Holland & N. Quinn (eds.) *Cultural Models in Language and Thought* (New York: Cambridge University Press), pp. 343–66.

Mendelson, A. L. & Papacharissi, Z. (2011) 'Look at us: Collective narcissism in college student Facebook photo galleries'. In Z. Papacharissi (ed.) *The Networked Self: Identity, Community and Culture on Social Network Sites* (Abingdon: Routledge), pp. 251–73.

Ng, T. H. (2012) Facebook Communication in Hong Kong: An Evolved ICQ Interaction in Bilingualism. Unpublished MA thesis, Chinese University of Hong Kong.

Page, R. (2012) *Stories and Social Media: Identities and Interaction* (Abingdon: Routledge).

Prensky, M. (2001) 'Digital natives, digital immigrants', *On the Horizon* 9(1): 1–6.

Rosenwald, G., & Ochberg, R. (1992) *Storied Lives: The Cultural Politics of Self-understanding* (New Haven, CT: Yale University Press).

Sebba, M. & Wootton, T. (1998) 'We, they, and identity'. In P. Auer (ed.) *Code-switching in Conversation: Language, Interaction and Identity* (London: Routledge), pp. 262–89.

Selfe, C. & Hawisher, G. (2004) *Literate Lives in the Information Age* (Mahwah, NJ: Lawrence Erlbaum Associates).

Silverstone, R. & Haddon, L. (1996) 'Design and the domestication of information and communication technologies: Technical change and everyday life'. In R. Mansell & R. Silverstone (eds.) *Communication by Design: The Politics of Information and Communication Technologies* (New York: Oxford University Press), pp. 44–74.

Tagg, C. & Seargeant, P. (2012) 'Writing systems at play in Thai-English online interactions', *Writing Systems Research*, 4(2): 195–213.

Thurlow, C. (2007) 'Fabricating youth: New media discourse and the technologization of young people'. In S. Johnson & A. Ensslin (eds.) *Language in the Media* (London: Continuum), pp. 213–33.

Warschauer, M., El Said, G. R. & Zohry, A. A. (2007) 'Language choice online: Globalization and identity in Egypt'. In B. Danet & S. C. Herring (eds.) *The Multilingual Internet: Language, Culture, and Communication Online* (New York: Oxford University Press), pp. 303–18.

Wellman, B. (2001) 'Physical place and cyber place: The rise of personalized networking', *International Journal of Urban and Regional Research*, 25: 227–52.

5
Entextualization and resemiotization as resources for identification in social media

Sirpa Leppänen, Samu Kytölä, Henna Jousmäki, Saija Peuronen and Elina Westinen

1 Introduction

Drawing on insights provided by linguistic anthropology, the study of multisemioticity and research in computer-mediated discourse (CMD), this chapter discusses how entextualization (Bauman & Briggs, 1990; Silverstein & Urban, 1996; Blommaert, 2005, pp. 46–8) and resemiotization (Iedema, 2003; Scollon & Scollon, 2004, pp. 101–3; Scollon, 2008) are key resources for identity work in social media. Three key arguments inspire and give direction to our discussion, each of them laying down touchstones for language scholars who wish to investigate identity in social media. First, for many individuals and social or cultural groups, social media are increasingly significant grassroots arenas for interaction and cultural activities (Androutsopoulos, 2011; Kytölä, 2012a, 2012b; Leppänen, 2012; Peuronen, 2011) which overlap, complement and intertwine in different ways with their offline activities. Importantly, social media encompass a range of diverse formats for social action, interaction and performance; thus they can be 'social' in quite different ways (see Baym, 2011, pp. 6–12) and offer various kinds of affordances for, and constraints on, identity performance.

Second, from an ontological and terminological perspective, we shift the focus here from 'identity' to acts and processes of *identification* and *disidentification*. We argue that in social media, identities are seldom assumed or transparent (or remain so); rather, they are performed in chains and skeins of activities and interactions. Identities are constructed in active processes of identification and self-understanding, seeking or eschewing commonality, connectedness and groupness (Androutsopoulos & Georgakopoulou, 2003; Blommaert, 2005, pp. 203–14; Brubaker & Cooper, 2000; Krzyżanowski & Wodak, 2008).

Third, we suggest that crucial resources for the performance of identity in social media are the closely related processes of *resemiotization* and *entextualization*. Communication in social media involves not only resources provided by language(s), but also other semiotic resources – textual forms and patterns, still and moving images, sounds and cultural discourses – as well as the mobilization of these in processes of decontextualization and recontextualization. The language of social media is thus woven from multiple and intertwined semiotic materials (see Kress & van Leeuwen, 1996, pp. 1–43; Jacquemet, 2005; Blommaert & Rampton, 2011) which are socially significant and culturally valuable to the immediate participants and groups involved.

As an illustration of the relevance and implications of these theoretical premises, we investigate four social media settings which provide different affordances for the performance of (dis)identification, and show how the participants in each of them draw in different ways and by different semiotic means on entextualization and resemiotization for specific social and cultural ends. First, however, we introduce and define the key concepts and orientations deployed for the purposes of our argument.

2   Key concepts and analytic orientations

In this chapter, we are defining social media broadly as online environments which enable social interaction (Baym, 2011; Fornäs *et al.*, 2002) between participants either synchronously, with an ephemeral output (e.g. chat channels, 'shoutboxes'), or asynchronously, often with more long-lasting 'end-products' (e.g. blogs, web discussion forums; see e.g. Kytölä, 2012a, 2012b). Thus, in our orientation, social media include, besides social network sites, other digital environments in which interaction between the participants constitutes an important part of their activities. Another key characteristic of social media is that they may constitute only one of the settings in which the participants or groups engage in shared activities – online activities may interweave with their activities in offline contexts (see, for example, Monaghan, this volume). The degree to which the interaction between the participants is organized can also vary. In some cases, the participants can, over time, organize themselves as relatively stable communities of practice (see e.g. Lave & Wenger, 1991; Eckert & McConnell-Ginet, 1992; Gee 2004). Alternatively, their activities can take place within more short-lived 'affinity spaces', stemming from shared interests, causes, lifestyles, activities and cultural products with short life spans or passing popularity

(Gee, 2004). Both long-lived communities of practice and more ephemeral affinity spaces can, however, offer their participants deeply meaningful arenas for shared social practice as part of a participatory, active 'prosumer' (producer + consumer) culture (Burgess & Green, 2009; Leppänen & Häkkinen, 2012).

The sociality of social media environments also shows in how their social and normative structures are jointly negotiated and enforced by the participants themselves (Leppänen, 2009; Kytölä, 2012b). In this sense, they exemplify what could be called 'post-Panopticon' sociality (e.g. Haggerty, 2006; Arnaut, 2012; Leppänen & Piirainen-Marsh, 2009), manifest in their lack of centralized mechanisms of control by 'those in power' and in a shift to forms of grassroots, 'bottom-up' and peer surveillance. These are often polycentric in that participants can orient to, and shift between, several competing and complementary orders of normativity (Blommaert, 2010, pp. 37–9).

As in any social environment, participants in social media need to reflexively conceptualize and performatively construct themselves, and navigate as particular kinds of personae in relation to their surroundings. Identity is thus both actively 'done' and contractually 'achieved'. Following Brubaker and Cooper (2000, pp. 14–21), we argue that such complex (dis)identification work is best conceptualized as a dynamic and multifaceted process involving affinity, alignment, emotional attachment and ideological notions of togetherness. First, it entails self-characterization of oneself *vis à vis* others and external characterization of oneself by others. This characterization can be either relational (with respect to the relationship to others) or categorical (as a member of a particular category). Second, identification includes a psycho-dynamic dimension in that individuals align emotionally with another person, category or collectivity. Third, identity also involves self-understanding, a practical perception of who one is and what one's role is in the social environment. Fourth, in identity performance, individuals seek – or eschew – commonality (what they share with others) and connectedness (ties linking them to others). Finally, commonality, and to a lesser extent connectedness, are also prerequisites for groupness, a sense of belonging to a group. Groupness requires that a particular social constellation believes that they actually share something (e.g. a sense of belonging to the same nation). In social media activities, it is the semiotic constructions and processes of indexing or eluding commonality, connectedness and groupness which are available for investigation. These processes will be central in our discussion in this chapter.

Another key argument here is that, in social media, entextualization and resemiotization are vital semiotic resources for identity performance, and useful analytical notions in understanding complex social media practices. These two concepts stem from different research traditions: entextualization originates in the nexus of anthropology and discourse studies (e.g. performance studies; Bauman & Briggs, 1990; Silverstein & Urban, 1996), while resemiotization was introduced within the research field of social semiotics (e.g. studies of multimodality; Kress & van Leeuwen, 1996; Iedema, 2003). For our exploration of social media activities, these research traditions and concepts offer a complementary analytic purchase. This is because both make it possible to trace the ways in which social media activities frequently and crucially build on the active recirculation and appropriation of complex multi-semiotic material.

More specifically, what the notion of entextualization offers the analyst is the identification and analysis of the trajectories and re-uses of language and textual material as resources in meaning-making (Bauman & Briggs, 1990, p. 73; Blommaert, 2005, pp. 46–8; Silverstein & Urban, 1996). Entextualization highlights how such recycling involves two related processes: decontextualization – taking discourse material out of its context – and recontextualization – integrating and modifying this material so that it fits in a new context. With entextualization in our analytical toolkit, it becomes possible to investigate how social media participants, through extracting 'instances of culture' (language forms, textual or other semiotic material) and relocating these in *their* discourses and repertoires, perform identity at the grassroots level of social media activities.

In these activities people are, following the original argument by Bauman and Briggs (1990, p. 76), active agents for whom entextualization is 'an act of control' through which they can claim a degree of social power. This power manifests in various ways: it shows in their access to the activity of entextualization, in the legitimacy of their claims to re-use the texts, in their competence in such re-use, and in the differential values attached to various types of texts. For the analysis of social media activities, these four issues of discursive power are of particular relevance: they imply that the investigation of entextualization is about discovering 'empirically what means are available in a given social setting, to whom they may be available, under what circumstances, for making discourse into text' (Bauman & Briggs 1990, p. 74).

The affordances of social media for the performance of identity through entextualization are aptly described by Kress and van Leeuwen

(1996, p. 34) as 'the new realities of the semiotic landscape'. With this statement, they point to processes of change taking place at different levels (the nation state, technology, and the economy) that not only have an impact on political and cultural boundaries but also on *semiotic boundaries*. Therefore, the second concept that we wish to introduce here for the study of (dis)identification in social media is resemiotization, the process of semiotic change in the circulation and flow of discourses across social and cultural boundaries.

While entextualization offers the analyst a tool for explaining how in social media activities discourse material originating elsewhere gets lifted out of its original context and is repositioned and remodified as a meaningful element in a new context, resemiotization focuses on the examination of the unfolding and re-articulation of meaning across modes and modalities, and from some groups of people to others (see Iedema, 2003, p. 41; Scollon & Scollon, 2004; Scollon, 2008). Further, whereas entextualization foregrounds the issue of social access, control and competence in textual 'work', resemiotization emphasizes the need for 'socio-historical exploration and understanding of the complex processes which constitute and surround' meaning-makings (Iedema, 2003, p. 48). Nevertheless, as in entextualization, so too in resemiotization there is a dialectical and dynamic tension between the patterns (cf. Iedema's 'schemes' [2003, pp. 43–4] or Bourdieu's 'homology' [1984, 1990]) carried over from earlier contexts, experiences or manifestations and the new forms and meanings that resemiotization gives rise to.

Although the concepts of entextualization and resemiotization are closely related, both are useful for the analysis of identity performance in social media, highlighting different aspects of the processual and multi-semiotic nature of meaning-making in social media activities. The examples from social media discussed in this chapter all include, alongside linguistic and textual forms and patterns of language(s), other semiotic means, and carry traces of socio-cultural action and complex discourse trajectories (see Scollon & Scollon, 2004; Scollon, 2008). From this perspective, our data samples are thus best seen as particular points, 'snapshots', in the cycle and process of entextualization and resemiotization.

3   Entextualization and resemiotization and (dis)identification in social media contexts

The four cases we discuss in this chapter all illustrate ways in which entextualization and resemiotization function as key resources for (dis)identification in different social media environments. We show how entextualization and resemiotization can involve a range of semiotic materials: linguistic, visual, textual and multimodal. More specifically, with our first example we look at the ways in which a close and delimited community of practice defined by shared and fairly stable activities and interactions construct their identities on Facebook, and how these online activities are contemporaneous and entwined with their simultaneous offline activities, with the online participants drawing on, and making use of, the community members' offline language uses. With the help of our second case, we move on to describe the ways in which identity work and cultural negotiation take place via the modification of mobile cultural emblems in a (sub)cultural online discussion in which the participants have shared cultural knowledge and interests (Christian metal music). Despite the prevalence of multimodality in many social media formats and sites, our third case – collectively maintained and monitored fan fiction discourses – shows how entextualization and resemiotization of textual material is also crucial in (dis) identification in social media. Finally, with the fourth case, we look at a multimodal YouTube video and discuss how identifications of both performers and audiences in videos of this kind involve the multimodal modification of text, sound and moving image.

3.1 'Soaking in God's presence' – linguistic entextualization and identification in a Facebook group

Our first example illustrates how social relations, activities and identities are performed on the Facebook page of a youth cultural group. The page belongs to a group of young Finnish Christians who share an interest in extreme sports. They form a community of practice whose members regularly participate in and organize events associated with extreme sports and teaching and studying the Bible. Although a shared physical space is essential to the community members for engagement in their sports activities, they also disseminate their experiences through digital communication channels (see Peuronen, 2011).

For this group, Facebook serves as a medium for sharing information on upcoming or ongoing events and provides a space for sending messages, for instance, regarding one's participation. Hence, through Facebook, a wider group of people can be familiarized with the community's activities. The status updates in the example below illustrate messages posted during an *Extreme Summer Camp* organized in 2011. Prior to these updates, the wall of this event had been filled with messages anticipating the camp, the first ones appearing four months before the actual event. In the following, we set out in Figure 5.1 the original Facebook posts,[1] followed by their translations into English (by Saija Peuronen).

118

1. Having a blast here also at night.
Sauna + moonlight swim =
brilliant case and extreme
enjoyment. Enthusiastic about
tomorrow's [moto]cross:)

2. Soaking in God's presence :)

3. Yes, 50 people here already.
We've started wakeboarding and
wind surfing, the sauna is warm
and there's real joy in the air :D

Figure 5.1 Finnish Christian group messages during Extreme Summer Camp

This example shows how heterogeneous linguistic resources are entextualized on the Facebook page in order to perform the community's offline camp activities online. Hence, the Christian extreme sports enthusiasts render their discourse extractable by 'lift[ing] it to a degree from its interactional setting and open[ing] it to scrutiny by an audience' (Bauman & Briggs, 1990, p. 73). By representing their material, lived reality online, the community members characterize themselves as young Christians, showing what they share and how they are connected with the group. Their membership in this particular community thus gives them access to, and socializes them into the use of, linguistic resources and their intended meanings, histories and ideologies (see Bauman & Briggs, 1990, p. 76).

Since the community combines two different socio-cultural frameworks – Christianity and extreme sports – which represent very different traditions, practices and values, the members necessarily draw on diverse linguistic and discursive resources that together form a heteroglossic repertoire (Peuronen, 2013). By making use of the meaning potential that the specific resources have, they manage to navigate within and between two different discursive realms. They actively engage in the social management of decontextualizing and recontextualizing linguistic and discursive elements (Bauman & Briggs, 1990, p. 74). This is possible through their knowledge of the appropriate contextual uses of these elements. In this example, the participants circulate linguistic and discursive constructs from one communicative space to another. Through this practice, they maintain 'simultaneous presence in a multiplicity of sites' (Jacquemet, 2005, p. 266). The use of different spaces of communication (offline and online) affects what is said, why something is said and how the message is understood. For example, the key phrase 'Soaking in God's presence' (line 2) refers to one of the camp's morning activities: when 'soaking', the participants gather together to pray silently by themselves, to contemplate God or simply to relax while listening to gentle songs of worship. The phrase has travelled with the community members to Finland from North America, where some of them have attended a Bible school and brought new concepts and practices with them. The concept of soaking has been adopted as part of the community's local activities and the members' habitual language use, and, eventually, it is used in their online communication as well. Therefore, the process of entextualization in this case includes the geographical, cultural, linguistic and discursive circulation of a specific communicative item. It has preserved its original English form, even though Finnishized derivatives, such as *soukkaus*, are also used by the community members.

The Facebook update was posted at 10:13 am, at the same time as the soaking activity took place (every morning from 10 to 11 am). However, when posted on Facebook, the specific meaning of this notion is most likely not shared by every reader of the page. Hence, although referring to a specific activity, the phrase could also be interpreted locally in the context of the Facebook page alone: there, it may function as an act of self-characterization that even 'outsiders' could recognize as denoting the group's commonality and its members' shared activity, culture and faith in God (Brubaker & Cooper, 2000, pp. 20–1).

Similar identification practices are illustrated by the two other messages in this example. In both of them, the participants perform camp activities by entextualizing them into the online context with heterogeneous linguistic and discursive resources. The two posters use resources available for them in different lexical registers (of youth cultures, religion and extreme sports). Since their extreme sports vocabulary does not contain standardized forms, varied uses of Finnish and English occur: they use terms such as *wakeboarding, purjelautailu* for wind surfing, and *crosseihin* for motocross. In addition, they report on their feelings about being involved in the community's activities with very positive and vivid expressions, such as *aitoa iloa ilmoilla* (real joy in the air), *innolla huomisiin crosseihin* (enthusiastic about tomorrow's motocross) and *Saunat + kuutamouinti = loistokeissi ja extremenautinto* (Sauna + moonlight swim = brilliant case and extreme enjoyment). The use of emoticons also emphasizes the positive tone of the messages. These updates aim to convey the posters' offline experiences and practices by transforming them into a different mode, that of online writing. By means of decontextualizing and recontextualizing the linguistic and discursive elements, the community members thus move from their immediate experience to mediated performance of their activities and identities on this particular social media site.

3.2   From pentagram to repentagram – visual emblems and renaming in cultural identification

As with our first case, two different socio-cultural frameworks or lifestyles are brought together in our second example. Here we explore how a visual cultural emblem related to Christian metal music on YouTube, a website built around uploads of videos, is appropriated and made sense of by members of the cultural group in question. Although YouTube is not a site explicitly aimed at enabling social networking, it is a social medium: on YouTube, participants not only share and watch videos, but also actively engage in reviewing the contents of videos and in discussing the issues emerging in and around them. In this case, however, the participants do not typically constitute a community of practice; rather, YouTube enables the emergence of an interest-based affinity space (Gee, 2004; Gee & Hayes, 2011) for participants interested in particular video genres and the cultural phenomena depicted in them. The structure of any YouTube subpage is another indication of its social nature: the video frame is immediately followed by audience comments on the same page.

The example in focus here is a video entitled *Great Christian metal bands*, compiled by a user named *pinoyoctopusgo*.[2] The video, made by editing audio clips and pictures and merging them together, presents its maker's favourite Christian metal artists. In this way, it is an example of resemiotization: visual material (band logos and photographs of band members) and audio material (extracts from Christian metal and rock songs) as well as text (band names, album names, and biblical extracts) are modified and fused together into a personalized representation of Christian bands. The video also exemplifies entextualization in that it is an outcome of a process involving the extraction of materials from elsewhere (e.g. band websites, CDs, mp3s, the Bible) and their recontextualization as part of the video maker's own audio-visual contribution. Importantly, these operations are not simply idiosyncratic and random acts: this is suggested by the fact that the video is presented as belonging to an evolving genre of 'My favourite bands' on YouTube.

The visual cultural emblem that is of particular interest in this video is a Christian metal band logo, a resemiotized object with a particular trajectory. The logo belongs to a Christian metal band *Impending Doom* (Fig. 5.2) and is shown in the video at the beginning of the 20-second time slot dedicated to the band (starting at 0:21).

In the video, the logo stands alone without any explanatory text or background graphics. While one aspect of its resemiotization is its trajectory from a pictorial logo to an element in an audio-visual video, another, and more complex, aspect of resemiotization in play here is the way in which the logo makes use of a visual form that refers to and evokes certain (sub)cultural contexts. Indeed, the logo is very similar to many other heavy metal band logos in that it uses dark colours and lines that cross each other to form a diagram (see Jousmäki, 2012, p. 220; Karjalainen *et al.*, 2009). In this case, the diagram resembles the notorious pentagram (Fig. 5.3) which, in the context of rock music, is associated with the non-Christian, 'black' metal music genre in general, and in particular with the anti-Christian or Satanic worldview of its

Figure 5.2 The repentagram   *Figure 5.3* A pentagram
© *Impending Doom. Reproduced with the band's permission.*

adherents. The video, however, offers the audience no explicit cues on how the pentagram-like diagram of the Christian band *Impending Doom* should be interpreted. As a result, it gives rise to a great deal of puzzlement in the discussion thread on the site. For example, one discussant, *DieToFleshNotSpirit*, initiates a long thread with the question 'what with the satanic star in the beginning aren't this bands christian?', thereby constructing Satanism and Christianity as incompatible with each other. To this s/he receives 18 replies, expressing reactions to the logo and offering various suggestions for its interpretation, including the following:

> @DieToFleshNotSpirit It's the Repentagram. Impending Doom took the pentagram and made it into the Repentagram, a Christian symbol. REDMAX777
> @REDMAX777 and... What does it mean?? franco802
> @franco802 It combines the words "repent" and "pentagram". It's basically a play on words that tells people the way to be saved: "repent" of your sins. REDMAX777

Another participant, *REDMAX777*, thus explains how *Impending Doom* transformed the pentagram into 'a Christian symbol' – and explicitly points to the central role of entextualization and resemiotization as means of self-identification for a Christian band seeking to build a bridge between their Christian values and the metal music community (Jousmäki, 2012). The ideological transformation of the symbol from non-Christian to Christian involved the addition of four sides to the original five sides of the pentagram as well as the renaming of the symbol with the lexical prefix 're-'. The choice of the word '*repent*agram', in turn, suggests that the band prioritizes repentance as the key to salvation (see Jousmäki, 2013). Thus, *Impending Doom* is finally interpreted by the discussants as having modified the pentagram for Christian purposes and for the purposes of Christian *metal* in particular, in order to characterize itself as a Christian metal band.

However, the outcome of these meaning-making operations is not simple or straightforward. This is clearly evinced by the prolonged discussion that ensues over what counts as 'Christian' and what does not, demonstrating that the 'participants reflexively examine the discourse as it is emerging' (Bauman & Briggs, 1990, p. 69). This discussion foregrounds the fact that the entextualization and resemiotization of an originally Satanic emblem as a Christian symbol is not unproblematic. One issue seems to be that some elements of the original non-Christian *scheme* may, nevertheless, have been transferred (Iedema, 2003, pp. 43–4) to the new Christian context, and hence many discussants remain uncertain whether the remodified emblem is a relevant and appropriate resource for identification or not.

3.3 'RANMA NO BAKA' – rewriting and genre modification as identity work on fan fiction sites

Our third example focuses on fan fiction sites as a particular social medium enabling interaction and shared cultural production (rewritings of, for example, the characters, plots and themes of popular films, TV series or novels) by fans. Although the crux of fan fiction is rewriting cult texts, fan fiction sites are also fundamentally social media environments, as they can only exist and thrive if these texts are read, commented on and discussed by readers. In this way, fan fiction sites build on interaction between the participants. Within the cultural and normative framework of fan culture, based on the fans' adoring attachment to cult objects, fan fiction sites thus evolve as, and constitute, social niches for particular, collectively created and monitored participatory cultures (Burgess & Green, 2009; Leppänen, 2009).

As in each case investigated in this chapter, in the fan fiction culture, active entextualization and resemiotization of semiotic resources are crucial for creating and maintaining a shared socio-cultural reality for individuals (Leppänen, 2012). What, however, distinguishes fan fiction from, for example, Facebook or YouTube discussions, is the amount of effort it often requires: many writers invest a great deal in their writing and painstakingly craft it in ways appreciated by members of these fan communities.

Fan fiction is essentially about the entextualization and resemiotization of textual resources of different kinds. Recognizable elements of the source text are decontextualized, modified and embedded within a new textual context. In this way, the new text can still appear to readers as a recognizable version of the original text. At the same time, these entextualized aspects of the source text, when integrated within the new text, make the fan fiction text a novel construction. Very often, entextualization and resemiotization are thus geared towards the creation of new imaginative interpretations of the source texts which are simultaneously appreciative of some of their aspects and critical or subversive about their other features (Leppänen, 2008).

In fan fiction, writers strive to create texts that constitute a bricolage in which objects are reordered and recontextualized 'to communicate fresh meanings' (Clarke, 1976, p. 177). In practice, bricolage can be achieved through a number of semiotic means. First, it can be created by fan writers when they draw on and mix resources provided by different languages and styles (e.g. English dialogue resembling the kind of talk typical of a particular TV series along with everyday, vernacular Finnish; see Leppänen, 2012). Second, bricolage can also be created through generic diversity. For example, the genre features of the source text can be modified, mixed and combined with features of other genres. Third, aspects of the contents and narrative of the source text – characters, settings and plot, for example – can be manipulated in various ways. A very common bricolage of this kind is one in which characters that originally populate different texts are brought together within fan fiction, often for the purpose of creating new romantic liaisons between them (Leppänen, 2008).

Here, the cross-over, combinatory and transformative aesthetics of fan fiction are briefly illustrated in Figure 5.4, a text submitted by a young Finnish woman.[3] The text entextualizes and resemiotizes linguistic and textual elements from several popular cultural discourses, including (at least) the Finnish *Moomin* stories and Japanese *Ranma ½* manga, and the television genres of cooking competitions and sports commentary. The left-hand column contains the original Finnish text and the column on the right its English translation (by Sirpa Leppänen).

The main characters here are Akane and Little My. Akane is the female protagonist of the Japanese manga series *Ranma ½*. Little My, in turn, is a tiny female character in the *Moomin* stories. The two characters resemble each other a great deal and this similarity has most likely been the stimulus for the writer to create the story. This is also noted by one of the characters here ('They must be sisters!'). The text depicts a scene in which the two cartoon characters are set against each other in a cooking competition, the performance-like

Kamala kokkisota	The horrible cooking competition
Erotuomari aloitti lähtölaskennan: "Paikoillenne, valmiit, kokatkaa!" "Noniin, kilpailijat saivat luvan aloittaa! He alkoivat availla kaappeja mielipuolisella raivolla! Minä olen teidän selostajanne, Ryouga Hibiki, ja selostan teille yksityiskohtaisesti jännittävän kokkisodan Akane Tendon (ah, Akane) ja Pikku Myyn välillä uskollisen asiantuntijatiimini avustuksella. [...] "Shampoo, mitäs sanot Akanen maustamistekniikasta? Liikaa vai liian vähän?" "Typerä tyttö liikaa pippuria laittaa. Ranman suu palaa!" [...] Akane tunki lusikan Ranman suuhun. Syntyi syvä hiljaisuus. Kaikki, kilpailijat mukaan lukien, tuijottivat tuota naamaa, joka sanoi: "Yääääääääkk! Kamalaa! HYI HYI HYI! Pahinta mitä olen koskaan maistanut!" "RANMA NO BAKA" mätks Kaikki (paitsi Akane): Macho macho man, I gotta be a macho man... Tuli Pikku myyn vuoro. Täsmälleen sama toistui. (Nodokan kommentti: "Kyllä he varmasti ovat sisaruksia!") [...]	The referee started the count-down: "Ready, steady, cook!" "Right, the competitors have permission to begin! They began to open cupboard doors with insane frenzy. I'm your commentator, Ryouga Hibiki, and will report to you in detail on the exciting cooking competition between Akane Tendo (ah, Akane) and Little My with the help of my faithful team of experts. [...] "Shampoo, what do you say about Akane's spicing technique? Too much or too little?" "The stupid girl too much pepper puts. Ranma's mouth will burn!" [...] Akane stuffed the spoon into Ranma's mouth. A deep silence followed. Everyone, including the competitors, stared at that face, which said: "Aaaaargh! Horrible! OH OH OH! This is the worst thing I have ever tasted!" "Ranma is stupid [Japanese]" smash Everyone (except Akane): Macho macho man, I gotta be a macho man... Then came Little My's turn. Exactly the same happened again. (Comment by Nodokan: "They must be sisters!" [...]

Figure 5.4 Fan fiction example text

quality of which is further accentuated by the fact that there is also a commentator who reports on the events as well as an audience – consisting of other *Ranma ½* characters who chip in with their own comments. As is typical of fan fiction as a whole, this text is linguistically and stylistically heterogeneous. It is mainly written in standard Finnish, but also includes one utterance in Japanese (RANMA NO BAKA ('Ranma is stupid') and another in English ('Macho macho man, I gotta be a macho man'). In the same vein, the text displays stylistic heterogeneity: the announcements by the sports commentator (e.g. 'Right, the competitors have permission to begin! They began to open cupboard doors with insane frenzy') simulate the register and style of live sports commentary. In addition, one of the character's comments ('Stupid girl too much pepper uses') resembles, in its syntactic distinctiveness, the idiosyncratic speech style of another famous fantasy character, Yoda from *Star Wars*. Likewise, the contextualization of the snippet from the famous song by Village People ('Macho macho man') adds yet another dimension of meaning to the text: *Ranma*, the main protagonist of the manga, who at times transforms into a woman, is urged here to be a man, and forget his other girly, non-macho persona.

What seems to have motivated this particular mélange of semiotic features is, first, that both its writer and audience are no doubt very familiar with the genres and particular discourses in question. Their lives are saturated by mediated popular culture – *Moomin* cartoons and films, Japanese manga and anime, and televised cooking competitions – as well as their languages, registers and styles. They recognize and enjoy the enmeshing of these in fan fiction, appreciate the craft of such art and can read between the lines, catching the (implied) meanings in sometimes quite subtle ways. They inhabit a cross-discourse, cross-media, cross-language discourse universe in which the creation and reception of media products is not a unidirectional act whereby the singular message/s of one particular media discourse is encoded by the sender and decoded and contemplated in the reader's or spectator's mind, but an active, interventional and heteroglossic activity (Leppänen, 2012). In this sense, fan fiction sites are social in a way that goes beyond the interactive dynamics of their participants' activities, one that involves a shared set of formal preferences, productive and interpretive conventions and of norms regulating how far and in what ways they can create and interpret their discourse.

Fan fiction is about claiming, gaining and being accepted as a member of a fan culture, about participation in communities created and maintained through shared practices, and about identification as a particular kind of person with particular kinds of alignments and values who strives to signal commonality and connectedness with a group of like-minded fans. What this means is that the entextualizations and resemiotizations fan writers make are also highly indexical and presuppose a certain social context with a shared normative order. Within such a context the choices made by the author in our previous example can become interpreted as playfully and respectfully interventional – and not, for instance, as dismissive about the cult texts they draw on.

This kind of affiliation with a shared indexical order is also frequently foregrounded in the discussion that fan fiction generates. For example, one of the discussants of the fan fiction text discussed above spells out his/her evaluation of the writer's choices as follows:

> I'm positively surprised that I could distinguish between My's and Akane's lines. I haven't followed Moomin for many years, and Ranma manga I have practically fast forwarded (many fanfics are in my opinion much more meaningful than the original work... as weird as that may sound). (Translated from Finnish by Sirpa Leppänen)

Acting as a 'post-Panopticon' grassroots gatekeeper, this commentator invokes here an authority position and makes it very clear that s/he is fully in the know about what makes good fan fiction. Commentary like this also shows that in fan fiction, writing in an appropriate way is considered a means for claiming and acquiring social capital and prestige in fan cultures.

Although at first glance it may seem that, in fan fiction, there are limitless possibilities for entextualization and resemiotization, it is also policed by quite specific norms (Leppänen, 2009). Thus, fan fiction is not merely free play, but, in the same way as all other human social spaces, it is regulated (Blommaert, 2005, 2010) by its own orders of normativity and mechanisms of control which constrain the discursive and identity options fans may utilize in them.

3.4 *Mammat Riivaa* – video and music as resources for entextualization and resemiotization in viral YouTube videos

Our fourth and final example deals with (the) entextualization and resemiotization of multimodal resources in a music video on YouTube. This video was created in the summer of 2011, when a Finnish rap artist, Ruudolf and his colleague, Karri Koira, transformed *Danza Kuduro*, the previous summer's tropical hit single[4] into a Finnishized version entitled *Mammat Riivaa* ('The chicks are harassing us').[5,6] Such YouTube videos are an increasingly popular genre; their popularity stems largely from the playful ways, typical of rap music on the whole, in which they adopt and modify music samples or the entire musical background of an existing cultural product. At the same time, thanks to the way in which this particular video plays with the cinematic and linguistic resources of the original music video, it is also quite a novel phenomenon (for a discussion of the typical features of Finnish hip hop, see e.g. Westinen, 2010).

The *Mammat Riivaa* video (see Figure 5.5), now with almost 1.57 million views on YouTube (27 November 2012), is a complex multi-semiotic product and a remodification of the original song consisting of music, moving images, dance and lyrics. While the background music and the

Figure 5.5 A screenshot of the official *Mammat Riivaa* dance video[7]

composition are exactly the same as in the original, every other aspect of the original video has been transformed. Firstly, its setting has been relocated from the Caribbean Sea to Finland, specifically to a Helsinki seaside suburb, Aurinkolahti ('Sunbay'). At the same time, this new setting remains ambivalent in that some of its semiotic features also link it with the original geographical context, the United States. These include, for example, the rapper Ruudolf's shirt, which bears an image of the US flag, and his cowboy-like straw hat. The connections between the two videos are further accentuated by the fact – known to his fans – that Ruudolf has Mexican-American roots and has studied in a Bible School in California. These facts, along with his explicit references to the United States (e.g. titles such as *Born in the U.S.A.* and *Florida Funk*) thus convey an image that his identity as a rapper is one that aligns with both Finland and the US.

In addition to the re-localization of the song, the dance performance in the original video has been transformed in the Finnish video. While *Danza Kuduro* features half-naked women dancing around the male singers, in *Mammat Riivaa* it is the two male rappers who do the dancing. Their choreography also differs a great deal from the original: in comparison to the professional gyrations in *Danza Kuduro*, the young Finnish men's dance looks quite home-made and amateurish. In another scene, the two dancing rappers are joined by a group of ordinary-looking young Finnish men. Amongst them, however, are some local hip hop and sports celebrities. This 'face-dropping' practice further emphasizes the local Finnish nature of the video.

Other levels of entextualization and resemiotization in *Mammat Riivaa* include the linguistic and the musical. *Danza Kuduro* is a bilingual Spanish-Portuguese song by Don Omar, a Puerto Rican reggaeton singer-rapper, and Lucenzo, a France-based artist of Portuguese origin. *Mammat Riivaa*, in turn, is a rap adaptation of this Latino song, and its lyrics are in spoken vernacular Finnish with some elements of English, as in the following example:

rapin suomen mestari in the place to be
('the Finnish rap champion in the place to be')

The idea behind the new lyrics, particularly the chorus, is what the Spanish (and Portuguese) words and sentences could sound like in the rap artists' own language, Finnish (see Table 5.1). The artists thus take advantage of a popular YouTube meme – the so-called 'mondegreen' technique – and create new 'misheard' lyrics on the basis of their

Table 5.1 *Mammat Riivaa* lyrics for choruses, with translations

SPANISH	its English translation	FINNISH	its English translation
La mano arriba	Put your hands up	mammat riivaa	the chicks are harassing
cintura sola	Moving only the hips	asfalttisoturii	the asphalt warrior
Da media vuelta	Turn half around	ne ottaa paidast kii	they grab my shirt
danza kuduro	Dance to Kuduro	tuu mun kanssa Ruudolf	come with me Ruudolf
No te canses ahora	Don't lose your breath now	ei anna taukoo	they don't allow a break
que esto solo empieza	Because this has just started	ne koiraa kauhoo	they doggy-paddle
Mueve la cabeza	Move your head	nyt poika saunoo	now the boy goes to sauna
danza kuduro	Dance to Kuduro	mun kanssa tuu jo	come with me

near-homophony with the original lyrics (see e.g. Leppänen & Häkkinen, 2012). However, *Mammat Riivaa* also differs in an important way from mondegreen videos. Unlike mondegreen videos that typically transform a commercial product into a personal, non-commercial fan product, in *Mammat Riivaa* the original music video is a commercial product transformed into *another* commercial video. The interventional practices of post-Panopticon social media are thus adopted here for commercial purposes.

The lyrics for the chorus of each song and their translations are presented in Table 5.1 (Finnish to English translations by Elina Westinen): The original party song gives explicit instructions on how to dance this tropical megahit. The Finnish version, in contrast, describes how the two Finnish rappers are constantly harassed and flirted with by girls wherever they go. In doing this, the new Finnish lyrics twist parts of the original lyrics, in the mondegreen fashion, for the rappers' own purposes. The clearest example of homophonic matching is with 'mano arriba' and 'mammat riivaa' – with the Spanish [-'ri:ba] sounding close to ['ri:va:] to the Finnish listener, since in Spanish, /b/ and /v/ are pronounced alike.

Homophonic 'translation' is one means by which lyrics can be localized and indexically grounded (Bauman & Briggs, 1990, p. 76) as meaningful to Finnish speakers – in other words, as something they can identify with as fans of Finnish rap. The same effect is also created by the artists' self-presentation and self-naming, and by cultural references which link the video content to Finland.

One of these references is 'the boy goes to sauna' which is, among other things, a quotation from a well-known contemporary Finnish sports song in which 'the boy' denotes an ice hockey championship trophy which the winning team takes to the post-match sauna when celebrating their victory. The cultural reference here is quite transparent to Finnish audiences, who are also likely to be able to appreciate the way in which it has been resemiotized in the context of this song to refer to the young men ('the boy(s)') who, even in a waterfront sauna, are harassed by young women swimming close by. Hence, this line is another illustration of complex meaning-making operations involving decontextualization, whereby a textual snippet has been lifted from a particular social event (the trophy in the sauna), its recontextualization in a new discursive context (a sports song) and finally its further recontextualization as an ingredient of another song (*Mammat Riivaa*), itself a multi-layered resemiotized cultural object.

The multiple levels of meaning of the Finnish video also show up in the comments made by the video's YouTube audience, who engage in a reflexive examination of its discourse (Bauman & Briggs, 1990, p. 69): among other things, they wonder whether *Mammat Riivaa* is meant for real or as pure parody. For example, the best-'liked' Finnish-language comment on the video (on 3 October 2012) includes the following statement: 'I heard that some Don Omar had made a parody of this', thus suggesting humorously that the original song is *Mammat Riivaa* and not *Danza Kuduro*. Ruudolf himself, however, claims that the song is no joke, but a serious interpretation of a piece which he likes (Sasioglu, 2012), the lyrics describing his life in which he is constantly pursued by young girls.

As has been shown above, in the video *Mammat Riivaa*, Ruudolf identifies both with Finland and the US. The video is thus characterized by translocality – it simultaneously aligns with the local and the global as meaningful co-ordinates (Leppänen *et al.*, 2009). As a cultural product, it also creates affordances for audience identifications which are equally translocal: as revealed, for example, by the commentary on the video, the audience orients to the song both as a product of a global music culture as well as of a localized music scene. In contrast, what Ruudolf himself dis-identifies with remains somewhat ambiguous. On the one hand, the lack of scantily dressed women on his video – a stereotypical characteristic of hip hop videos and a prominent feature of Don Omar's video – could be read as an act of disidentification with the mainstream American hip hop videos and their apparent sexism. On the other hand, the Finnish lyrics tell a different story of rappers being constantly surrounded and admired by women, no doubt with the additional implication of bragging, an essential part of hip hop culture on the whole. In these ways, the entextualization and resemiotization processes to which the original video is subjected imply that the identifications of its audiences remain divided and polycentric.

4 Discussion

In this chapter, we approached social media as environments which enable social activities, interaction, and the emergence and sharing of an active, 'prosumptive' participatory culture, regulated by 'post-Panopticon' grassroots normativities. Our focus was on (dis)identification, and we argued that processes and practices of entextualization and resemiotization play a key role in it. As an illustration of both the convergent and divergent ways in which identity performances take place in social media, we looked at four different types of remodifications of social media discourses: of linguistic material on Facebook, visual material on YouTube and its discussion threads, textual interventions on fan fiction sites, and multimodal resources in YouTube rap videos.

In our analyses of these cases, we aimed to demonstrate the kinds of semiotic means that are available in each social media setting, to whom they are available, how they are mobilized by participants in identity performances, and with what kinds of meanings and effects. Considering that the semiotic landscape of social media is essentially multimodal, we paid attention not only to uses of language(s) but also to multiple other semiotic means which carry traces of socio-cultural actions and complex discourse trajectories, by drawing on, making use of, reinterpreting and resemiotizing features, text and discourses which originate and have travelled from elsewhere.

Importantly, we demonstrated how it is specifically these semiotic resources that are crucial in (dis)identification and meaning-making performances and in orientation to or evasion of commonality, connectedness and groupness. In all of the social media environments examined here, mobilization of these resources helped identify the participants as legitimate members of the particular group or community. For example, such identity performances were achieved by the participants in each social media setting by their self-selection as legitimate participants in the social media activities in question, and by demonstrating competence in responding to or crafting the discourse in appropriate ways. This was further enhanced by the reactions and responses of other participants, guided by the normative and socio-cultural set-up of the particular environment.

More specifically, in a close-knit youth group, unified by their Christian faith and interest in extreme sports, the members' Facebook updates recorded lived reality online. Through this means, they were able to characterize themselves as members of a young Christians' community, showing what they share and how they are connected with the group. Their membership in this particular community of practice gives them access to, and socializes them into, a particular usage of linguistic resources and their intended meanings, histories and ideologies. In this process, the decontextualization and recontextualization of particular language uses was shown to be a significant social resource for the participants.

In the YouTube discussions centring on cultural emblems, similar processes of self- and other-identification, connectedness, commonality and groupness were also identified. On the one hand, the transidiomatic (Jacquemet, 2005) mobilization of cultural symbols and the comments and discussion on them clearly functioned as a means for the participants in these social media activities (Christian metallers) to identify both themselves and others as members of this specific cultural group. Within the communal context afforded by the YouTube discussion threads, they can share with one another their interest in particular cultural practices, ways of language use and discursive resources. On the other hand, these social media activities also foregrounded disidentification and ambiguity. The case of the entextualization and resemiotization of a non-Christian symbol as a new kind of Christian band logo which would link the band not only with Christianity but also with metal music was shown to be only partly successful. The participants in this social media group had trouble shedding the original non-Christian aspects of the symbol. Hence, the identification potential of the processes of entextualization and resemiotization was not realized fully, as the commentators could not take on board all the meanings conveyed by the appropriated symbol.

The entextualization and resemiotization of globally available popular cultural material were also argued to be crucial resources for creating and maintaining a shared socio-cultural reality on online fan fiction sites. Self- and other-identification, connectedness, commonality and groupness were shown to be dependent on a consensually established and monitored discourse practice, in which the recontextualization of other texts and textual material as well as playful (but normatively regulated and policed) appropriations of linguistic, stylistic, generic and contents features of source texts are means for claiming membership and mutual respect in fan cultures.

In our final example, we discussed an interventional Finnish rap video, based on another music video of trans-Atlantic origin, which sought a balance between the non-commercial YouTube meme culture and commercial popular music culture. In this case, it was shown how entextualization and resemiotization were used by the rap artists to create a cultural object which oriented both towards the global genre of rap music culture and the local music scene and setting, as well as the very local concerns of the young rappers themselves. These semiotic meaning-making operations were shown to provide affordances for the artists and their audiences to identify themselves as members of a translocal and polycentric music culture in which the knowledge of the source product and its localization are important parameters for connectedness, commonality and togetherness.

In conclusion, we wish to argue that the kind of semiotic resources that are available to participants in social media activities can be empowering as well as delimiting: they can provide new opportunities for identification, agency and social action, in which the capacity to use a range of semiotic resources can play a key role, and they can also impose new divisions, hierarchies and exclusions. In addition, our analyses in this chapter highlight the ways in which micro-level discourse practices are linked and contribute to global social and cultural processes of change, and have considerable relevance to new kinds of identifications and communality which do not always have a national, ethnic or local basis. In this way, this chapter provides insights into processes of sociolinguistic, discursive and semiotic diversity as aspects of participatory socio-cultural practices in social media that are manifest in all corners of the globe where people have access to and interest in engaging with others through these media.

Notes

1. Reprinted with the permission of these participants.
2. The link to the video is www.youtube.com/watch?v=bcWuO9MmJn4 (accessed 23 November 2012).
3. The link to the fan fiction text is www.fanfiction.net/s/3420979/1/Akane_vs_ Pikku_myy_eli_kamala_kokkisota (accessed 23 November 2012).
4. The link to the video *Danza Kuduro* is www.youtube.com/watch?v=rUFgacK 8sZ0 (accessed 23 November 2012). Danza Kuduro actually samples largely on a bilingual Portuguese-English song entitled 'Vem Dançar Kuduro' (Let's Dance Kuduro), by Lucenzo, featuring France-based American rapper Big Ali – a song which was published earlier the same year, in 2010.
5. A translation which would precisely capture the meaning of the Finnish concepts 'mammat' and 'riivaa' is difficult to form. 'Mammat' referred earlier to middle-aged women, often in a derogatory way. Nowadays, the word can refer neutrally to young women, young mamas (but not necessarily to 'mothers' in any way). 'Riivaa' has the literal meaning 'be possessed' in English, but here it has to do with young women harassing, bugging, pursuing and being obsessed by these young male rappers.
6. The link to the video *Mammat Riivaa* is www.youtube.com/watch?v=yO_ hPCYhVX8 (accessed 23 November 2012).
7. Reprinted with the permission of Ruudolf.

References

Androutsopoulos, J. (2011) 'From variation to heteroglossia in the study of computer-mediated discourse'. In C. Thurlow & K. Mroczek (eds.) *Digital Discourse: Language in the New Media* (Oxford: Oxford University Press), pp. 277–98.

Androutsopoulos, J. & Georgakopoulou, A. (eds.) (2003) *Discourse Constructions of Youth Identities* (Amsterdam: John Benjamins).

Arnaut, K. (2012) 'Superdiversity: Elements of an emerging perspective'. In K. Arnaut, J. Blommaert, B. Rampton & M. Spotti (eds.) Special Issue of *Diversities*, 14(2): pp. 1–16.

Bauman, R. & Briggs C. L. (1990) 'Poetics and performance as critical perspectives on language and social life', *Annual Review of Anthropology*, 19: 59–88.

Baym, N. (2011) *Personal Connections in the Digital Age* (Cambridge: Polity Press).

Blommaert, J. (2005) *Discourse: A Critical Introduction* (Cambridge: Cambridge University Press).

Blommaert, J. (2010) *The Sociolinguistics of Globalization* (Cambridge: Cambridge University Press).

Blommaert, J. & Rampton, B. (2011) 'Language and superdiversity', *Diversities*, 13(2): 3–21.

Bourdieu, P. (1984) *Distinction. A Social Critique of the Judgment of Taste* (Cambridge, MA: Harvard University Press).

Bourdieu, P. (1990) *The Logic of Practice* (Cambridge: Polity Press).

Brubaker, R. & Cooper, F. (2000) 'Beyond "identity"', *Theory and Society*, 29: 1–47.

Burgess, J. & Green, J. (2009) *YouTube: Online Video and Participatory Culture* (Cambridge: Polity Press).

Clarke, J. (1976) *Resistance Through Rituals: Youth Subcultures in Post-War Britain* (London: Hutchison).

Eckert, P. & McConnell-Ginet, S. (1992) 'Think practically and look locally: Language and gender as community-based practice', *Annual Review of Anthropology*, 21: 461–90.

Fornäs, J., Klein, K., Ladendorf, J., Sundén, J. & Svennigsson, M. (2002) 'Into digital borderlands'. In J. Fornäs, K. Klein, J. Ladendorf, J. Sundén & M. Svennigsson (eds.) *Digital Borderlands: Cultural Studies of Identity and Interactivity on the Internet* (New York: Peter Lang), pp. 1–47.

Gee, J. P. (2004) *Situated Language and Learning: A Critique of Traditional Schooling* (New York: Routledge).

Gee, J. P. & Hayes, E. (2011) 'Nurturing affinity spaces and game-based learning', *Cadernos de Letras (UFRJ)* 28, July 2011. http://www.letras.ufrj.br/anglo_germanicas/cadernos/numeros/072011/textos/cl2831072011gee.pdf (accessed 23 November 2012).

Haggerty, K. (2006) 'Tear down the walls: On demolishing the panopticon'. In D. Lyon (ed.) *Theorizing Surveillance: The Panopticon and Beyond* (Devon: Willan), pp. 23–45.

Iedema, R. (2003) 'Multimodality, resemiotization: Extending the analysis of discourse as multi-semiotic practice', *Visual Communication*, 2(1): 29–57.

Jacquemet, M. (2005) 'Transidiomatic practices: Language and power in the age of globalization', *Language & Communication*, 25: 257–77.

Jousmäki, H. (2012) 'Bridging between the metal community and the church: Entextualisation of the Bible in Christian metal discourse', *Discourse, Context and Media*, 1(4): 217–26.

Jousmäki, H. (2013) 'Spiritual quest and dialogicality in Christian metal lyrics', *Journal of Religion and Popular Culture*, 25(2): 273–86.

Karjalainen, T-M., Ainamo A. & Laaksonen, L. (2009) 'Occult, a tooth, and the canopy of the sky: Conceptualizing visual meaning creation of heavy metal bands', *Design and Semantics of Form and Movement, Conference Proceedings*, pp. 20–32, http://www.northumbria.ac.uk/static/5007/despdf/designres/2009proceedings.pdf (accessed 23 November 2012).

Kress, G. & van Leeuwen, T. (1996) *Reading Images: The Grammar of Visual Design* (Abingdon: Routledge).

Krzyżanowski, M. & Wodak, R. (2008) 'Multiple identities, migration and belonging: 'Voices of migrants''. In C. R. Caldas-Coulthard & R. Iedema (eds.) *Identity Trouble: Critical Discourse and Contested Identities* (Basingstoke and New York: Palgrave Macmillan), pp. 95–119.

Kytölä, S. (2012a) 'Multilingual web discussion forums: Theoretical, practical and methodological issues'. In M. Sebba, S. Mahootian & C. Jonsson (eds.) *Language*

136 *Leppänen et al.*

Mixing and Code-Switching in Writing: Approaches to Mixed-Language Written Discourse (New York: Routledge), pp. 106–27.

Kytölä, S. (2012b) 'Peer normativity and sanctioning of linguistic resources-in-use: On non-Standard Englishes in Finnish football forums online'. In J. Blommaert, S. Leppänen, P. Pahta & T. Räisänen (eds.) *Dangerous Multilingualism* (Basingstoke and New York: Palgrave Macmillan), pp. 228–60.

Lave, J. & Wenger, E. (1991) *Situated Learning: Legitimate Peripheral Participation* (Cambridge: Cambridge University Press).

Leppänen, S. (2008) 'Cybergirls in trouble? Fan fiction as discursive space for negotiating gender and sexuality'. In C. R. Caldas-Coulthard & R. Iedema (eds.) *Identity Trouble: Critical Discourse and Contested Identities.* (Basingstoke and New York: Palgrave Macmillan), pp. 156–79.

Leppänen, S. (2009) 'Playing with and policing language use and textuality in fan fiction'. In I. Hotz-Davies, A. Kirchhofer & S. Leppänen (eds.) *Internet Fictions.* (Newcastle upon Tyne: Cambridge Scholars Publishing), pp. 62–83.

Leppänen, S. (2012) 'Linguistic and discursive heteroglossia on the translocal internet: The case of web writing'. In M. Sebba, S. Mahootian & C. Jonsson (eds.) *Language Mixing and Code-Switching in Writing: Approaches to Mixed-Language Written Discourse* (New York: Routledge), pp. 233–54.

Leppänen, S. & Häkkinen, A. (2012) 'Buffalaxed super-diversity: Representing the Other on YouTube'. In K. Arnaut, J. Blommaert, B. Rampton & M. Spotti (eds.) Special Issue of *Diversities* 14(2), pp. 17–33.

Leppänen, S. & Piirainen-Marsh, A. (2009) 'Language policy in the making: An analysis of bilingual gaming activities', *Language Policy*, 8(3): 261–84.

Leppänen, S. Pitkänen-Huhta, A., Piirainen-Marsh, A., Nikula, T. & Peuronen, S. (2009) 'Young people's translocal new media uses: A multiperspective analysis of language choice and heteroglossia', *Journal of Computer-Mediated Communication*, 14(4): 1080–107.

Peuronen, S. (2011) '"Ride hard, live forever": Translocal identities in an online community of extreme sports Christians'. In C. Thurlow & K. Mroczek (eds.) *Digital Discourse: Language in the New Media* (Oxford: Oxford University Press), pp. 154–76.

Peuronen, S. (2013) 'Heteroglossia as a resource for reflexive participation in a community of Christian snowboarders in Finland', *Journal of Sociolinguistics*, 17(3): 297–323.

Sasioglu, M. (2012) 'Rap-artisti Ruudolf uskoo onnellisiin loppuihin' ['Rap artist Ruudolf believes in happy endings'] *Helsingin Uutiset*, 20 March 2012, http://www.helsinginuutiset.fi/artikkeli/99326-rap-artisti-ruudolf-uskoo-onnellisiin-loppuihin (accessed 23 November 2012).

Scollon, R. (2008) 'Discourse itineraries: Nine processes of resemiotization'. In V. Bhatia, J. Flowerdew & R. Jones (eds.) *Advances in Discourse Studies* (Abingdon: Routledge), pp. 233–44.

Scollon R. & Scollon, S. W. (2004) *Nexus Analysis: Discourse and the Emerging Internet* (New York: Routledge).

Silverstein, M. & Urban, G. (eds.) (1996) *Natural Histories of Discourse* (Chicago: The University of Chicago Press).

Westinen, E. (2010) 'The linguistic and discursive construction of hip hop identities: A view on Finnish rap lyrics'. In M. Palander-Collin, H. Lenk, M. Nevala, P. Sihvonen and M. Vesalainen (eds.) *Proceedings of the Dialogic Language Use 2: Constructing Identity in Interpersonal Communication* (Helsinki: Société Néophilologique), pp. 251–62.

Part II
The Construction of Community on Social Media

6
CoffeeTweets: bonding around the bean on Twitter

Michele Zappavigna

1 Introduction

This chapter explores how we use social media to communicate our experience of the world and bond with others by forming communities of shared values. Microblogging services such as Twitter and Weibo are a form of social media allowing users to publish streams of length-delimited posts to internet-mediated audiences. As such they afford new kinds of interpersonal interaction via the conversation-like exchanges that occur (Honeycutt & Herring, 2009). An example of a length-delimited post (hereafter 'micropost') is the following. It contains one of the most common patterns in microblogging, an expression of thanks for personal endorsement:

@Tim I love #coffee too

This post is addressed to Tim using the @ symbol before the name, a construction which can also function as a reference to the person (e.g. @Tim makes great coffee), and contains a hashtag, the # symbol, which acts as a form of metadata labelling the topic of the post so that it can be found by others. This chapter will consider microposts such as this in terms of how they illuminate the way microblogging as a practice creates alignments around shared quotidian experiences by conferring upon the private realm of daily experience a public audience. The kind of personal expression of the everyday that we see in microposts has never been subject to real-time mass dissemination in the way that we are currently witnessing on Twitter. This chapter focuses on one such personal domain, coffeetalk, that is, discourse relating to coffee as consumed in everyday life.[1] I will consider this discourse from two simultaneous perspectives: affiliation (personae aligning into communities of value) and identity (personae enacting particular evaluative dispositions).

Alongside a multitude of other choices in fashion and taste, how you take your coffee is part of how you construe your social identity and align with others. Indeed some marketers claim that 'Coffee is the easiest way to figure out who is a member of your "tribe"' (Bosman, 2006). It is a tribe that likes to talk: the beverage has a semiotic history that has long associated coffee with communal spaces and egalitarian conversational practices. European coffeehouses of the seventeenth century were sites 'where commoners and aristocrats alike could meet and socialize without regard to rank' (Gaudio, 2003, p. 670). This early association of coffee with conversation has continued into contemporary times where 'Let's get a coffee' has come to stand for 'Let's have a chat' usually as 'an ostensibly "private," casual interaction in a "public," institutional venue that is "privately" owned' (Gaudio, 2003, p. 672).

With the development of social media there has been additional blurring of the public and private realms with people making reference to their coffee consumption while 'chatting' via microblogging services. For example, on Twitter, the private morning coffee has become a public ritual displayed to a potentially vast ambient, internet-mediated audience:

> enjoying my morning cup of coffee – yum
> Oh how I love coffee =) first thing in the morning

Microposts such as the above regularly announce that the microblogger has consumed their morning 'cup of java' and/or declare the user's love of coffee. Just as consuming a cup of coffee in a coffeehouse involves interpersonal and social dimensions beyond the experiential (i.e. beyond the act of drinking), posting about coffee is much more than informational: it allows people to build community. This chapter will focus on this interpersonal dimension of microblogging, specifically on 'rallying affiliation' (Knight, 2010) in microposts celebrating shared enjoyment of coffee. I begin by looking at the nature of communication and affiliation on a microblogging site, Twitter. I then outline the model used for analysis of the coffee tweets – Martin and White's (2005) Appraisal theory – which focuses on the evaluative devices employed by language users in aligning with other users and texts. My analysis shows how couplings of experiential and evaluative meanings in discourse work to align personae around shared values.

2 The language of micro-blogging

Exploring affiliation in microblogging requires understanding how language is being used via this channel to enact communal bonds. Descriptions of microblogging usually imply that it is a form of conversation involving some kind of 'conversational exchange' (Honeycutt & Herring, 2009). It is variously described as 'lightweight chat' (Starbird *et al.*, 2010, p. 242), as 'prompting opportunistic conversations' (Zhao & Rosson, 2009, p. 251), as 'a specific social dialect, in which individual users are clearly singled out and engaged in a conversation' (Grosseck & Holotescu, 2009) and as constituted by 'dialogue acts' (Ritter, Cherry & Dolan, 2010, p. 172). Microblogging is clearly a highly social activity involving communicative practices in which conversational reciprocity is central. For example, the most common 3-gram (3-word pattern) in HERMES, a 100 million word corpus of microposts, was the interpersonal pattern, *THANKS FOR THE*, with users thanking each other for retweeting or mentioning them (Zappavigna, 2012).

Some studies have suggested that microblogging has a largely phatic function. Malinowski introduced the notion of 'phatic communion' as a way of describing communication in the service of establishing or solidifying bonds of companionship rather than serving 'any purpose of communicating ideas' (2004 [1948], p. 250). If conceived in this way, microblogging functions as what Makice (2009), using a computer metaphor, calls 'linguistic ping'.[2] Just as a computer on a network can be pinged, we may think of microbloggers declaring to their audience, 'I'm still here!'. Thus we might interpret a micropost announcing in the author's first tweet of the day that they have just consumed a great cup of coffee as telling their networked audience that they have just come online for the day. This notion may be extrapolated to relationships formed via social media as part of an overall 'phatic media culture', where 'content is not king, but "keeping in touch" is' and where 'the text message, the short call, the brief email, the short blog update or comment, becomes part of a mediated phatic sociability necessary to maintain a connected presence in an ever expanding social network' (Miller, 2008, p. 395). The extent of this function across microblogging platforms is likely to vary since, for example, status updating on Facebook, within a semi-private network of peers, encourages different forms of expression to the more public networking seen with Twitter (Page, 2012).

The affiliation in operation in microblogging may thus be seen as 'ambient' in the sense that microbloggers as individuals do not necessarily have to interact directly in order to align around a common value. Instead they may signal their alignments indirectly by displaying particular patterns of evaluation, or they can do so directly through resources such as hashtags (e.g. #coffee) that are used to signal the evaluative target of a post (see below for detailed discussion). Language is resplendent with resources for negotiating community such as naming practices, slang and all kinds of variation across phonology, grammar and semantics that characterize different personae and groups (Martin, 2010). However, the language used in social media, particularly microblogging, is under significant interpersonal pressure since users are faced with expressing highly interpersonal meanings in a very constrained context. Microblogging posts are limited to 140 characters and they are posted in a fast-moving environment in which posts can easily be missed by an intended audience. Users therefore have to draw on existing resources in new ways, or develop new resources such as the hashtag. In addition, meanings that might otherwise be expressed paralinguistically must be expressed via other means, such as through the use of punctuation or capitals.[3]

3   Ambient affiliation

This chapter draws on work from systemic functional linguistics in considering how associations between interpersonal and ideational[4] meanings operate to negotiate values in discourse and enact social bonds. The perspective relies upon a social semiotic lens on language as a resource for making meaning (Halliday, 1978). The social semiotic perspective means that I am interested in alignments construed in discourse as a way of understanding communities of socially constructed personae, rather than in how we might group 'individuals' (for example, grouping microbloggers on criteria such as geographic location). In other words, I am interested in 'persons and personalities communing in discourse' (Martin, 2009, p. 563) rather than individuals interacting in groups.

To adequately account for the particular semantic domain considered in this chapter (coffee), the theory used must also acknowledge the semiotic power of bonding icons (Stenglin, 2004) as devices for unification. The concept of iconization, as understood in this context, is a semiotic process whereby interpersonal meaning is condensed and ideational meaning discharged. In other words, it foregrounds the interpersonal (coffee as solidifying relationships) and backgrounds the ideational (coffee as a beverage). Posts about coffee are not just relaying ideational content, they are proposing interactive bonds. Consider, for example, the following micropost, most likely a first post of the morning for this user:

Got my morning cup of #coffee, ready to start my day off!

Rather than simply informing other users that the microblogger has consumed a cup of coffee, the main function of this post is to propose a bond. It can be seen as inviting its audience to align around the bond of enjoying a morning coffee and invokes related associations of coffee with promoting productivity and wakefulness. Due to the powerful cultural impact of iconization, these apparently positive properties of caffeine have great influence on the daily practices of many people. This semiotic influence results from 'the heady association between coffee, conversation and companionship encountered in the coffee-houses' (Ellis, 2004) more than on any psychopharmaceutical reality.

4 Evaluative language in ambient affiliation

Evaluation is a domain of interpersonal meaning where language is used to express attitudes and to adopt stances about other texts. This section explains Appraisal theory (Martin & White, 2005), the model used to analyse evaluative language in the microposts considered in this chapter. Evaluation is an important resource for construing solidarity:

> Feelings are meanings we commune with, since we do not say what we feel unless we expect the person we are talking with to sympathize or empathize with us. We express feelings in order to share them ... to build relationships; where we misjudge the situation and get rebuffed, then a sense of alienation sets in. (Martin, 2002, p. 196)

For example consider the following micropost that offers a highly emotional expression in relation to coffee:

7:00 in morning. No sleep all coffee lol I live it love it ! Yea boy!

This post is typical of the highly evaluative style that the channel encourages (Zappavigna, 2012). The widespread tendency towards using evaluative language in microblogging means that it has become an interesting data source for exploring collective emotive trends, often using some form of automated sentiment analysis (natural language processing methods used in computer science to automatically detect evaluative language in texts) to investigate public reaction to world events (Gruzd, Doiron & Mai, 2011; Thelwall, Buckley & Paltoglou, 2011). Applications of sentiment detection using social media include prediction of the stock market based on 'Twitter mood' (Bollen, Mao & Xiao-Jun, 2011).

Appraisal theory models choices in evaluative meaning using system networks. System networks are networks of interrelated options that are organized paradigmatically, in terms of 'what could go instead of what', rather than syntagmatically in terms of structure (Halliday & Matthiessen, 2004, p. 22). They are an alternative to modelling language as a catalogue of structures. This kind of systemic orientation to meaning arose out of the Firthian tradition in linguistics which asserted the need for a distinction between structure and system, that is, between syntagmatic and paradigmatic relations in language (Firth, 1957).[5] Figure 6.1 provides examples of each region of appraisal as a system network,[6] following Martin and White (2005). The network specifies ATTITUDE,[7] the way in which we construe evaluative orientation in discourse, as a choice between AFFECT (expressing emotion), JUDGEMENT (assessing behaviour) and APPRECIATION (estimating value). The orientation is modified by the way the text either excludes or includes other voices via the ENGAGEMENT system through the choice between monoglossia and heteroglossia. In addition, the evaluation may be upscaled or diminished via GRADUATION systems. The examples in the network shown in the boxes are tweets from the Obama Win Corpus, a corpus of tweets about Obama collected in the 24 hours after he won the 2008 US presidential elections (Zappavigna, 2011). Each example illustrates a type of appraisal and the network may be further specified to greater levels of delicacy depending on the kind of analysis for which it is being used.

Depending on the target and source of the evaluation, lexis such as 'good' can work within any of the ATTITUDE systems. Consider JUDGEMENT working along moral parameters targeted at behaviour in the following tweet:

Thank god is the weekend, time off for **good** behaviour

and AFFECT construing emotion:

I feel really **good**, finally reached the 1,000 followers who wanted both!!

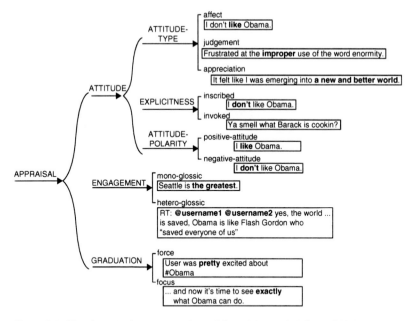

Figure 6.1 The Appraisal system – adapted from Martin & White (2005)

or APPRECIATION expressing an aesthetic assessment about an entity:

> Got to have some best friend time tonight, pack a few boxes and drink some **good** wine. Going to bed content.

The model of evaluative language briefly outlined here offers a useful way of analysing the kinds of emotions and stances that are adopted in microposts; however, this is only half of the picture and we need to consider how such evaluation is used to construe values about the world that we then share with one another. This is the topic of the next section.

5 Affiliation and coupling

While Appraisal theory provides a way of modelling how evaluative language functions, understanding how we align around shared values means that we need to model how we adopt stances about particular things. How do evaluative meanings associate themselves with particular ideation in our discourse and how does this result in producing particular configurations of social bonds? In adopting a social-semiotic approach to this question, this chapter considers how interpersonal meaning co-patterns with ideational meaning in microposts. The theoretical basis of this approach is the concept of 'coupling' introduced by Martin (2000) and taken up by Zhao (2010, 2011) and Zappavigna, Dwyer and Martin (2008) for looking at textual relations:

> Coupling concerns the temporal relation of 'with': variable x comes with variable y. To put it another way, it is the relation formed between two semiotic elements at one given point in time within the logogenetic timeframe. Coupling can be formed between metafunctional variables (e.g. ideational and interpersonal), between different semiotic resources (e.g. image and verbiage) and across strata (e.g. semantics and phonology). (Zhao, 2011, p. 144)

Zhao (2011) argues that cultures incline toward stable coupling patterns when viewed from the perspective of a particular timeframe (e.g. a historical perspective). This modelling perspective is akin to Bakhtin's (1986) work on speech genres as stable patterns of utterance.

In a similar vein, Knight's (2010) model of affiliation, developed through analysis of conversational humour, describes 'communal identity as discursively negotiated in text' in terms of coupling (Knight, 2010, p. 43). The model considers how communities form as people rally around, defer or reject different values construed in language (Knight, 2008). According to Knight, 'we discursively negotiate our communal identities through bonds that we can share, and these bonds make up the value sets of our communities and culture, but they are not stable and fixed' (Knight, 2010, p. 43). Put simply, in order to adopt an evaluative stance, around which we might affiliate (or not), we must construe attitudes *about* ideation (people, places, things etc.). For example, the following micropost construes an aesthetic assessment of coffee made in a particular establishment:

> @user They have fantastic coffee as well!!

The coupling involved may be indicated as shown below, where 'reaction' is a kind of appreciation involving an aesthetic response to something:

> [ideation: coffee / evaluation: appreciation: reaction]

This is the convention that will be adopted throughout the chapter, with the square brackets signalling that the contents are part of the particular coupling of meaning. These associations that build up between patterns of evaluation and patterns of ideation offer a kind of bottom-up approach to defining communities of shared feelings, a tendency that I will refer to as their 'coupling disposition'.

6   The Coffeetweets corpus

The microposts included in the Coffeetweets corpus were extracted from Twitter, the dominant microblogging service currently in operation. Twitter allows users to post messages of 140 characters or less to the general internet or to a set of users who subscribe to a user's message stream, known collectively as 'followers' (see Page, this volume). These microposts are referred to as 'tweets' and are presented to the user in reverse chronological order as an unfolding feed of content. The content is public and searchable unless the user actively makes their account private. Tweets may be accessed, sent and received via a variety of methods such as the web, email, SMS, and third party clients, often running on mobile devices. A tweet may also incorporate links to micromedia (small-scale multimedia) and shortened aliases of longer hyperlinks intended to conserve characters within the constrained textual environment, for example:

I checked in at Starbucks Coffee (200 Running Hill Rd) on #Yelp http://bit.ly/adzBJN

The hyperlink in this tweet points to the complete web address (www. yelp.com/biz/starbucks-south-portland) that the microblogger has used to 'check-in', a common social media activity where users indicate their real-time geographic location, usually by updating this information via a third party service on their smartphone.

The Coffeetweets corpus was derived from HERMES, a 100 million word corpus of tweets (approximately 7 million tweets) (see Zappavigna, 2012, for a corpus-based analysis of this larger corpus). HERMES was collected using the Twitter Streaming Application Programming Interface (API)[8] and filtering for English tweets. It contains randomized tweets based on the algorithm used by Twitter for sampling. The Coffeetalk subcorpus included all tweets containing the string 'coffee'.

The ranked frequency wordlist for the corpus shows a number of items, also seen in HERMES, indicative of the interactivity of Twitter that was flagged at the beginning of this chapter:

- @: the 'at' character is usually used to address a tweet to another user. (N=1, freq.= 8922)

- #: the hash character is used to mark a hashtag, typically to indicate the topic of a tweet. (N=13, freq.= 2351)
- RT: two characters that refer to a 'retweet', the act of republishing another tweet within your own tweet. (N=19, freq.=1850)

It is interesting that these three items, which are dependent on the mode of communication (we would not expect these in a corpus containing communication via other CMC channels), are also items that work in the service of interactivity. It seems that users have worked creatively and collaboratively to create additional resources that allow them to more effectively commune in the constrained environment.

All of these items are examples of resources for bringing voices from other texts into a tweet, working in cooperation with ENGAGEMENT resources in the discourse semantics. As we will see later, the #coffee hashtag plays an important role in aligning users into communities of shared values about coffee.

7   Rallying affiliation: bonding around the bean

We will now focus upon a particular affiliation strategy, rallying affiliation (Knight, 2010). This strategy involves communing around a shared bond by negotiating couplings of evaluation and ideation in discourse. Rallying affiliation was very common within the Coffeetweets corpus with many posts deploying coffee as an icon around which to unite through accumulating APPRECIATION, for example:

> Damn, that's **good** coffee, @User. I suggest you get some and put it in you.

These might be described as tweets displaying couplings of the following kind:

> [ideation: coffee / evaluation: positive appreciation: positive reaction]

These posts positively appreciated coffee with reference to its aesthetic dimensions. They were complemented by posts aligning users around AFFECT resulting from pleasure in drinking coffee, characterized by couplings of [ideation: coffee / evaluation: affect: happiness/satisfaction/ desire]. For example:

> coffee and cigarettes, **love** it!

JUDGEMENT was generally infrequent in the corpus and was more likely to be used for condemning than rallying:

> @Starbucks bought 65 perccent of their coffee from **ethically** traded sources. That number is too low for me! Make it 100!

In terms of GRADUATION,[9] there was a clear pattern toward upscaling ATTITUDE via the intensifying lexis, for example:

> coffee is **SO** good!
> Illy coffee might be the **best** coffee on earf. Of **all** times.
> @User I try **really** hard to only have **really** great coffees, I research **a lot.**

Since HERMES and the Coffetweets corpus are composed of randomized posts it is not possible to consider the exchange structure of interactions about coffee. However, because instances of rallying affiliation abound on Twitter it was relatively straightforward to retrieve a relevant example via the service's search interface. The exchange shown in Table 6.1 is of an interaction that unfolded following a 'good coffee' bond proposed in the first tweet (1). The indents in the first column indicate a direct reply to a post via an @mention (directing tweet at a user with their username preceded by the @ symbol) and the unfolding of rows represents the sequencing of posts in time. The posts which follow the initial bond proposal (2–12) involve instances of accumulating positive appreciation targeted at coffee (evaluation shown in bold). The couplings in these posts (shown in the second column in Table 6.1) are complemented by markers of solidarity such as smiley emoticons and inscribed agreement (e.g. AMEN!, AGREED!!!!). This attitudinal communion is enhanced by the tendency toward upscaled GRADUATION realised both lexically and orthographically (via repetition of exclamation marks and caps font). The users are rallying around the values that they share about coffee, forming a small ambient community. In the section which follows we will consider the increase in scope of such affiliation when it is marked with a hashtag.

8   Rallying via hashtagging

While the Coffeetweets corpus does not preserve conversational links between tweets, the semiotic alignments enacted are nevertheless apparent. Many posts contain a typographic convention deployed by users to indicate that their tweet is associated with other tweets on the same notional topic. This convention is known as the 'hashtag'.

Table 6.1 Couplings involved in rallying affiliation in a Twitter interaction

	Tweet	Coupling
1	Have I mentioned that **coffee** is sooo **good**!?	[Ideation: coffee /evaluation: positive reaction]
2	@User1 agreed,, I'm **enjoying** my **cup** right now.. **mmmm caffine**	[ideation: cup (of coffee) / evaluation: positive reaction] [ideation: caffeine / evaluation]
3	Not **into coffee**, but give me a vat of tea in the mornings and I'm a **happy** gal!	[ideation: coffee / evaluation: invoked negative reaction] [ideation: microblogger / evaluation: happiness]
4	@User1 have I mentioned that **coffee** is sooo **good**!?	[ideation: coffee / positive reaction]
5	@User1 just about to make my second cup before waking DD, I **heart** this **time of morning**:)	[ideation: time of morning / evaluation: positive reaction]
6	@User1 **cafe mocha** is my **weakness**!	[ideation: café mocha / evaluation: negative judgement invoking positive reaction]
7	@User1 amen. **coffee** should be **the 5th major food group**.	[ideation: coffee / evaluation: invoked positive valuation]
8	@User2 **It's number one on my list**!;)	[ideation: coffee / evaluation: positive valuation]
9	@User1 AMEN!	
10	@User 1Amen to that! Cup # 2 for me now:)	
11	@User1 oh i **love coffee**...	[ideation: coffee / evaluation: positive affect]
12	@User1 AGREED!!!! And pouring another cup right now!:)	

Hashtags are a form of conversational tagging that emerged through community use on Twitter (Huang, Thornton & Efthimiadis, 2010). They are a form of social tagging or folksonomy (Vander Wal, 2007) that may derive from internet relay chat (IRC) conventions for naming channels (#channelname). The # character marks the label that a user has assigned to a tweet. For example, #coffee in the following post indicates that the tweet is about coffee:

I hate being 'twired' where I am awake because of stimulants, but actually tired. #coffee #sleep

The label means that that other users interested in coffee can find the post even though this lexical item does not occur in the body of the tweet. They may do this by searching for the tag via the search interface that Twitter provides, or, if they are likely to have an ongoing interest in the tag, they may elect to subscribe to a feed of tweets containing this tag: a process known as following the tag. In this way hashtagging increases the interactivity of microposts by rendering them a form of 'searchable talk' (Zappavigna, 2011). The three most common hashtags in the Coffeetweets corpus are shown in Table 6.2.

Hashtags can thus function to coordinate mass expression of value by focusing rallying affiliation around a particular ideational target (e.g. #coffee) and aligning users into 'overlapping communities of attitudinal rapport' (Martin, 2004, p. 323). They typically function as a way of marking the ideational component of a coupling in a tweet – for example the following post construes the coupling [ideation: coffee/ evaluation: affect: happiness] (evaluation shown in bold):

I **love** #coffee

Here the hashtag marks coffee as the ideational centre[10] of the potential affiliation. In this way hashtags indicate the ideation around which other users (adopting this hashtag) might rally.

Posts containing similar hashtags can be seen to form ambient communities of value, that is, particular orientations toward a particular ideation. The general idea is shown in Figure 6.2 where tweets marked #coffee form an ambient affiliative network populated by couplings about coffee,

Table 6.2 The most frequent hashtags in tweets containing COFFEE

Freq.	hashtag	Example	Function
141	#coffee	Good morning, Twitterverse! Today's as good day.... Enjoy in the morning a delicious #coffee	Indicates coffee as the ideational focus of the post.
109	#fb	Peanut butter, with honey & sliced banana on toast with coffee. Quickie breakfast of champions=p #fb	Used by third party application to automatically import the post into Facebook.
56	#ff	#FOLLOW @User1! She is soo insightful and loves coffee!: D #FF #F4F	Indicates the post is part of the 'Follow Friday' (FF) meme where microbloggers promote other users.

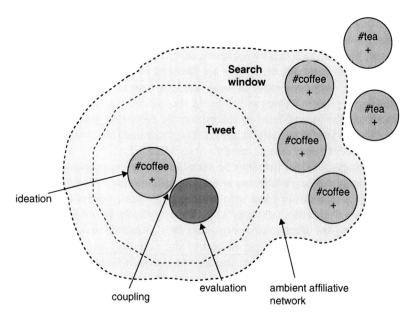

ideation

coupling   evaluation   ambient affiliative
                               network

Figure 6.2 Tweets marked with the hashtag #coffee forming an ambient affiliative network

distinct from those for example about '#tea'. The + symbol is used in this figure to suggest a kind of semiotic charging: by adding the hashtag to an instance of ideation we make it more available to be evaluated.

9   Coffee bonds and identity

Since patterns of coupling align personae into communities (Martin, in press), the kind of ambient communities characterized by rallying affiliation that have been suggested in this chapter may be approached from the perspective of identity. The general tendencies in the patterns of coupling seen in the Coffeetweets corpus suggest two broad identities enacted in relation to coffee. These identities may be compared in terms of their 'coupling disposition'. The first is a Coffee Connoisseur who generates aesthetic assessments via APPRECIATION regarding the quality of the coffee they are drinking. The coupling pattern typifying this identity is [ideation: coffee / evaluation: appreciation: positive reaction]:

> @User thanks very much, I'm looking forward to tasting all the **amazing** coffees we have coming in through the Synesso, and Aurelia.

The sun is shining. I am off to Donington Market to stock up on **rare** and **exotic** coffee blends.

Ditto! RT @User: Just had an Allagash Black. **Fantastic! Notes of roasted coffee, chocolate, and fruity Belgian yeast.**

Agnate identities include wine and chocolate connoisseurs and the more generalized 'foodie', or more ideologically charged 'food snob'. The Coffee Connoisseur personae also tend to construe couplings such as [ideation: life / evaluation: appreciation: reaction] that contribute to a 'fine life' bond, with the positive prosody targeted at coffee seeming to have spilled over into other aspects of daily life. For instance this might involve positive APPRECIATION of the day to come (APPRECIATION in bold):

What a **beautiful** day!! Sun is shining (first time in weeks!), coffee tastes so **good** and pancakes for breakfast:) I couldn't be happier! <3

Back in Milwaukee, I so love it here..**great** coffee, **lovely** people, **great** shopping...this is gonna be a **wonderful** day:)

The other identity prevalent in the corpus is a more humble Coffee Addict addicted to consuming coffee in order to survive the day. This persona tends toward construing AFFECT:

Did I ever tell you I **HATE** mornings? **Wish** I could wake up and have a cup of coffee before the chaos started!

*leans my hot head on the cold counter, watching the coffee pot fill and **groaning** at the thought of another long day*

In these examples the iconized coffee bond works with another common bond, a 'hard life' bond relating to the negative affect engendered by life's minor irritations. This latter bond is very common in microposts about everyday experiences (see Zappavigna, 2012, for examples of this bond in relation to the Fail meme).

The complaints made by the Coffee Addict persona are symptomatic of a shift in social relations where microblogging has afforded users previously unavailable opportunities to complain about the details of their lives to a large audience. Complaining itself can invoke solidarity via the potential for evoking commiseration in relation to shared irritations. For example, consider the common bond shared by the following tweets inscribed in the hashtag #needcoffee [ideation: microblogger / evaluation: affect: desire]:

> I hate waking up at 6am everyday. Ughh #needcoffee

> I'm so out of it this morning. #needcoffee or #moresleep

> I want to fast forward to 3:30, to where I'm laying in bed, taking a nap. #needcoffee

> Getting out of bed can be so difficult some days...its one of those days #needcoffee

> I feel like a zombie. #ineedcoffee

> Well that was a "fun" morning commute..gggrrrr #INeedCoffee

Related n-grams included, I NEED COFFEE (n=10) and NEED MORE COFFEE (n=41), for example:

> Whyy am I soo tired this morning?:/ Ugg **I need coffee**!!

> Snow again this morning. 2 kids with fevers. Flat tire. Shivering dog. I think I **need more coffee.**

These types of posts typically express frustration at minor concerns such as lack of sleep the night before or how early in the morning the Coffee Addict has gotten out of bed. This kind of pattern was also seen more generally in the HERMES corpus where common semantic domains of complaint were work, school and sleep, often within a single tweet:

> 18 hours of no sleep. I have to go to work and i`m still going out tonight. FAIL!

Thinking synoptically about these identities we might map them onto two axes:[11] an ideational dimension along the vertical axis and an interpersonal dimension along the horizontal axis (Figure 6.3). In the upper right quadrant is the Coffee Connoisseur who tends to present a 'good coffee' bond with the couplings involving appreciation and also the 'fine life' bond instantiated as positive appreciations of daily life. In the lower left quadrant is the Coffee Addict persona characterized by proposals of the 'need coffee' and 'hard life' bonds, both of which are instantiated by couplings involving negative affect. The dotted lines

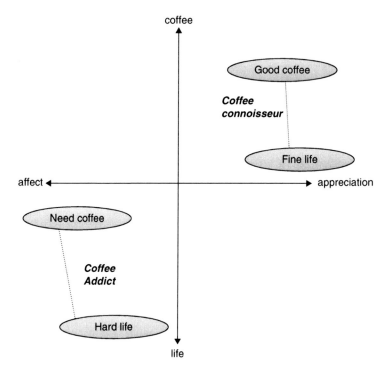

Figure 6.3 Bonding tendencies of two coffee-related personae

between the bonds indicate that they form part of a 'bond complex' in the sense that they are typically co-construed by these personae.

This topological perspective affords us a view of the polarization of these two subject positions in terms of their differing coupling dispositions. We may think about these identities more relationally along a cline of affiliating personae (Martin, in press) subclassified by the range of bond complexes they tend to enact.

While the particularities of the organizing principles that might describe how personae align and de-align as we engage in social life remain elusive, the impact they have on our lives is intuitively apparent. This impact is humorously depicted in a cartoon picture of a grumpy-looking cat, replicated across the internet, which reads 'Before my morning coffee ... I might as well be a dog'. The simple humour readily underlines how patterns of alignment, such as rallying around morning coffee, are intimately involved in both the construction of identity and group boundaries. As Martin (in press) notes, 'Personae are only ever personae as affiliating members of a group'.

10   Conclusion

Social media such as microblogging allow us to connect with common travellers who share our values. With mobile computing and using resources such as smartphones to access social media, we can share experiences online relatively seamlessly at the same time as engaging in our daily activities. Social media render online interaction 'searchable' in a way and to an extent that has never been seen in history. It is now possible, using metadata such as hashtags, to find the values people are sharing about both daily minutiae (e.g. what someone feels about their morning coffee) and about important world events. This means that we can track the kinds of communities that form as people rally around shared concerns.

This chapter has discussed rallying affiliation in microblogging in order to explore how such communities form. I have considered the kinds of bonds that are negotiated when microbloggers post 'coffeetweets'. The perspective on how these bonds are enacted in discourse involves considering how couplings of ideation and evaluation work to align personae around shared values. I have also shown how hashtagging operates to allow ambient affiliation around common ideational targets. This is a novel gaze on community, with the organizing principle of affiliation being an emergent bonding around searchable topics rather than direct interaction.

Affiliation is about more than connecting; it is about negotiating meanings within genres of language use. Thinking about affiliation and microblogging in this way overcomes some of the problems that researchers have recognized regarding defining what constitutes a virtual community. By analysing how people use language to share values, and considering their language from a functional perspective, we have a way of viewing community in unfolding discourse semantics rather than solely approaching community via less subtle variables such as geographic location or links between profiles. Indeed, some studies suggest that reciprocity in the 'following' relationship on Twitter is not prevalent (Kwak *et al.*, 2010) and that the 'follow' relation itself does not necessarily imply direct interaction between people. They argue instead that 'we need to find the hidden social network; the one that matters when trying to rely on word of mouth to spread an idea, a belief, or a trend' (Bernardo, Romero & Wu, 2008). I argue here that the 'hidden' network is a semiotic network of bonds and bond complexes. The analysis of rallying affiliation undertaken in this chapter is a small step towards understanding the linguistic strategies available to personae in electronic discourse for construing community.

Notes

1. That is, both the social media equivalent of casual conversation over coffee and more general discourse about coffee produced by coffee drinkers and their associates.
2. 'Ping' in networking refers to a way of detecting if there is a valid communication path between two or more computers: one computer sends out a message and the other replies with an identical copy.
3. However the medium does afford new meaning potential not possible in face-to-face communication and it is possibly not very productive to continue thinking of online communication as the poor cousin of spoken discourse.
4. It should also be noted at this point that the distinction being made between an ideational focus on information and an interpersonal emphasis on social connection should not be conceived in binary terms, since language makes multiple kinds of meaning simultaneously. Within systemic functional linguistics this concurrent meaning potential is referred to as the metafunctions of language: an ideational function of enacting experience, an interpersonal function of negotiating relationships, and a textual function of organizing information (Halliday & Matthiessen, 2004). A functional account of language aims to take into account these three dimensions when approaching any instance of meaning.
5. These ideas originate in Hjelmslev's (1961 [1943]) conception of paradigmatic relations, in turn influenced by Saussure's (1983 [1916]) distinction between syntagmatic and associative relations.
6. The network adopts the convention whereby capitalized labels above the arrows indicate different systems of meaning, and the lower-case labels at the end of each path mark features within systems. A square bracket represents a choice between two options in a system (an 'or' relation), while a brace represents simultaneous choices (an 'and' relation).
7. Appraisal terminology is shown in small caps to differentiate it from commonplace terms.
8. The API is the language that software tools use to communicate with Twitter's backend database.
9. For a study in graduation systems see Hood (2010).
10. Examples with evaluation or evaluation and ideation coupled together were possible as hashtags but were usually deployed for humorous effect given the relative absurdity of anyone searching for a tag such as #ilovecoffee or #awesome.
11. For examples of this kind of topological modelling of personae in another domain, see Martin, Zappavigna and Dwyer (in press), inspired by work in Legitimation Code Theory (Maton, forthcoming).

References

Bakhtin, M. M. (1986) *Speech Genres and Other Late Essays* (Austin: University of Texas Press).

Bernardo, H., Romero, D. M. & Wu, F. (2008) 'Social networks that matter: Twitter under the microscope', *First Monday* 14(1). http://firstmonday.org/

htbin/cgiwrap/bin/ojs/index.php/fm/article/view/2317/2063 (accessed: 24 January 2013).

Bollen, J., Mao, H. & Xiao-Jun, Z. (2011) 'Twitter mood predicts the stock market', *Journal of Computational Science*, 2(1): 1–8.

Bosman, J. (2006) 'This Joe's for you?' *The New York Times*, http://www.nytimes.com/2006/06/08/business/media/08adco.html?pagewanted=all&_r=0 (accessed: 24 January 2013).

Ellis, M. (2004) *A Cultural History of Coffee* (London: Weidenfeld and Nicolson)

Firth, J. (1957) *Papers in Linguistics 1934–1951* (London: Oxford University Press).

Gaudio, R. P. (2003) 'Coffeetalk: Star-bucks™ and the commercialization of casual conversation', *Language in Society*, 32: 659–91.

Grosseck, G. & Holotescu, C. (2009) 'Indicators for the analysis of learning and practice communities from the perspective of microblogging as a provocative sociolect in virtual space'. Paper presentend at the 5th International Scientific Conference eLSE – eLearning and Software for Education conference, Bucharest 9–10 April 2009.

Gruzd, A., Doiron, S. & Mai, P. (2011) 'Is happiness contagious online? A case of Twitter and the 2010 Winter Olympics'. Paper presented at the the 44th Hawai'i International Conference on System Sciences (HICSS), Kauai, Hawai'i.

Halliday, M. A. K. (1978) *Language as Social Semiotic: The Social Interpretation of Language and Meaning* (London: Edward Arnold).

Halliday, M. A. K. & Matthiessen, C. M. I. M. (2004) *An Introduction to Functional Grammar*, Third edition (London: Arnold).

Hjelmslev, L. (ed.) (1961[1943]) *Prolegomena to a Theory of Language* (Madison, WI: University of Wisconsin Press).

Honeycutt, C. & Herring, S. (2009) 'Beyond microblogging: Conversation and collaboration in Twitter'. Paper presented at the Proceedings of the Forty-Second Hawai'i International Conference on System Sciences (HICSS-42), Los Alamitos, CA.

Hood, S. (2010) *Appraising Research: Evaluation in Academic Writing* (Basingstoke and New York: Palgrave Macmillan).

Huang, J., Thornton, K. M. & Efthimiadis, E. N. (2010) 'Conversational tagging in Twitter'. In *Proceedings of the 21st ACM Conference on Hypertext and Hypermedia* (Toronto: ACM) pp 173–8.

Knight, N. (2008) '"Still cool…and american too!": An SFL analysis of deferred bonds in internet messaging humour'. In N. Nørgaard (ed.), *Systemic Functional Linguistics in Use*. Odense Working Papers in Language and Communication (Odense: University of Southern Denmark, Institute of Language and Communication), pp. 481–502.

Knight, N. (2010) 'Wrinkling complexity: Concepts of identity and affiliation in humour'. In M. Bednarek & J. R. Martin (eds.), *New Discourse on Language: Functional Perspectives on Multimodality, Identity, and Affiliation* (London: Continuum), pp. 35–58.

Kwak, H., Lee, C., Park, H. & Moon, S. (2010) 'What is Twitter, a social network or a news media?' In *Proceedings of the 19th International Conference on the World Wide Web* (Raleigh, NC: ACM), pp. 591–600.

Makice, K. (2009) 'Phatics and the design of community'. In *Proceedings of the 27th International Conference Extended Abstracts on Human Factors in Computing Systems* (Boston: ACM), pp. 3133–6.

Malinowski, B. (2004 [1948]) *Magic, Science and Religion and Other Essays* (Lavergne, TN: Kessinger).

Martin, J. R. (2000) 'Beyond exchange: APPRAISAL systems in English'. In S. Hunston & G. Thompson (eds.), *Evaluation in Text: Authorial Stance and the Construction of Discourse* (Oxford: Oxford University Press), pp. 142–75.

Martin, J. R. (2002) 'Blessed are the peacemakers: Reconciliation and evaluation'. In C. Candlin (ed.) *Research and Practice in Professional Discourse* (Hong Kong: City University of Hong Kong Press), pp. 187–227.

Martin, J. R. (2004) 'Mourning: How we get aligned' *Discourse and Society*, 15(2–3): 321–44.

Martin, J. R. (2009) 'Realisation, instantiation and individuation: Some thoughts on identity in youth justice conferencing', *DELTA: Documentação de Estudos em Lingüística Teórica e Aplicada*, 25: 549–83.

Martin, J. R. (2010) 'Introduction: Semantic variation'. In M. Bednarek & J. R. Martin (eds.) *New Discourse on Language: Functional Perspectives on Multimodality, Identity, and Affiliation* (London: Continuum), pp. 1–34.

Martin, J. R. (in press) 'Heart from darkness: Apocalypse Ron', *Revista Canaria de Estudios Ingleses (Special issue on Evaluative Uses of Langauage: the Appraisal System)*.

Martin, J. R. & White, P. R. R. (2005) *The Language of Evaluation: Appraisal in English* (Basingstoke and New York: Palgrave Macmillan).

Martin, J. R., Zappavigna, M. & Dwyer, P. (in press) 'Users in uses of language: Embodied identity in Youth justice conferencing', *Text & Talk*.

Maton, K. (forthcoming) *Knowledge and Knowers: Towards a Realist Sociology of Education*. (Abingdon: Routledge).

Miller, V. (2008) 'New media, networking and phatic culture', *Convergence: The International Journal of Research into New Media Technologies* 14(4): 387–400.

Page, R. (2012) *Stories and Social Media: Identities and Interactions* (Abingdon: Routledge).

Ritter, A., Cherry, C. & Dolan, B. (2010) 'Unsupervised modeling of Twitter conversations'. In *Human Language Technologies: The 2010 Annual Conference of the North American Chapter of the Association for Computational Linguistics* (Los Angeles: Association for Computational Linguistics).

Saussure, F. (1983) *Course in General Linguistics* (La Salle, IL: Open Court).

Starbird, K., Palen, L., Hughes, A. L. & Vieweg, S. (2010) 'Chatter on the red: What hazards threat reveals about the social life of microblogged information'. In *Proceedings of the 2010 ACM Conference on Computer-supported Cooperative Work*, pp. 241–50.

Stenglin, M. (2004) Packaging Curiosities: Towards a Grammar of Threedimensional Space. Unpublished manuscript, University of Sydney, Sydney.

Thelwall, M., Buckley, K. & Paltoglou, G. (2011) 'Sentiment in Twitter events', *Journal of the American Society for Information Science and Technology*, 62(2): 406–18.

Vander Wal (2007) Folksonomy coinage and definition, http://vanderwal.net/folksonomy.html (accessed: 24 January 2013).

Zappavigna, M. (2011) 'Ambient affiliation: A linguistic perspective on Twitter', *New Media and Society*, 13(5): 788–806.

Zappavigna, M. (2012) *Discourse of Twitter and Social Media: How We Use Language to Create Affiliation on the Web* (London: Continuum).

Zappavigna, M., Dwyer, P. & Martin, J. R. (2008) 'Syndromes of meaning: Exploring patterned coupling in a NSW youth justice conference'. In A. Mahboob & N. Knight (eds) *Questioning Linguistics* (Newcastle: Cambridge Scholars Publishing), pp. 103–17.

Zhao, S. (2010) 'Intersemiotic relations as logogenetic patterns: Towards the restoration of the time dimension in hypertext description'. In M. Bednarek & J. R. Martin (eds.), *New Discourse on Language: Functional Perspectives on Multimodality, Identity, and Affiliation* (London: Continuum), pp. 195–218.

Zhao, S. (2011) Learning Through Multimedia Interaction: The Construal of Primary Social Science Knowledge in Web-based Digital Learning Materials. Unpublished manuscript, University of Sydney, Sydney.

Zhao, D. & Rosson, M. B. (2009) 'How and why people Twitter: The role that micro-blogging plays in informal communication at work'. *Proceedings of the ACM 2009 International Conference on Supporting Group Work, Sanibel Island, FL.*

7
Audience design and language choice in the construction and maintenance of translocal communities on social network sites

Caroline Tagg and Philip Seargeant

1 Introduction

This chapter explores how multilingual users perceive their audience on semi-public social network sites (SNSs), and how these perceptions shape users' language choices as they construct and maintain translocal communities. It does so by building upon a widely used framework for understanding style choices in spoken interaction: Bell's 'audience design' (1984). Bell's model posits that a speaker's stylistic choices can in great part be shaped by their attempts to accommodate to their addressees and to others present in the exchange, and this basic principle also holds for online contexts. However, the particular affordances of communication via SNSs are likely to result in interesting differences between the type of audiences perceived by someone posting on an SNS such as Facebook, and the audiences which Bell's model describes for spoken interaction. Firstly, unlike either conversational or broadcast talk, the type of interactions that typically take place on SNSs are conducted via the written mode, and yet at the same time they exhibit much of the interactivity and informality that is often found in speech. Secondly, given that they sit somewhere between personal conversation and public broadcasts, SNSs can be described as 'semi-public' forums in the sense that a user's audience, while often large, diverse and unseen, generally comprises people they know. Given this noisy environment, we argue that audience design strategies are crucial for SNS users as they seek to target individuals and communities from within the wider audience. Moreover, within multilingual communities, language choice becomes an important element of audience design strategies.

Although Bell argues that the notion of 'audience' underlies other factors shaping style and language choices in spoken interaction – chiefly topic and setting – consideration must also be given to the range of technological and social variables that shape practices in online communication (Herring, 2007). For analytic purposes it is useful to divide the elements that combine to constitute online communicative practice into different categories. In multilingual online exchanges of the sort we focus on in this chapter, three elements combine to create a communicative dynamic which is specific to the way people interact and manage relationships on SNSs. These are: (1) a form of audience design (the ways in which users tailor their posts to the expectations of their imagined readership), which often involves or is related to (2) issues around language choice (decisions over which code, variety, register and script to use), which together play a part in the construction and maintenance of (3) the 'translocal' community (the context in and towards which the communication is performed). The notion of *translocality* – a term used to describe the negotiation of locally defined meanings which occurs when diverse local practices and values are brought together (Blommaert, 2010) – is useful here because of the dispersed or diffuse communities that are possible on SNSs, and which are often the context for multilingual interactions. These three elements have combinatory effects, but each of them also consists of other factors. So audience design in SNS interactions among translocal communities involves language choice, but is not limited to it (other strategies and motivating factors are also involved); likewise language choice in SNS interactions by translocal communities can be related to audience design but is also influenced by other issues (such as speaker biography); and finally, the maintenance and creation of translocal communities via SNS interaction is facilitated by language choice and audience design, but also by other communicative means (e.g. patterns of indexicality). This chapter focuses predominantly on the audience design element of this triad, in order to map how style choices influenced by perceptions of the nature of the audience operate within the context of SNS interactions, and how this element then combines with the others to create a particular communicative dynamic.

The chapter begins with a brief overview of audience design in relation to style in speaking (Bell, 1984, 2001), focusing on defining the roles identified in spoken interactions and exploring the extent to which this model is sufficiently dynamic to describe the interactions that occur via SNSs. It then discusses the ways in which interaction via SNSs resembles and differs from spoken interaction, and the implications of these differences for the way audiences are likely to be perceived and managed. The chapter then lays out a modified audience design framework for SNSs as they currently operate, using case study data from multilingual exchanges via Facebook (which at the time of writing [early 2013] is the most used and high-profile SNS). It concludes by discussing how audience design combines with language choice in the construction of translocal communities on Facebook.

2 Audience design in spoken interaction

Bell's original audience design framework can be seen as an attempt to address the question of why a speaker says something *this* way on *this* occasion (as phrased by Bell, 2001, p. 139); that is, as a way of understanding speakers' stylistic choices. It originally emerged from his reflections on how the same New Zealand newsreaders varied their pronunciation when reading the news on different radio stations, suggesting that they were imagining different audiences for each station; and this observation came to be seen as relevant to everyday spoken interactions. The framework needs to be viewed in the context of contemporary studies of style, which tended to follow Labov's seminal observation that style varied according to the amount of attention paid to one's speech (1966). Bell drew attention to the crucial way in which audiences – and, importantly, different members of an audience – shape a speaker's style. Drawing on Bakhtin's (1930s/1981) notion of addressivity, the framework reflects earlier models which emphasize the role of the audience (Clark & Carlson, 1982; Garfinkel, 1967; Goffman, 1981; Sacks, Schegloff & Jefferson, 1974) and also has parallels with speech accommodation theory which, in its basic form, explores the ways in which speakers converge with or diverge from interlocutors (Giles & Powesland, 1975).

At the centre of Bell's model is the speaker, whose utterances are shaped in response to his/her perception of, and orientation towards, the people who occupy three main audience roles: addressee, auditor, and overhearer. The addressees are participants in an interaction who are 'oriented to by the speaker in a manner to suggest that his or her words are particularly for them, and that some answer is therefore anticipated from them, more so than for the other ratified participants' (Goffman, 1975, p. 260). The remaining participants are the 'auditors', who are not directly addressed but whose involvement in the exchange is 'ratified': considered by the speaker to be 'taking part' (Clark & Carlson, 1982). The final category, the 'overhearers', are not ratified participants, but the speaker is nonetheless concerned with pre-empting the assumptions and hypotheses that this group may draw from an utterance (Clark & Carlson, 1982, p. 344).

Bell held that an addressee will exert more influence over speaker style than an auditor, who in turn has more effect than an overhearer (1984, 2001). In practice this may depend on how a speaker perceives the people involved and the power relationships that pertain – so that, for example, the presence of a child's mother as an overhearer may encourage the child to use standard forms, regardless of who the child is directly addressing (Youseff, 1993). Another criticism levelled against Bell's model is that it is overly 'responsive' in that speakers are posited as reacting in predictable ways to pre-determined audiences (Finegan & Biber, 2001). The criticism can be countered in part by emphasizing the fact that roles are not pre-determined but allocated by the speaker. In other words, speakers can be seen as active agents who simultaneously construct and respond to their audiences. As we shall see, this element of audience design may be particularly pertinent to semi-public SNSs where the particular individuals who will read and respond to a post cannot be guaranteed and so, as with broadcast speech, a potential audience must be imagined into being (Litt, 2012).

Also important in challenging the suggestion that audience design is necessarily reactive is Bell's (1999, 2001) development of his notion of 'initiative style shift'. While addressing an audience, speakers will also accommodate to non-present third parties – either groups to which the speaker belongs or to those they do not – through 'initiative' style shifts which, by transposing meanings from other contexts, serve to shape rather than simply respond to the current situation (cf. Rampton's notion of 'crossing' [1995]). As Bell (2001, p. 165) explains, responsive and initiative style shifts must be seen as 'two complementary and coexistent dimensions of style'. The emergent nature of norms on email and on sites such as Facebook (McLaughlin & Vitak, 2011) may make it likely that users will take the initiative and be seen to 'shape' rather than 'respond to' the online context in ways that may go on to become 'institutionalized' by an online community.

If presented as a dynamic process during which participants actively target, shape and re-shape their listenership, audience design allows us to probe the complexity of self-presentation and the various strategies this involves (Goffman, 1990[1959]). It has long been recognized that people are active producers of their own identities, and that linguistic resources form part of the repertoire of ways in which they bring their identities into being (see, for example, Eckert's [1989] classic observations regarding 'jocks' and 'burnouts' at American high schools). However, people do not act the same way in front of everyone, but vary their performances according to the context, their own communicative purposes, and their audience (Baker, 1991). Bell's framework, by drawing attention to the fact that different members of the same audience may encourage speakers towards different styles, highlights the complex ways in which speakers must sometimes vary their presentational strategies within one exchange or context. As we shall see, this type of dynamic has implications for the application of the framework to SNSs, given that SNS audiences have often been described in terms of a more pervasive 'context collapse' (Marwick & boyd, 2010).

The framework – with its highly interpersonal focus and its recognition of the imagined nature of all audiences and the inherently dialogic nature of communication (Bakhtin, 1930s/1981) – has immediate advantages for understanding interactional patterns and language choice on an SNS such as Facebook, where a largely unseen and varied audience must be imagined, constructed and targeted by users. However, the extent to which the model can be applied to multilingual Facebook data lies with the differences between spoken and online written interaction, particularly that taking place via SNSs. In the following sections we detail these differences and their implications for a model of audience design.

3   The affordances of social network sites

The way in which Facebook users construct and engage with their perceived audience(s) will differ to some extent from similar processes in spoken interactions, due to the ways in which they exploit the affordances that characterize online, networked communication in general and SNSs in particular. In this section, we describe the affordances of online communication and their implications for the strategies that online users can employ in targeting others. We then look at the specific affordances of Facebook and how users are likely to perceive the make-up of their online audience.

We start with a word about 'affordances' (Gibson, 1986, p. 127), as the term is of central importance for understanding how the possibilities and potential constraints offered by an SNS shape the communication that takes place there. Specifically, we use the term to refer to users' interpretations of what is made possible by the technology, based on their own technical competence and communicative intent (Lee, 2007, pp. 226–7). Given the rapidly evolving nature of online communication software and sites such as Facebook, the ways in which users engage with and negotiate these affordances have a significant influence over the structure of their communication and the language resources they employ.

3.1   The affordances of online communication and addressivity strategies

Since the 1990s, online communication has been understood as embodying several characteristics typically associated with speech: namely interactivity, informality, playfulness and close community (Danet, 2001; Ferrara, Brunner & Whittemore, 1991; Rheingold, 1994). In this context, perhaps the most striking characteristic of online communication is that it is predominantly written rather than spoken (although not by any means entirely). As documented in the early literature on computer-mediated communication (Baron, 1998; Crystal, 2001), participants are often separated in time and space; there tends to be opportunity for more asynchronous communication; online messages tend to have more permanence than speech; and, rather than the paralinguistic features such as gesture and prosody that accompany face-to-face interaction, users instead draw on visual resources of page format, symbol, image and, in multilingual interactions, script-mixing (Tagg & Seargeant, 2012; Warschauer, Said & Zohry, 2007). Given the 'speech-like' nature of much interaction online, these graphic resources are often seen as compensating for the lack of gesture and so on in facilitating intimate and interpersonal communicative functions (Androutsopoulos, 2013). These resources can all have implications for the audience design strategies available to users in addressing other participants.

A speaker in a face-to-face interaction has various resources on which to draw for making role assignments explicit. Specifically, Clark and Carlson (1982, p. 346) suggest that participants can be addressed, ratified or excluded through one or a combination of the following: 'physical arrangement, conversational history, gestures, manner of speaking, and linguistic content'. Resources which rely on the immediate physical space – such as the physical arrangement of the participants – are not available to Facebook users who are separated in time and space and communicating through the written channel, and thus other strategies need to be employed to offset this. Other paralinguistic resources – such as gestures – can be compensated for by graphic resources such as emoticons or changes in font. In addition there are user-generated symbols aimed at addressing posts: for example the '@' sign can be used to tag an individual in a post (often with the aim of drawing the attention of the individual, who is notified by Facebook, to the post). Other resources – such as conversational history, manner of speaking, and linguistic content – find their parallels on Facebook.

The various strategies for audience design used on SNSs are likely to be as follows. Note that the strategies range from the very explicit (direct address) to the implicit (style).

- Direct address strategies (use of the @ sign; photo- or post-tagging;[1] use of groups or lists)
- Other structural affordances (e.g. dividing messages into separate posts)
- Style (level of formality; degree of vagueness or explicitation) and language choice (including language, script and dialect choice; and switches between them)
- Content of post (topic; degree to which content can be described as public or private)

As an example of the strategies used, we have looked elsewhere at the use of 'photo tagging' by a translocal Thai community to draw Friends' attention to a post (Tagg & Seargeant, 2012). A practice had emerged within this community whereby they tagged each other specifically in photos of food in order to elicit exclamations of jealousy from other members of the group. The practice was tied to their ongoing shared interest in cooking (i.e. a common cultural interest which had taken on a ritual symbolic value for the group's identity), and the fact that the participants in the exchange were geographically dispersed and clearly unable to try the food themselves. In this way, a straightforward and fairly direct audience design strategy of photo tagging is enhanced by the participants' shared interactional history, online and offline, and plays a direct role in the maintenance of their sense of community.

Other examples of how these strategies operate in practice are given below as the audience design framework is laid out. Firstly, however, the particular affordances of Facebook, and their implications for how audience is perceived on the site, are described.

3.2   Affordances and audience on Facebook

Facebook is a social media platform where users create profiles (now displayed as personal 'timelines') and then establish and traverse links with networks of other users, or 'Friends'. Friends tend to comprise people with whom users have existing, offline relationships, rather than those they meet online (boyd & Ellison, 2008, p. 211). There are various options for communicating within Facebook. Status updates – short messages resembling broadcasts – are seemingly 'undirected' in so far as the motivating principle is that of 'pull' rather than 'push' (boyd & Marwick, 2011, p. 11), in the sense that users are not obliged to read others' posts but free to choose which to engage with. Status updates appear in Friends' newsfeeds and Friends can then comment on them, thus instigating a conversation. There are also options within Facebook for more private conversations: private messages sent to people's inboxes or public messages which appear on their 'walls' (a 'wall' is a page within each user's profile where their recent activity is listed, presented since 2011 in the form of a 'timeline'). In general, however, the audience for most Facebook posts can be described as 'semi-public', in the sense that, although a user decides who to friend and generally does so on the basis of pre-existing relationships, they can never be entirely sure who amongst their Friends are reading their posts and who are going to respond to them. To an extent then, as with broadcast audiences, the 'readership' is invisible (boyd & Marwick, 2011; Litt, 2012). Furthermore, given that users are likely to friend people from various phases and parts of their lives – family, current friends, former lovers, colleagues – what in day-to-day life would normally constitute a number of different contexts are brought together as one large 'conflated' audience, a phenomenon known in the literature as 'context collapse' (Wesch, 2008; Marwick & boyd, 2010). Whilst such collapses of context are not unknown in spoken interactions – such as when a pupil addresses a teacher in a classroom of peers (Ladegaard, 1995) – on Facebook the issue of self-presentation has the potential to be much more problematic than in most spoken contexts.

The unseen, semi-public nature of Facebook audiences and the need to negotiate collapsed contexts has implications for the kinds of audience design strategies that users may choose to adopt. One response may be simply to avoid communicative topics or language practices that are likely to exclude some groups or be considered inappropriate for or by them. For example, Takahashi (2010) suggests that topics discussed on the Japanese SNS Mixi are constrained by users' desire not to offend; i.e. users normalize their behaviour due to the fact that they are engaging in something which has the status of public discourse. In contrast, users may develop highly nuanced self-presentation strategies in an attempt to target and address particular audiences within the semi-public site (boyd & Marwick, 2011). Some of these are described below.

There are various structural options for audience design embedded into the site itself, such as the development of an 'audience selector' function so that each status update can be restricted to a particular 'group' or 'list' of Facebook Friends (Google+ operates a similar system with its use of 'circles'). However, boyd and Marwick's (2011) research suggests that certain groups, for example American teens, prefer in general not to rely on these structural affordances for negotiating privacy, in part because they are not seen as 'foolproof' (p. 21) and in part because the point of status updating is to be 'performing for others to see' (p. 23). Instead, the teens in boyd and Marwick's study choose to use social and linguistic practices to signal boundaries, to target other users, and exclude others. For multilingual groups, language choice is another audience design strategy. For example, in their study of the photo-sharing site Flickr, Lee and Barton (2012) report the case of Chinese user Kristie using Chinese characters in her name (rather than Romanizing it) so as to 'connect quicker and better' (p.138) with other Chinese users.

As mentioned previously, the implication of an invisible, semi-public, and converged audience is that Facebook users are constructing their audience as much as they are targeting it. By varying the audience design strategies they adopt, users not only respond differently to the audience before them but actually put together or construct an audience from amongst the wider potential readership – an audience that could conceivably comprise a user's colleagues for a work-related post, locally based friends when announcing plans for a night out, and others of the same nationality for a domestic politics update. As French Facebook user, Pauline, told us, 'My postings always refer to something I've experienced, and so they're linked with the people who share that experience. The language I choose is related to that too'.

In the next section, we introduce the three multilingual Facebook users – Eva, Pauline and Kaija – and look at examples of their addressivity strategies to posit a framework of audience design on Facebook.

4 Dataset

The data we are using here consist of three case studies which have been chosen partly because of the users' highly multilingual online experiences, and partly because of the nature of the translocal communities to which they belong. The research study from which these examples have been taken had as its broader aim an exploration of how English as a lingua franca is being used in online contexts to bring together multinational communities across Europe, and how it is used within the wider language ecologies of these communities. The three participants in this particular subset are all European, female, and aged in their early 30s at the time of data collection (in 2010). They are all regular users of Facebook, are connected to people from various national and linguistic backgrounds, and all use English as well as other languages on the site.

- **Eva** is a Dutch university lecturer who was born in 1979. She currently lives in the Netherlands. She speaks English and some Danish, French and German, as well as her native Dutch. Being married to an Englishman and having spent three years in the UK doing doctoral research, she uses English daily in various contexts. She also uses Facebook on a daily basis. At the time of the study, she had 463 Friends from a range of national backgrounds, including Japanese, Polish, Greek, French, Brazilian and Slovenian, but assumed that her 'active circle' comprised around 20 people from the Netherlands, Britain and the USA. Eva mainly uses English on Facebook, although she also uses Dutch when she deems it appropriate.
- **Pauline** is a French Master's student in Paris who was born in 1980. She speaks advanced English, intermediate Danish and some German, as well as her native French. She says that she loved English 'from the start' at school, took an undergraduate degree in English, and now tries to use English every day, though often in a receptive, 'passive' way. She spent a month in Scotland and another month in Lancaster, and also spoke English when living in Denmark from 2000–2005 and in Prague for two years after that. She uses Facebook 'almost every day, sometimes several times a day'. At the time of the study, she had 257 Friends, from various countries including Brazil, the Czech Republic, Denmark, Germany, Japan, Nepal, the Netherlands, Togo and the UK. Of these, her active circle numbers around 30–40 from 'France and Europe, plus a few from the US'. She reports that she uses French and English 'fairly equally' on Facebook – 'French with my family and English with most of my friends'. Her mood and the content of her posts also determines her language choice but, as indicated in the quote from her above, it is difficult to separate those factors from consideration as to who she is addressing. She also says that her love of language also determines her language choice: 'Since I like playing with words, sometimes I'll choose the language that allows me a pun'.
- **Kaija** is a Finnish researcher and policy analyst who was born in 1977. She speaks fluent English, everyday Dutch and Spanish, some French and a little Swedish, as well as her native Finnish. Based in Helsinki, she uses English every day for work and with her Dutch partner and some friends, and has been a regular visitor to the UK

for five years. She uses Facebook daily and updates her status two or three times a week. At the time of the study she had 188 Friends, from a range of European countries, including the Netherlands, the UK, Spain, Greece, the USA and Canada. Of these, her active circle is quite small – around ten people, mainly from Finland, the Netherlands, and the UK. Kaija mainly uses English on Facebook. Although she told us that, 'as a rule', she tends to use English in status updates, 'When I comment on someone else's post I use Finnish for my Finnish friends and English for all others'.

For this study we draw on a number of exchanges taken from these participants' Facebook 'walls'. In each case, the exchange develops through the Comment function in response to a status update posted by one of the participants. The exchanges have been translated and 'explained' by the participants themselves where necessary, and the analysis also includes commentary from the participants on their own and their interlocutors' motivations for various language choices (for practical reasons, Eva was interviewed while the others completed written questionnaires). These explanations are taken as attempts at self-rationalization, with all the caveats that post-hoc reflections bring. At this stage, the aim is not to generalize across SNS use, even with respect to these participants' long-term SNS use; instead, the data are used to illustrate a framework with potential implications for a more general understanding of SNS interactions.

5   Audience design framework for interaction on Facebook

Having provided contextual background to the various factors involved, this section posits a modified audience design framework for understanding language choices in multilingual interactions on Facebook. The epistemic basis for the proposed categories comprises three factors: (a) the site architecture (outlined above), particularly as it shapes addressivity both through inbuilt structural devices and explicit recommendations from the site or the community that use it; (b) top-down categorization of the nature of audience on SNSs, in the form of legislation prescribing how audience is to be understood and what is and is not socially acceptable (discussed later in the chapter); and (c) empirical observation of the interactions taking place on Facebook and how shifts in style or language choice correlate with different audiences. The latter is the most important basis for our audience design model, but what people do is in part determined by what is made possible or encouraged by the architecture and by people's awareness of, and responsiveness to, top-down regulation from both the site owners and the state.[2]

Bell's participant categories (speaker, addressee, auditor and over-hearer) do not map neatly onto a communicative situation like Facebook which combines elements of a public broadcast with a potential reader-ship characterized by a collapse of the offline contexts in which the users also interact. Facebook participants can instead be divided into five cat-egories which reflect the semi-public and performative aspects of inter-action on the site. The basis for the first three categories lies primarily in our empirical observations, with the latter categories emerging from speculations based primarily on the legislation and site architecture.

a. Poster of the message (= speaker)
b. Addressee
c. Active Friends
d. Wider Friends
e. The internet as a whole

Participants in interactions can be in different groups at the same time, or they can shift from one to another as the conversation unfolds. For example, the role of 'poster' applies not only to the user who initiates a conversation when they update their status, but also to addressees or members of the active audience who respond to the initial post with a comment. In the following sections, we explore the addressivity strate-gies and patterns of interaction evident in our participants' multilingual interactions as they navigate these different aspects of their audience. Throughout our analysis we highlight (a) the complex way in which status updates subtly target different groups simultaneously, and (b) the 'node-oriented' communities interactively constructed in the com-ments that build up from a status update.

5.1 Addressees

Status updates can be directly or indirectly targeted at a particular indi-vidual (although this happens infrequently) just as comments within the conversational thread that develops from a status update can be directed to the initial poster or another 'commenter'. In this section, we look at the interactive patterns that emerge from these various choices.

Following the 'pull' principle, status updates are most likely not directed at a particular person, but this does on occasion take place. Consider, for example, this status update from Pauline. After an announcement regarding her travel plans, Pauline switches to French to recite a slogan about her hometown. Pauline informed us during interview that this was an intertextual 'hint' to a university friend, Sophie, who came from the same town and who had a keyring emblazoned with this slogan. Following various comments from other people responding to Pauline's announcement, Sophie notices the hint.

Example 1

1 Pauline	is enjoying the sun in Lille before going to Bressuire for the weekend. Deux-Sévrien, c'est trop bien!! :)
	It's good to be from Deux-Sèvres!!
...	
6 Sophie	ah ah! t'as kiffé le porte-clé, hein!
	Ah ah! You liked the key ring, didn't you!

In this instance, therefore, a statement which is directed at one level to anyone who receives her status updates in their newsfeed also operates as a more private, one-to-one communiqué by means of the use of a fragment of shared, localized cultural knowledge in a local language. This example illustrates a more general pattern that emerges when users simultaneously address different groups from within their active circle of Friends.

Before moving on to the category of active Friends, it is worth looking at direct address within the comments, and in particular the interesting communicative dynamic that emerges when subsequent commenters address the poster. In this example (again from Pauline), David and Kate address their comments back to Pauline, with little sign that they are engaging with each other. Pauline addresses both individually, using a variety of strategies: the sending of two separate comments (turns 4 and 5), language choice (English to David, French to Kate), a vocative ('Kate'). What thus develops is a series of one-to-one communications within the comment thread.

Example 2

| 1 Pauline | is back. or is she? |

| 2 David | you never can tell |

| 3 Kate | tu es dispo vendredi à midi? |
| | *Are you free on Friday at noon?* |

| 4 Pauline | here and there at the same time... |

| 5 Pauline | Kate, la réponse est oui. je suis même dispo à 11h30 :) |
| | *Kate, the answer is yes. I'm even free at 11.30 :)* |

Pauline's language choices may in part be motivated by accommodation to her interlocutor's choices (although it is interesting to note that Kate does not similarly accommodate to the language of her original post), but they also serve to target the intended recipient and to distinguish a particular thread in the exchange. This is further illustrated in the following exchange where participants discuss the latest Twilight film (*Eclipse*). In turn 6, Kaija uses vocatives to distinguish her response to Wouke from her response to Tiina and Riina (T&R), but she also switches from English to Finnish to mark the change of topic within the second response.

Example 3

1 Kaija   experienced the Eclipse and realised that she'd been batting for the wrong team all along. *go team Jacob* :)!

2 Wouke   I didn't see the movies but I just read the second book and am all confused now. Time for the third.

3 Tiina   Hoo! That's quite a change! Interesting... – Shall have to experience it myself. ;)

4 Riina   ohoh! Mitenkähän mun mieli muuttuu..tarkoitus mennä kattomaan pe. Tiina, tuu mukaan jos pe sopii ?
          Oh! Might I change my mind ... meaning to see on Fri. Tiina, come with me if Fri suits you?

6 Kaija   Wouke: It is all ok – the third book is a real treat and it will all turn out fine in the end :)
          T&R: I simply just could not resist all that wolf action;).
          Kaykaahan kattomassa pe – jo odotatte la iltaan niin voin tulla teidan kanssa kattomaan uudestaan ...
          Do go see on Fri – and if you wait until Sat evening then I can come with you to see again.

What seems to happen less often is that people posting comments will engage directly with each other (rather than with the initial poster). Indeed, emerging norms appear to encourage people not to 'clog' Friends' newsfeeds with lengthy private conversations (McLaughlin & Vitak, 2011, p. 306). The exchange below took place within the comments on Eva's status update. Her two former students (Julia and Josie) eventually rebuke themselves for carrying on a private conversation within her status update; the notion that norms are being impinged on is (humorously) reinforced when Eva switches into her former teacher role (and into Dutch) to reprimand them (turn 18).

Example 4

6   Julia   you gettin' married ? :D

7   Eva   @Julia: got married in February :) See my photos!

8   Julia   :D Niceee :D little late, but congrats !! Xx

9   Josie   juuuuules you didn't know Eva was married??

10   Julia   No :$... I do now !! :D

11   Josie   goh ....

12   Julia   pshhh xP

13   Josie   let's not put spam on Eva's profile too

14   Julia   yeah... I was thinking that too :P Sorry Eva :P
...
18   Eva   @Julia & Josie: het is net al.sof jullie weer in mijn klas zitten :)
              @Julia & Josie: it is just like you are in my class again :)

This communicative dynamic – whereby commenters tend not to interact with each other in the communicative space opened up by a status update but with the initial poster – leads to the potential emergence of what might be called 'node-oriented' communities, ones characterized by a lack of direct interaction between all members. These Facebook communities are brought together not around a shared interest or collective action (as is the case in a community of practice) but around a mutual Friend, and this is affirmed in their patterns of interaction. The potential for the emergence of this kind of community will become more evident in the next section, where we look at the complex ways in which users target particular groups from their active circle of Friends.

5.2   Active Friends

When status updates are not targeted at individuals, they can to an extent be said to function as undirected 'broadcasts' to be consumed by Friends if and when they choose. In the case of these undirected broadcasts, however, it appears that posters have in mind a group or groups from what they consider to be their active circle, those Friends who tend to respond regularly to posts and who can therefore be expected to respond to a new status update. For example, Kaija tends 'to think of my close, "active" circle of friends when I post my messages' [the scare quotes are hers], whilst Eva says 'I now know who responds a lot and I tend to think of that circle of people when I write something'. The active circle resembles, to some extent, the auditors identified in spoken interactions (Bell, 1984) although, as an audience for 'broadcast' status updates, active Friends differ from Bell's auditors in that there is not also a direct addressee. The participation of a user's active Friends is 'ratified' not only in the general sense that they have been accepted onto the poster's list of Friends, but also that they have the necessary background knowledge to understand a particular post. For example, Kaija's highly contextualized reference to the latest Twilight film (she 'experienced the Eclipse and realised she'd been batting for the wrong team all along') serves to target those among her active circle with an interest in and knowledge of the series and the culture that has grown up around it. The strategies used by Kaija to target this group include implicit signals of topic choice and (lack of) explicitation. Other strategies used to target groups within an active circle of Friends are more direct, such as tagging their names on a photo or in a post.

Our interest, however, is in the use of language choice alongside these other strategies. Awareness of language choice as an addressivity strategy is evident in the participants' own accounts of who they target with which language: Pauline says that she uses 'French with my family and English with most of my Friends', a pattern similar to that of Kaija (Finnish for her family circle, English for wider Friends), while Eva claims 'The only times I post in Dutch is when I really don't think it will be of any use to any foreigners (like when I was on Dutch telly last week)'. In other words, these Facebook users perceive some distinction between a local, nationally defined community (which in this case comprises either Dutch, French or Finnish speakers who also speak English) and other non-local groups which may not speak the participant's local language but with whom they use English as a lingua franca. Thus, for example, when Pauline writes as status update: 'Fac 'em all!', this is clearly designed for English-speaking French nationals among her close friends in that it incorporates a multilingual English/French pun related to her own personal circumstances (although non-French-speaking English speakers may access the phrase on another level). As Pauline explained, the phrase is a play on an English expletive and a reference to the university *faculté* ('faculty' or 'school') where she was having problems registering.

In contrast to Pauline's status update, which non-English-French bilinguals cannot access on the same level, our participants' audience design strategies also enable them to address different language-speaking groups on a more equal basis. For example, in Eva's status update below – in which she indirectly laments the fact that her husband is away on a business trip – she simultaneously addresses her active circle of Friends (which includes people from a wide range of linguistic, cultural and national backgrounds) and those within that circle familiar with Dutch cultural traditions – in this case, those featuring 'Sinterklaas'.

Example 5

1 Eva   is missing a certain man (hint: it is not Sinterklaas)

2 Stefan   So it could still be me.. ;)

3 Eva   Oh yes it could be! ;)

4 Mary   Is it James? I am missing him too!

5 Eva   Oh yes, I miss him too! Gosh, I miss more men than I even realised!

6 Anne   Zwarte Piet!

In this exchange both Dutch and non-Dutch speaking Friends respond to the message about Eva's husband's absence – Mary, for example, mentions her own travelling husband, James – but the bilingual Dutch-English speakers can take on board the full effect of the post, as it were – Anne, for example, asks if Eva is missing Sinterklaas's helper, Zwarte Piet ('Black Pete'). Thus, the use of code-switching into Dutch in this instance does not exclude close Friends of Eva's who are unfamiliar with Dutch traditions (they are still able to understand the meaning on a certain level), but the mention of 'Sinterklaas' suggests that the message is simultaneously being tailored towards the Dutch speakers among her active circle. If a 'community' can be said to be emerging or its identity being performed through such interactions, it is therefore one character-ized by members' shared connection to Eva and an orientation around her post, rather than a mutual appreciation of the topic discussed.

5.3 Wider Friends

When targeting an active circle of Friends, and particular groups within it, posters are likely also to have their wider circle of Friends in mind.

These are, in Bell's terms, the 'overhearers' or, in internet terms, 'lurkers' (Androutsopoulos, 2013). Accommodation to Facebook overhearers may manifest itself in language choice, and we argue elsewhere that the use of English (as global lingua franca) is often motivated by a general awareness of one's wider, multilingual audience on Facebook (Seargeant, Tagg & Ngampramuan, 2012). The present dataset, however, suggests that where our participants use English to ensure the diverse individuals that make up their active Friends have access to the post, they may use other strategies to exclude more peripheral Friends. We saw above that Eva's announcement that she 'is missing a certain man' with the hint that 'it is not Sinterklass' was simultaneously designed to include two groups in her active Friends; what we did not mention was how the highly intimate and contextualized update would serve to exclude more distant acquaintances on her Friends list. Referring to 'a certain man' instead of making an explicit reference to her husband, by name or otherwise, allows the post to be meaningful to those who know her relationship status, but not to others. In other words, other addressivity strategies may become a way of obscuring meaning and excluding others (boyd & Marwick, 2011), as with overhearers in spoken interaction (Clark & Carlson, 1982, p. 345), even where the post is in English.

However, it follows that privacy concerns in front of a wider, semi-public audience may encourage a switch from English into a local language. In the following exchange, for example, both Eva and Nina use English as part of a lengthy, largely English language, thread of comments. In turn 5, Eva uses the acronym, BV, for *borstvoeding* ('breast-feeding'). When Nina responds (turn 15), she also switches to Dutch to discuss what could be described as a personal issue, or perhaps one not seen as appropriate for Facebook. Given that most of the people responding to the status update speak Dutch, the switch may represent a concern for 'overhearers', although other factors may be involved: greater ease in discussing a complex issue in a native language; the fact that the two have an offline history of discussing the issue in Dutch, and so on.

Example 6
1 Eva   has found her mojo again!
....

4 Nina   enjoy it! Ive lost mine too.....

5 Eva   Is it hidden under BV-stress?
...

15 Nina @ Eva: hidden onder slaapgebrek en fysieke uitputting en de
vierde borstontsteking in 4.5 maanden. Heb nu besloten de
'dames' op early retirement te sturen. Kan me nu al verheugen op
de grote hoevelheden alcohol die ik kan gan nuttigen;)
*@Eva: hidden under sleep deprivation and physical exhaustion
and the fourth mastitis in 4.5 months. Have decided to send the
'ladies' on early retirement. Already looking forward to the great
amounts of alcohol I shall be consuming ;)*

5.4 The internet as a whole

Beyond people's circles of Friends, their awareness of the internet
as a whole may (to varying extents) influence what and how a user
posts. Online networked communication is automatically recorded
and archived, and is thus both more permanent and more replicable
(easily copied) than spoken conversation. Online exchanges often also
constitute what Zappavigna (2011) calls 'searchable talk', in that posts
can be accessed through search engines (although the capacity of this
depends to an extent on the SNS and user settings). In part because of
these affordances, networked discourse is characterized by scalability
(boyd & Marwick, 2011); that is, it is visible to a potentially very great
number of people. The fact that Facebook users are contributing to a
wider internet discourse characterized by permanence, replicability,
searchability and scalability may constrain some users' posts, according
to their awareness of possible content leakage (boyd & Marwick, 2011,
p. 19) outside Facebook and their individual concerns over privacy. In
fact, in certain contexts the existence of this possible public audience
is having profound effects on the status of utterances produced on
SNSs. There have been a number of notable instances of people getting
into trouble by not taking into consideration the potentially public
nature of their online posts. Following the riots that took place in a
number of British cities in August 2011, for example, several people
were convicted of 'inciting violence in a public place' on the basis of
messages they posted to Facebook.[3] The case with the highest profile
to date, however, is from Twitter rather than Facebook: this is the so-
called 'Twitter joke trial'. In January 2011, during heavy snowfall in
Britain and shortly before he was due to fly from Doncaster Sheffield
airport, Paul Chambers tweeted 'Crap! Robin Hood airport is closed.
You've got a week and a bit to get your shit together otherwise I'm blow-
ing the airport sky high!' Chambers claimed the tweet was a joke, and
there was never real concern among the authorities that his intentions
were serious, but his trial centred around the extent to which the tweet

constituted a 'public' menace, akin to making a terrorist threat in a public place.

There are various implications of court cases such as these. Although it is evident that official institutions such as the judiciary and the police are still struggling to decide how to deal with these 'semi-public' new ways of communicating/broadcasting, it is clear that there is some discrepancy between how they have chosen to view this form of communication so far (very much as public offerings) and how utterances on social media are perceived by users themselves (often apparently as private messages). However, as such stories abound in the public news media, they are likely to have greater influence on how users themselves perceive their audience, and the ways in which they thus tailor what they say and how they say it. Even if posts are never accessed by a future or unintended audience, the perception that they might be seen may well shape a user's choices.

To conclude, our modified audience design framework suggests to some extent that addressees will have a greater effect on the poster's language choice and expression than unknown readers across the internet, about which users may have only a vague notion. However, the basic tenet underlying the model is that the various audience roles will simultaneously shape language choice and other stylistic features as, in boyd and Marwick's (2011, p. 24) words, users negotiate how to 'express themselves privately in situations where they assume that others are watching'; and that who a user predominantly orients towards at any one time is not static nor pre-determined but will shift in the course of an interaction.

6   Conclusion: audience design, language choice and translocal community

Having laid out a possible formalization of the ways in which audience can be perceived on Facebook and the kinds of audience design strategy available to users in addressing individuals and groups, we now return to the question of how audience design combines with language choice in the construction and maintenance of communities. Audience design is founded on the insight that one constructs an idea of the audience – and in broadcast or certain non-face-to-face contexts, imagines the audience into being – for the purpose of giving context to one's utterances. As such, it is an important element in constructing or maintaining the community: it is an aspect of constructing the links between yourself and those in your network, and of building these links around shared cultural and linguistic practices. In effect, positing an audience (through the decisions one makes about style, language choice, topic of conversation and so on) is a key element in the social organization that constitutes the patterns of community relationship enacted online. Audience design works by drawing on shared practices which are part of the dynamics which constitute community relations, and at the same time enacting and elaborating upon these practices. In this sense, online audiences are imaginings of the poster's understanding of a community's practices.

Our main focus in this chapter has been how the use of the linguistic resources employed by multilingual groups – constructed by and oriented around a central node – facilitates translocal interactions on Facebook. That is, while interactions on Facebook can be grounded in a shared locality (such as when Kaija's friends discuss going to see a film), the online site also has the potential for bringing geographically dispersed people together into the same communicative space: for all the users in our data, their active circle was made up of people from a variety of national backgrounds, currently living or staying in diverse locations. Rather than conceptualizing Facebook as an abstract global space isolated from people's offline localities, however, the notion of translocalization allows us to see the site as a space where various, often globally dispersed, local practices meet in processes which involve the mobilization and reinterpretation of locally defined meanings (Blommaert, 2010). An example of this can be seen in the indirect reference to Eva's husband and the joking around Sinterklaas in Example 5, both of which refer to different scales of local knowledge but in a context which is not grounded in (i.e. limited to) a particular locale.

The potential for an SNS to facilitate translocal communities is not novel in the history of internet communication, and language researchers (such as Androutsopoulos, 2006) have described the ways in which chat rooms and special-interest forums bring together geographically dispersed individuals to form what can be described as communities of practice characterized by mutual interest in a joint enterprise (Wenger, 1998). However, SNSs such as Facebook generate potentially novel forms of community, in part because of the complex way in which users construct and address different groups within the semi-public space, and due to the fact that the resultant interactions are often oriented not around topic but around social connections.

In its role as a global lingua franca, English facilitates the formation of translocal communities for the simple reason that the language allows posters to target various language-speaking groups, either across active or wider circles of Friends. We would also argue that English can sometimes function as a marker of inclusivity; that is, the use of English signals that a particular post is intended for a general audience (Seargeant *et al.*, 2012). In contrast, local languages can function as a strategy for addressing a particular language community and/or for marking a post as more private. To take another example which illustrates this, turns in the following interaction are marked as part of the public thread through English, and as more private in Danish.

Example 7
1 Pauline: is enjoying the sun in Lille before going to Bressuire for the weekend. Deux-Sévrien, c'est trop bien!! ☺
             It's so good to be from Deux-Sèvres!

2 Jens: gotta love'em weekend trips. hvordan går det ven?
             How are you my friend?

3 Pauline: det gaar fint, tak! havd med dig, ven? [*It's going well, thank you! How about you, my friend?*] hey, not everyone can take off to Costa Rica when they get itchy feet, so weekend trips it is for me... ;-)

But participants in our data used language choice in more complex ways than a simple formula whereby 'English = global' and 'local languages = local' would suggest. We have seen throughout the examples how the mixing of English with local languages in the same post allows participants to target bilingual groups (such as Pauline's 'fac 'em all!') and to address and navigate multiple audiences, as when Eva claimed to be missing 'a certain man' and then hinted 'it is not Sinterklaas' (Example 5). As described above, commenters from Eva's active circle were able to respond to different parts of the post, depending on their access to the languages and cultural knowledge. Perhaps more exclusive, in posts like this, is the vague, highly contextualized language used ('a certain man') which serves to exclude those not familiar with Eva's life. A similar point can be made with respect to Kaija's mention of the Twilight film (Example 3), which excludes through the choice of topic. In these cases, despite the use of the lingua franca, groups are targeted through other means – topic, vague language, contextualized reference.

Thus, the 'community' that fleetingly comes together in the online space opened up by a status update tends to be made up of people whose chief connection is their close attachment to the status updater, the 'node'. In the case of our participants, these people are often from different parts of the poster's life and thus from various geographical locations who do not necessarily have contact offline. As Eva says of her active Facebook Friends: 'I think that particular circle was created through the use of Facebook'. As noted above, the fact that these communities are brought together primarily by their mutual friendship with the initial poster (and not by a shared interest or engagement with the group as a whole) leads to the interaction patterns noted throughout this chapter, whereby commenters address the initial poster and display a lack of engagement towards each other.

This, then, is one particular pattern of social organization – facilitated by the affordances of the site and managed by, among other things, the strategies of audience design employed by participants. It is still emergent, in the sense that the affordances of the site and the practices developing around them are relatively recent and in a constant state of adaptation. Yet, despite this emergent nature, users appear already to be using complex strategies of addressivity to shape the communicative space and navigate the potentially limitless audience that exists in the semi-public forum of online social network sites.

Acknowledgements

Many thanks to Mel Evans, Susan Hunston and Ruth Page for providing feedback on early drafts of this chapter.

Notes

1. Facebook offers a feature whereby users can be tagged in photos (through a link to their profiles). Originally designed to identify people in photos, it can alternatively be used to draw a particular individual's attention to a photo in which they may not appear. Since 2009, Facebook has also enabled users to tag other users in their status updates or comments through the use of the @ sign.
2. There is an interesting difference between the status of legislation as a foundation for our model and empirical investigation in that empirical investigation identifies what people actually do (how awareness of the audience actually influences their style), while top-down legislation identifies what people are supposed to do (how it is meant to influence their style), but in many cases does not, and thus legislation is necessary.
3. Prosecutions of Facebook users during the August 2011 British riots include the following: www.bbc.co.uk/news/uk-england-hampshire-18536940; www.bbc.co.uk/news/uk-england-sussex-15789186.

References

Androutsopoulos, J. (2006) 'Multilingualism, diaspora, and the internet: Codes and identities on German-based diaspora websites', *Journal of Sociolinguistics*, 10(4): 520–47.

Androutsopoulos, J. (2013) 'Code-switching in computer-mediated communication'. In S. C. Herring, D. Stein & T. Virtanen (eds.) *Handbook of the Pragmatics of CMC* (Berlin: Mouton de Gruyter), pp. 667–94.

Baker, J. (1991) *Gender Trouble* (London: Routledge).

Bakhtin, M. (1930s/1981) *The Dialogic Imagination* (Austin: University of Texas Press).

Baron, N. S. (1998) 'Letters by phone or speech by other means: The linguistics of email', *Language and Communication*, 18: 133–70.

Bell, A. (1984) 'Language style as audience design', *Language in Society*, 13: 145–204.

Bell, A. (1999) 'Styling the other to design the self: A study in New Zealand identity making', *Journal of Sociolinguistics*, 3(4): 523–41.

Bell, A. (2001) 'Back in style: Reworking audience design'. In P. Eckert & J. R. Rickford (eds.) *Style and Sociolinguistic Variation* (Cambridge: Cambridge University Press), pp. 139–69.

Blommaert, J. (2010) *The Sociolinguistics of Globalisation* (Cambridge: Cambridge University Press).

boyd, d. m. & Ellison, N. B. (2008) 'Social network sites: Definition, history, and scholarship', *Journal of Computer-Mediated Communication*, 13(1): 210–30.

boyd, d. m. & Marwick, A. E. (2011) 'Social privacy in networked publics: Teens' attitudes, practices, and strategies'. Paper given at 'A Decade in Internet Time: Symposium on the Dynamics of the Internet and Society', Oxford, September 2011.

Clark, H. H. & Carlson, T. B. (1982) 'Hearers and speech acts', *Language*, 58(2): 332–73.

Crystal, D. (2001) *Language and the Internet* (Cambridge: Cambridge University Press).

Danet, B. (2001) *Cyberpl@y: Communicating Online* (Oxford: Berg).

Danet, B. & Herring, S. (eds.) (2007) *The Multilingual Internet: Language, Culture, and Communication Online* (Oxford: Oxford University Press).

Eckert, P. (1989) *Jocks and Burnouts: Social Identity in the High School* (New York: Teachers College Press).

Ferrara, K., Brunner, H. & Whittemore, G. (1991) 'Interactive written discourse as an emergent register', *Written Communication*, 8: 8–34.

Finegan, E. & Biber, D. (2001) 'Register variation and social dialect variation'. In P. Eckert & J. R. Rickford (eds.) *Style and Sociolinguistic Variation* (Cambridge: Cambridge University Press), pp. 235–67.

Garfinkel, H. (1967) *Studies in Ethnomethodology* (Englewood Cliffs, NJ: Prentice-Hall).

Gibson, J. J. (1986) *The Ecological Approach to Visual Perception* (Hillsdale, NJ: Lawrence Erlbaum).

Giles, H. & Powesland, P. F. (1975) *Speech Style and Social Evaluation* (London: Academic Press).

Goffman, E. (1975) 'Replies and responses', *Language and Society*, 5: 257–313.

Goffman, E. (1990[1959]) *The Presentation of Self in Everyday Life* (London: Penguin).

Goffman, E. (1981) *Forms of Talk* (Philiadelphia: University of Pennsylvania Press).

Gumperz, J. (1967) 'On the linguistic markers of bilingual communication', *Journal of Social Issues*, 23(1): 48–57.

Herring, S. (2007) 'A faceted classification scheme for computer-mediated discourse', *Language@Internet*, 1.

Labov, W. (1966) *The Social Stratification of English in New York City* (Washington, DC: Centre for Applied Linguistics).

Ladegaard, H. J. (1995) 'Audience design revisited: Persons, roles and power relations in speech interactions', *Language & Communication*, 15(1): 89–101.

Lee, C. K.-M. (2007) 'Affordances and text-making practices in online instant messaging', *Written Communication*, 24: 223–49.

Lee, C. & Barton, D. (2012) 'Multilingual texts on Web 2.0: The case of Flickr. com'. In M. Sebba, S. Mahootian & C. Jonsson (eds.) *Language Mixing and Code-switching in Writing: Approaches to Mixed-Language Written Discourse* (London: Routledge), pp. 128–45.

Litt, E. (2012) 'Knock, knock. Who's there? The imagined audience', *Journal of Broadcasting & Electronic Media*, 56(3): 330–45.

Marwick, A. E. & boyd, d. m. (2010) 'I tweet honestly, I tweet passionately: Twitter users, context collapse, and the imagined audience', *New Media & Society*, 13: 96–113.

McLaughlin, C. & Vitak, J. (2011) 'Norm evolution and violation on Facebook', *New Media & Society*, 14: 299–315.

Rampton, B. (1995) *Crossing: Language and Ethnicity among Adolescents* (London: Longman).

Rheingold, H. (1994) *The Virtual Community: Finding Connection in a Computerised World* (London: Secker and Warburg).

Sacks, H., Schegloff, E. & Jefferson, G. (1974) 'A simplest systematics for the organisation of turn-taking for conversation', *Language*, 50: 696–735.

Seargeant, P., Tagg, C. & Ngampramuan, W. (2012) 'Language choice and addressivity strategies in Thai-English social network interactions', *Journal of Sociolinguistics*, 16(4): 510–31.

Tagg, C. & Seargeant, P. (2012) 'Writing systems at play in Thai-English online interactions', *Writing Systems Research*, 4(2): 195–213.

Takahashi, T. (2010) 'MySpace or Mixi? Japanese engagement with SNS (social networking sites) in the global age', *New Media & Society*, 12(3): 453–75.

Warschauer, M., El Said, G. R. & Zohry, A. (2007) 'Language choice online: Globalisation and identity in Egypt'. In B. Danet & S. C. Herring (eds.) *The Multilingual Internet: Language, Culture, and Communication Online* (Oxford: Oxford University Press), pp. 303–18.

Wenger, E. (1998) *Communities of Practice: Learning, Meaning and Identity* (Cambridge: Cambridge University Press).

Wesch, M. (2008) Context collapse, http://mediatedcultures.net/projects/youtube/context-collapse.

Youssef, V. (1993) 'Children's linguistic choices: Audience design and societal norms', *Language in Society*, 22(2): 257–74.

Zappavigna, M. (2011) 'Ambient affiliation: A linguistic perspective on Twitter', *New Media & Society*, 13: 788–806.

8
Youth, social media and connectivity in Japan

Toshie Takahashi

1 Introduction

Children and young people these days are born and grow up in an incredibly rich global media environment. They engage with multiple media such as mobile phones, the internet, digital television and game consoles in their everyday lives. They have constant complex online and offline interactions with others via social media. In Japan, for example, since 1999, people have been buying mobile phones with the i-mode service through which they can access the internet. Over the past ten years, young people have been able to watch television and video, listen to music, play games, take photographs and access the internet entirely via their mobile phones. To describe people in their late 20s who have grown up adept at manipulating their mobile phones (even without looking at them), the Japanese term *oyayubibunka* (literally, thumb culture) is often used. As they tend to communicate with each other in writing rather than speech, the mobile phone is called *kei-tai* (portable device) rather than 'phone'. As well as texting and emails, they also access information, images, and culture nationally and transnationally via social media, using both Japanese sites such as Mixi and Line[1] and American sites such as Facebook and Twitter.

In this chapter, I investigate Japanese young people's relationships with social media in everyday life, partly using data from my ethnography in the media-rich Tokyo Metropolitan Area in Japan, conducted between 2000 and 2013. The ethnography has underscored the salience of culturally specific concepts for understanding communication practices in Japanese society. By recontextualizing these emic concepts, I open a window for wider comparative research into the cross-cultural validity of non-Western conceptual categories, thereby introducing these ideas into the Western literature on media and communication. The specific focus in the chapter is on one key dimension of 'audience engagement' (Takahashi, 2009), that of *connectivity*. As a primary aim of social media is to facilitate social networking, 'connectivity' is one of the most important dimensions of audience engagement with social media among young people (Ellison, Steinfield & Lampe, 2007). In the literature on the topic in Western contexts, notions of the 'always-on' culture (Baron, 2008) and 'constant connection' (Livingstone, 2009) have been much discussed, and today's children and young people are referred to as the 'constant contact generation' (Clark, 2005). American clinical psychologist Sherry Turkle initially offered a positive perspective on technology but, concerned about young people growing up with an expectation of constant connection, she has since investigated the powerful psychological influences of mobile communication and social media on young people who 'connect' with each other all day rather than 'communicate' (Turkle, 2011):

> Their digitalized friendships – played out with emoticon emotions, so often predicated on rapid response rather than reflection – may prepare them, at times through nothing more than their superficiality, for relationships that could bring superficiality to a higher power, that is, for relationships with the inanimate. They come to accept lower expectations for connection and, finally, the idea that robot friendships could be sufficient unto the day. (Turkle, 2011, p. 17)

In contemporary society, where mobile phones and social media are embedded into people's everyday lives, 'constant connectivity' can likely be seen as a universal phenomenon. If this is the case, the question arises as to why young people constantly engage with social media, and whether the reasons are the same across different cultural contexts. Couldry (2012) suggests that when investigating media culture we should take into account social, as well as economic and political needs:

> Social needs can be said to shape media cultures where the need for general social contact, or the specific need to socialize with one's peers (at work, in a particular cultural formation, or simply those of the same age), shapes distinctive forms of media production or consumption... Today's mobile phone-based youth cultures are of great interest, but they must be understood always in relation to local dynamics. (Couldry, 2012, p.175)

In this chapter I will investigate constant connectivity as a *universal phenomenon with cultural specificity*, approached within the context of the local dynamics of everyday life in Japan. In communication studies, children and young people are often thought of in one of two ways: pessimistically as vulnerable objects of media industries or optimistically as creative subjects. I will investigate Japanese youth engagement with social media beyond the dichotomy between utopia and dystopia for young people. The chapter begins with a discussion of the methodological approach, focused on the question: 'why do young people engage with media?' I then discuss the notion of connectivity in relation to the following concepts: *uchi*, the full-time intimate community, *kuuki*, high context culture and low context culture, and *uchi* creation/recreation. These will be explained and discussed in terms of the developing social media environment in the Japanese context, with the aim of showing how cultural values and community relations within Japan relate to Japanese young people's engagement with social media.

2 Methodology

In order to answer the question of 'why young people engage with media' I have conducted a series of ethnographic studies on youth and media over the last ten years in Japan. The initial body of research was an ethnography of Japanese engagement with media and ICT in the Tokyo Metropolitan Area since 2000. The primary fieldwork for this was conducted from April 2000 to December 2001. I chose informants in their 20s and 30s (and members of their immediate families if they shared a house) who lived in media-rich environments. I worked with 30 families, totalling 84 people (aged between 0 and 73), including 34 children and young people (aged between 0 and 29) (Takahashi, 2009). This primary fieldwork was followed by a further series of empirical studies on youth and media in Tokyo, which involved observation and interviews with some of the original subjects, as well as with new participants (Takahashi, 2008, 2010, 2011). In order to overcome the problems associated with the reliable interpretation of results in previous ethnography work, triangulation was achieved using multiple sources, methods and/or investigators. These included group and in-depth interviews, participant observations, street interviews, diaries and surveys.

In order to investigate specifically the role of social network site (SNS) use in Japan, I examined two different SNSs in the Japanese context from April 2007 to January 2008. The first of these was Mixi, which was the most popular SNS in Japan during that period; the other was

MySpace, which was at that time the most popular SNS in the world. I worked with 15 Mixi users aged between 18 and 24 years old, all of whom were college students in the Tokyo Metropolitan Area. Eight of these used only Mixi, while seven used both Mixi and MySpace (see Takahashi, 2010). In order to update this data and to expand the scope of the investigation into youth and digital media, I also conducted further ethnographic work, both longitudinally with the previous informants and also with a wider range of participants.

Since April 2009, I have been working with a further 28 informants aged between 11 and 21, focusing on digital media such as mobile phones, PC and digital television, in the Tokyo Metropolitan Area. My informants are from a variety of social backgrounds, with different experiences of living abroad and family organization. I used snowball sampling to recruit my informants for a number of reasons: firstly, in order to investigate the role of social media within the various social connections of the informants, I needed to gain an invitation into their social groups; secondly, as my informants were children and young people, I had to gain their trust before they felt comfortable talking about their private lives. For both these reasons, using a system of chain-referral sampling was the most effective. I observed these informants' everyday lives in front of the screen settings (both PC and mobile phones) as well as their on-screen everyday lives through social media (Mixi, Line, Facebook and so on). I conducted semi-structured, conversational, in-depth interviews, using a digital recorder in front of their PCs and mobile devices, as well as informal interviews. The interview questionnaires included questions about social media, mobile phones, emailing and other forms of interaction in their everyday life both online and offline. I interviewed them individually as well as in the company of close friends in order to observe their actual interactions, relationships and the structure of their social groups.

To arrive at a theorized interpretation of my data, I followed Glaser and Strauss's (1968) grounded theory approach. This is a qualitative research methodology that stresses the emergent over a pre-determined theory construction strategy – for instance, through the use of emic concepts arising from the data to develop the analytic codes and categories, instead of applying etic or *a priori* conceptions. After this stage of open coding,[2] I went back to my data again and again, constantly re-coding them in terms of other and higher dimensions of theory. I made sure to identify not only categories and concepts common to a majority of my informants, but also those which were apparently aberrant yet significant to me in the light of the broader concerns and scope of my research. This focused coding process underwent several stages of re-coding and further analysis, leading to increasingly general theorizing.

In the rest of this chapter, I focus on *connectivity*, which emerged from the fieldwork as the most relevant dimension of audience engagement. I take an emic approach, first exploring connectivity in relation the Japanese concepts of *uchi* and *kuuki* (defined below), as well as observations by Japanese researchers about 'the full intimate community', and then looking at how these play out as Japanese young people move from local SNSs such as Mixi to global sites Twitter and Facebook.

3 The full-time intimate community

The children and young people I interviewed in Japan never switch off their mobile phones. Even while they sleep, they put their mobile phones next to their pillows. In bed just before they fall asleep, they check Mixi, Line, Facebook, Twitter and emails via their mobile phones, and as they sleep they continue to receive messages via social media through these devices. They often check their mobile phones and some-times reply during the night, although some may not remember this engagement the next morning. Here, for example, is Akari, a 19-year-old female college student:

Akari: I put my mobile phone in vibration mode under the pillow when I'm asleep.

Researcher: Don't you wake up when you receive messages in the middle of the night?

Akari: I do. But I don't even remember opening or replying to the messages.

Others even engage with mobile phones and connect with their friends while they take a bath.

One of the most popular early studies on youth and mobile phones in Japan, by Ichiro Nakajima, Keiichi Himeno and Hiroaki Yoshii (1999), suggests that mobile phones create a 'full-time intimate community' with close friends, boyfriends and girlfriends. The researchers claim that:

People who live in the city, who have gained their autonomy and have broken the hold of the village type of community, create a 'full-time intimate community', where they reinforce their connectivity with their close peer groups whom they frequently meet, and where they feel a 24 hour a day psychological togetherness. (Nakajima *et al.*, 1999, p. 90)

Nakajima *et al.* (1999, p. 89) suggested that mobile phones 'have the function to divide friends into two different groups'. While the internet creates 'community directed outward (*soto*)' where people seek new social relationships with strangers, mobile phones (in the pre-smart-phone era where mobile telephony was not integrated with mobile internet access) create 'community directed inward (*uchi*)' where people search for their total and exclusive commitment with close friends. Following this work, many researchers working in this field, both inside and outside of Japan, refer to the concept of the 'full-time intimate com-munity', and have recontextualized it into their own social and cultural settings. The more that mobile phones with internet access and smart-phones become embedded in people's everyday lives, the more people have mobile access to social media, and thus the 'full-time intimate community' (Nakajima *et al.*, 1999) or 'always-on intimate communi-ties' (boyd, 2010) are being formed both in terms of text messages on mobile phones and of social media interactions facilitated by mobile devices (Takahashi, 2010). In this chapter I build upon early theoriz-ing concerning the influence of mobile technology on communication patterns and community relations in Japan, and extend it to the use of social media via mobile devices which are becoming such a key feature of young people's lives today.

4 Social media and Japanese emic concepts: *uchi* and *kuuki*

4.1 *Uchi* and mobile SNSs

The Japanese concept of *uchi* has been notably investigated by Nakane (1967) in her influential comparative research on Japan, China and India in the 1960s. In searching for the most enduring, unchanging and thus essential or definitive feature of Japanese society, Nakane looks towards relationships which, she argues, are the one phenomenon of Japanese society and culture that have not changed since Japan's modernization. *Uchi* has several meanings in the Japanese language: it is used to refer to inside, the house, family or that belonging to either of these. But *uchi* also, importantly, refers to a sense of belonging together in family or social groups. Each member of an *uchi* is, essentially, an individual, and so the internal nature of the group is not homogenous. The members of the group occupy the same *ba*/space (equivalent to Giddens's [1984] 'locale'); but simply sharing a locale does not, Nakane argues, constitute a social group but merely makes a 'crowd'. Thus the 'group' must be constructed, and this is done through a 'strong, everlasting bond' (for example, life-long living in one village with a close-knit community). These bonds can be created only through 'unification' and 'internal structure'. Unification, the becoming 'as one', is achieved through emotional bonds, built up through constant face-to-face communication in the locale. In the locale there is no private space for the individual, only space for the 'group'; an individual has no independent existence, only the group exists. Within the group, opinions, beliefs, values and philosophies must be shared to create internal homogeneity.

The internal structure of the *uchi* emerges through its 'tangibility', the constant sharing of the locale and constant face-to-face interaction. To overcome the inherent instability inevitably arising from individual difference within the group, 'group consciousness' must constantly be raised and fostered and this is done through, for example, the daily recitation in some offices of the company philosophy. Such 'consciousness-raising' exercises serve to reinforce belongingness to the group and stamp out individualism, and the hierarchy existing within the *uchi* serves to maintain ties of interdependence between members. The degree of unity of an *uchi* is a function of the contact over time and the passion or intensity of the active reinforcement of the internal structure.

According to Nakane, it is belonging to an *uchi* which gives a person their 'social capital' (the commodity of social interaction) and without this, an individual is nothing. If someone leaves the locale, they lose their social capital as it does not extend beyond space – *uchi* is intrinsically connected to the locale. Thus the *uchi* requires a person's total and exclusive commitment; they cannot leave it nor belong to an alternative *uchi*.

Writing in the pre-internet age, Nakane (1967) discusses the constant sharing of the locale and constant face-to-face interaction as fundamental for the internal structure of *uchi*. In the internet age, mobile phones and other mobile devices enable 'ubiquitous and permanent connectivity' (Castells *et al.*, 2007, p. 248), while social media enable people to connect with their friends and colleagues beyond traditional time-space constraints. In my research I have investigated how the internal structure of the *uchi* has emerged not just through face-to-face interaction in spatial localities, but also through constant mediated interaction via SNSs and mobile phones in non-spatial localities. Mobile SNSs allow young people to disembed from their immediate spatial locations to connect with their friends beyond time-space constraints, and thus to reinforce social intimacy and maintain the new forms of *uchi* to which they currently belong. Thus young people create and maintain multiple *uchi* through their constant complex online and offline interactions in their social worlds (Takahashi, 2008, 2010).

4.2 *Kuuki* and *kei-tai* natives

Alongside *uchi*, the concept of *kuuki* is also useful for understanding Japanese young people's online connectivity. It is associated with the Japanese critic Shichihei Yamamoto (1977) and was then developed by Yoichi Ito in communication studies. Ito (2009) gives the following definition:

> *Kuuki*, the Japanese linguistic equivalent of *air*, refers to the *atmosphere of a situation* to which all those involved are expected to pay respect. At the heart of the kuuki process is some kind of mechanism that aggravates a situation in a way that those involved in the issue are compelled to comply with the position put forth. This idea is widely used in Japan to describe what happens in various settings, from small groups to business to political contexts, in which people are said to be under the influence of the kuuki process or sprit... Translations are always imprecise, but kuuki is often compared to *ideology, zeitgeist, climate of opinion,* and *spiral of silence*... In relatively collectivist cultures like Japan, in which harmony is privileged, those who are insensitive to kuuki and say or do things that create disharmony tend to be disliked by other group members and are alienated or isolated... Compared with ideology, kuuki is more changeable or fluid because it heavily depends on the situation. As a situation changes, kuuki should change accordingly. (Ito, 2009, pp. 573–4; italics in the original)

Yohei Harada (2010) replaced the widespread term 'digital natives' (Prensky, 2001a, 2001b) with '*kei-tai* natives' thus emphasizing the relative uniqueness of the situation for the Japanese young generation where the mobile phone (*kei-tai denwa*) is absolutely central to their engagement with digital technology. The generation of young people up to their late 20s have been dependent on mobile phones since they were in junior high school and high school, and typically it is easier for them to write via mobile phones than computers. Referring to the *kuuki* theory, Harada claims that mobile phones have revived traditional village society in Japan. As young people constantly connect with each other via their phones, they feel the same kind of commitments and obligations as Japanese people who lived in small villages in the pre-modern era used to. Then, if someone did something wrong, he or she would be were ostracized by their community. In the digital age, this is intensified with constant connectivity via mobile phones. Harada (2010) suggests that there is now nowhere one can go to avoid such ostracism. There are strict implicit rules among young people such as the need for immediate responses to emails and constant comments on others' blogs or SNSs within *uchi*. As this suggests, social media *uchi* is by no means unproblematic for Japanese users. In the next section, I consider how moves between different SNSs reflect Japanese struggles with *uchi* and *kuuki* online.

4.3   Early use: Mixi and MySpace

I had initially investigated the differences between the uses of Mixi and MySpace and recontextualized the concept of *uchi* in contemporary Japanese society. The research found that while Japanese young people participated in Mixi as *uchi* to gain a sense of 'ontological security' (Giddens, 1990, 1991), they participated in MySpace to disembed from Japan *uchi* and connect with non-Japanese people in order to have a chance to express themselves in an environment free from Japanese cultural norms. They connected with each other in the local *uchi* to which they belong and used to belong (Haythornthwaite, 2001; Gross, 2004) on Mixi, while they connected with *soto* – outsiders to their local *uchi* – on MySpace.

My research also revealed that use of Mixi was not just 'about us', following the stereotyped picture of Japanese with its groupism, but equally about the 'me' who is embedded in the multiple *uchis*. In this respect, users reflexively and contextually create and recreate their identities through complex connectivity with information, images, people, social groups and communities on SNSs. Thus, while MySpace use is not simply all about me, and Mixi use is not simply all about us, the findings of my ethnography suggest that MySpace is about me *and* them, while Mixi is about me *with* them. Japanese young people reflexively create and recreate themselves in everyday life via their use of SNSs, to-ing and fro-ing in the spectrum between two different sets of cultural values.

Mixi was not, however, perceived by my informants as a space where they could freely express their opinions personally within their small *uchi*. Recently, young people have developed a psychological problem, the so-called 'Mixi *tsukare*' (fatigue). They are too sensitive to the *kuuki* (the atmosphere of a situation) among *maimiku* (the equivalent of 'Friends' on Facebook) who are from different backgrounds and have different identities. They are thus reluctant to write anything important, and even stop writing their diaries because they are afraid that someone might be offended or cannot share their experiences or feelings. Within the traditional *uchi*, opinions, beliefs, values and philosophies must be shared to create internal homogeneity. As people belong to multiple *uchi* in contemporary society, they show different faces and play different roles within each *uchi* in order to maintain internal homogeneity. However, the more that different *uchi* integrate on Mixi and the walls of each *uchi* become transparent (compare this with the notion of 'context collapse' discussed in the Introduction), the more my informants fear their different faces might be revealed and they will thus lose their real voice in the intensified *uchi*. As they come to register too many *maimiku* from different *uchis*, they can only write inoffensive things in the compound *uchi*, of a kind which anyone can accept. Partly as a reaction to this, Japanese young people are now transferring from Mixi to Twitter and Facebook to seek two different spaces where they can freely express themselves.

Harada indicates that a 'network divide' (p. 248) has emerged between people who restrict the scope of their action within the network of their local friends via Japanese SNSs such as Mixi and GREE, and those who open up the scope of their action to connect with people in the wider world via Facebook – making connections beyond locality, education level and generation. While the former constantly connect only with local friends via Mixi, the latter constantly connect with both local friends via Mixi and foreign friends and business people via Facebook. This is supported by surveys which suggest that, while Mixi remains one of the most popular Japanese SNS in Japan (used by 26.1% of the population), other international sites are rapidly catching up, with 24.5 per cent of the population (up from just 8.3% in 2011) now on Facebook and 26.3 per cent on Twitter (compared to 15.5% in 2011) (Impress R&D, 2012a).

Given the spread of engagement across different sites and services, Tadamasa Kimura (2012) has investigated the different levels of pressure to interpret *kuuki* that exist in different communication media. Mixi, Facebook and Twitter have become the most popular social media sites in Japan because they have different functions: Mixi as community (*Gemeinschaft*), Facebook as society (*Gesellschaft*) and Twitter as connection. Kimura suggests that the reason for the recent popularity of Twitter in Japan is that there is no obligation to reply to others' messages immediately, which is different from Mixi and emails via mobile phones. He writes that '140 characters seem to be too limited in terms of self-expression and information transmission media. However, in Japan, where people feel pressure to interpret *kuuki*, we perceive that on Twitter there is no room to be over-solicitous, which compares favourably with emails via mobile phones' (p. 206).

When I interviewed Japanese young people in 2009, they were mainly using Mixi. However when I interviewed them again in 2012, because of Mixi *tsukare* (fatigue), most of them were communicating with others via Facebook, Twitter and Line (the social messaging service introduced in 2011; see below for further discussion), although they still kept their Mixi accounts. One of the most influential Twitter critics, Daisuke Tsuda, identifies the reasons for the popularity of Twitter in Japan as being due to '"*Yurui* (loose)" ties and *kuuki* feeling' (Tsuda, 2009, pp. 40–1):

> With services that require agreement between users, such as '*mai-miku*' of Mixi [the equivalent of the mutual acceptance of friend requests on Facebook], it is no easy task to escape from the ties of obligation of real interpersonal relationships... While such SNSs enable us to construct strong relationships, these real interpersonal relations have become fetters for users, and it [Mixi] tends to be a fixed, closed space where users feel constrained within the fetters of the site and structure of the relationships it makes possible.

The increasing popularity of Twitter over Mixi among Japanese users may therefore be understood as a shift from Japanese closed social media to American open social media. In the next section I introduce the concepts of *high context culture* and *low context culture* in order to help analyse the use of Twitter in Japan.

5   High context culture and low context culture: the case of Twitter

The American cultural anthropologist Edward T. Hall (1976) investigated high context culture and low context culture in the 1970s and this work is still influential in the field of intercultural communication studies, social linguistics and business. In communication studies, Steinfatt (2009, pp. 278–9) introduces this binary concept as follows:

> In a high-context culture, the significance intended by a message is located largely in the situation; the relationships of the communicators; and their beliefs, values, and cultural norm prescriptions... High-context cultures usually emphasize politeness, nonverbal communication, and indirect phrasings, rather than frankness and directness, in order to avoid hurt feelings. They emphasize the group over the individual and tend to encourage in-groups and group reliance. Messages in many high context conversations are ambiguous,

with multiple possible interpretations that may drift into vagueness, seemingly indefinite in form and imprecise in thought... In a low-context culture, the meanings intended by a message are located in the interpretations of its words and their arrangement. These are carefully selected in an attempt to express those meanings clearly and explicitly... Low-context cultures often place a high value on the individual, encouraging self-reliance. The predominant culture of the United States provides an example in which the presumed need is minimal for context surrounding a message in order to understand it.

Within this framework, the United States can be understood as a low context culture while Japan can be identified as a high context culture. Bearing in mind that these concepts were developed in a pre-internet age, I will now examine and recontextualize them in the current era, in relation to the advent of social media.

The US-based microblogging service Twitter, representing low context culture (in that it originates from – and draws upon norms from – the cultural communicative practices of the US), involves users communicating with each other within a 140 character limit. Hiro, a 21-year-old male college student, has moved from Mixi to Twitter because of Mixi fatigue. He has over 1000 followers on Twitter and constantly interacts with others. However, his Twitter account sometimes experiences *enjo* (becoming flooded by comments). He explained that his posts attract criticism because 'I can't explain the context within 140 characters'. On Twitter, where one can only write the content with very little or no context, some users who do not share their interlocutor's context might interpret posts wrongly and others might be upset by perceived rudeness in writing style. This leads to criticism and then a flood of comments.

As a high context culture, Japanese people tend to communicate depending on the situation and context. They often markedly change their language and communication styles (and sometimes their opinions) depending on their relationships with others, and the influence of variables such as their age (older or younger) and status (senior or junior, occupation). When Hiro shows his identity in his profile in Twitter as a college student and expresses his opinion frankly and directly within 140 characters, he could be easily criticized by others because of a lack of politeness and the use of indirect phrasings.

It is true that the internet enables us to communicate with others directly beyond differences of age, gender and status. However, once people communicate with others using their real identity on the internet, the same social norms that exist in face-to-face communication in

Japan can become reinforced in mediated online communication. Kazu, an 18-year-old high school boy, said, 'I write very politely and follow the implicit rules on the BBS and other sites where strangers can read my messages. I think I shouldn't be rude to strangers. I always think "what should I wear" on the internet depending on how well I know the people with whom I am communicating'.

However, not all Japanese Twitter users are like Kazu, who is aware of the online context and adapts to Japanese social norms and changes the way in which he interacts with others depending on the sites he is using. Some young Twitter users believe that only their close friends – who they have as their followers – can read their tweets, and forget that in fact anyone can read their comments on the site. They thus tend to write their opinions frankly and directly, as if they were within a small closed *uchi*. Kaori, for example, who is an 18-year-old female college student, has two different Twitter accounts, one for college and the other for her hobby, *biwa* (Japanese lute). About using these she says:

> Kaori: I can say anything on Twitter. I use real names when I'm tweeting about what happens in my university in Twitter because only my friends read it.
> Researcher: But other people never read it?
> Kaori: I use a nickname for my Twitter account. So I'm OK!

Teenagers who tweet about drinking, cheating in exams or not paying for tickets on trains, because they want to get attention from their friends, are often criticized very severely by others and get flooded by comments. This can lead to social punishments such as suspension from school or losing their jobs. Due to this, they have become more conscious and aware that, on Twitter, others from *soto* can suddenly invade what they have been treating as an extension of their *uchi*.

6   Impression management: Facebook and bricoloage

In an earlier study on SNSs (Takahashi, 2010), I identified 'bricolage' (Levi-Strauss, 1966) as one of the most important dimensions of audience engagement with SNSs among young people. Bricolage is 'the re-ordering and re-contextualization of objects to communicate fresh meanings, within a total system of significances, which already includes prior and sedimented meanings attached to the objects used' (Clark, 1976, p. 149). Through creatively re-arranging and combining a variety of sources and images, Japanese young people create/recreate their self-identity by means of 'impression management' (Goffman, 1990[1959]): 'A profile on a social networking site is an opportunity to present yourself, as you really are, or as you would like to be' (Dwyer, 2007, p. 5). On Facebook, Japanese users do this by, for example, uploading many photos (and sometimes decorating them with stars or hearts by using the photo function of mobile phones), and by tagging each other in order to present themselves as active and popular. Hikari, for example, an 18-year-old female college student, told me that 'I use Facebook to show "*reajuu* [I live life to the fullest]". But if I keep looking at Facebook, I feel depressed. I feel jealous because everyone looks happy, especially when I feel down'. Before Japanese people began using Facebook, they mostly interacted with others anonymously on the internet. However, on Facebook, people have to (or at least are encouraged by the site to) communicate with each other using their real identities. Some Japanese young people feel uncomfortable writing their comments in such an open space using their real identity. They prefer to send messages or chat one-to-one rather than write comments on someone's wall. They also create many different groups by means of the privacy settings that the site provides, and communicate with each other inside these closed groups. Thus they tend to use Facebook for impression management in order to connect with *soto* as well as members of their *uchi*.

The above sections show how some Japanese young people connect with *soto* as well as *uchi* via Facebook and Twitter, and have to navigate different styles of communication in doing so. Others, on the other hand, prefer to connect with their *uchi* via a more recent form of Japanese social media, Line, where they are able to separately maintain different *uchi* and feel security within a small, bounded online community. In the final section of the chapter I will discuss the use of Line and '*uchi* creation/ re-creation'.

7 Line and *uchi* creation/recreation

Although Mixi had begun to provide a service enabling users to reorganize *maimiku* in order to keep each *uchi* separate, Japanese users seem to have chosen recently to leave Mixi for a new communicative online space, Line. The *Social Media Research Report 2012* (Impress R&D, 2012a) shows 21.3% of Japanese internet users, and nearly half of all young internet users, use Line. The *Line Users Research Report 2013* (Impress R&D, 2012b) reports the rapid growth of Line users and emphasizes that the site is particularly popular among smartphone users, with more than half of young smartphone users using Line in Japan. According to the later report (Impress R & D, 2012b), Line users communicate by belonging both to small groups with less than ten people in them, and to large groups such as their school class, their clubs and social circles, which will have between 31 and 50 people in them. Statistics suggest that they are likely to interact predominantly with only two or three people within these groups, and that 74.1 per cent of people tend to interact with less than five people. They communicate amongst each other both one-to-one as well as via intra-group communications such as group chat.

Line facilitates patterns of constant communication by showing the time at which each member reads their messages, thus providing pressure for an immediate response, in much the same way that Mixi does. In this way, traditional Japanese social norms continue to be reinforced by 'emotional bonds' and 'constant communication' as Nakane suggested back in the 1960s, and some of my informants have already expressed 'Line fatigue'. Nevertheless, there are three main reasons for Line's current popularity among young people in Japan: it is free of charge, it operates as a closed space, and it enables the sharing of emotional feelings by the use of 'stickers'. With respect to the first of these, most young users communicate through Line free of charge via mobile phones because Line uses the internet rather than phone lines. Users can therefore send messages or make calls without any additional charge, similar to Skype. Secondly, Line enables people to create different levels of groups and keep constant intra-group communication within each closed space. They create and reorganize their multiple *uchi* separately through online and offline communication in their everyday life, by moving their communication space from Mixi to Line. They feel security within each closed communication space, where opinions, beliefs, values and cultural norms are shared and which allows them to avoid any form of invasion or attack from *soto* as happens on open social media such as Twitter.

Finally, my fieldwork since 2000 has revealed the way that many Japanese young people frequently exchange *emoji* (emoticons) and animated decorative images via mobile phone. When young people receive texts or emails *without* accompanying images, they worry that their friends may be angry with them; or they become angry with their friends because of a perceived lack of thoughtfulness to themselves as receivers. For example, in Figure 8.1, Mika – a 19-year-old female college student who belongs to 33 groups of many different sizes and constantly communicates with ten groups at the same time – sends an image of a bear, which functions as an expression of politeness and a form of indirect phrasing showing her love and respect to others (Figure 8.1).

Risa sent a message saying simply 'Noisy!' because her group was exchanging messages constantly and this meant her mobile phone kept

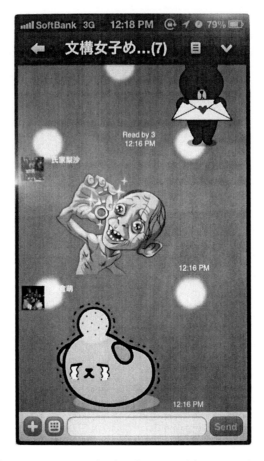

Figure 8.1 Intra-group communication: Japanese girls communicate using both Japanese and Western stickers unaccompanied by text

vibrating during class. This wasn't meant to signal that she was actually angry though. The other members responded immediately at 12:16 pm, and Mika then sent the message, 'Sorry, sorry', followed by:

Mika: (Mika sends a bear sticker – the bear is holding a letter to show her love – thus indicating that she is asking Risa to forgive her.)

Risa: (Risa sends a sticker of Gollum from *Lord of the Rings* to tell her 'OK'. The Gollum's gesture of holding the ring is similar to the OK sign in Japan.)

Moe: (Moe sends a *Mameshiba* sticker – the image shows a figure with an injured head who is crying, which indicates Moe's sympathy for how Risa's message made Mika feel.)

As Mika explained to me, stickers were used for similar reasons (Figure 8.2) in the following exchange between her friends.

Yurika, one of the group members, sent a message saying 'I have my dance presentation now. I will do my best'.

Risa: (Risa sends a Minnie Mouse sticker to show her feelings, 'That sounds good! I love it!')

Figure 8.2 Intra-group communication: Japanese girls often find that they can mimic verbal communication better through images and stickers rather than texts

Risa: Yurika, Love you ♡
Saki: Good luuuuuuck!!!
Saki: (Saki sends a Colonel Sanders sticker to show her love and wishes of good luck)

The two examples above illustrate how Japanese girls constantly connect and communicate with each other using a combination of texts, emoticons and images. Japanese images emphasize politeness and humbleness which is preferable in Japanese communication style, while Western images, which attract an additional charge,[3] represent something special and fun.

Through negotiating the interpretation of Western and Japanese consumer cultural products among *uchi* members, these Japanese young people share their own cultural values and reinforce their social intimacy and emotional bonds, and thus they reflexively create and recreate multiple *uchi* on Line.

8 Conclusion

In this chapter, I have investigated constant connectivity in social media in the Japanese context. In order to understand Japanese communication and cultural specificity, I have explained some Japanese emic concepts such as *uchi*, *kuuki* as well as the high/low context culture distinction. At the time of writing in 2013, Japanese young people are changing their communication habits by moving from Mixi to Facebook, Twitter and Line. On the one hand, Line enables them to create and maintain different levels of *uchi* within their small closed communication space via mobile phones. By reinforcing the emotional bonds within each *uchi*, a collective identity has emerged through constant intra-group online and offline communication. On the other hand, Facebook enables them to connect with distant others transnationally. As they have to show their real identity on Facebook, they create their own self-image as active and popular individuals by, for example, posting many photos which are tagged by other friends. Thus they use Facebook for 'impression management'. Some of them use Twitter to connect with *soto* following the content rather than motivated by relationship to the communicators. There are yet others who tweet more exclusively with close friends and followers. An individual identity has also emerged through constant connectivity with both multiple *uchi* and *soto* on 'an individual-centred network' (Castells *et al.*, 2007) via multiple social media. Thus Japanese young people reflexively create and recreate their self-identity which has emerged as a complex result of the interaction of both collective and individual identity partly through social media management.

'Global' social media such as Facebook and Line enable them to connect with non-Japanese people transnationally. Line has become popular mainly in Asia and Spanish-speaking countries and, as of July 2013, had 200 million users over 230 countries worldwide, with 80 per cent of users outside of Japan (Line, 2013), while Facebook had one billion users all over the world. The affordances of stickers and images of Line are helpful in their struggle against differences of languages and cultures which they may encounter in transnational communication. Mika, for instance, communicates with her Syrian friend (who lives in Japan) and her Thai friend (who lives in Thailand) by using stickers in her everyday life.

Mika:	The stickers are good because I can communicate with foreigners in Japanese and they are not good at Japanese. We can understand each other with stickers on Line more than by emails or other social media.
Researcher:	Don't you have miscommunication with stickers? They might interpret the meaning of stickers differently?
Mika:	No. Because I choose only simple stickers, like a smile or angry face. Everyone can understand the meaning.
Researcher:	I see. But then do you choose different stickers for non-Japanese from your Japanese friends?
Mika:	Yes. I choose very different stickers.

As well as selecting words and languages, they use universal images in order to show their care and emotions to 'distant others'. Although Turkle (2011) is concerned about superficiality in 'digitalized friendships – played out with emoticon emotions' (p. 17), I believe young people do not just connect but also 'communicate' with each other with text, emoticons and images which enable them to create emotional bonds, thereby enriching online communication. These social media maintain connectivity and social intimacy with 'distant others' through their interactions. By frequently interacting with 'distant others' via social media, 'others' are gradually embedded into their local everyday life. Through these interactions a small global *uchi* can thus emerge, just as a small local *uchi* emerges through frequent face-to-face interactions with 'local others'. In these contexts, social intimacy and emotional bonds with 'others' are developing, and 'distant others' are becoming affectively 'close *uchi* members'. The notion of global *uchi* which I have proposed may be a very small *uchi* but it may be an irreplaceable locus for its members. A sense of 'global *uchi-ism*' may constitute an '*uchi* membership' wherein people have social intimacy, emotional bonds, ontological security and moral responsibility with significant members in their privatized global *uchi* (Takahashi, 2009). Social media created by both Western and non-Western communication styles could provide mutual communication time-space to create global *uchi* through constant transnational connectivity and emotional bonds beyond languages and cultural context. Japanese young people reflexively create and recreate themselves and *uchi* through their constant engagement with social media in the global world.

Notes

1. The first SNS in Japan, SNSGocoo, was started in 2003: GREE and Mixi were then launched in 2004. Line was launched in 2011 by NHN Japan, which is an independent corporation within the Korean internet company, NHN. NHN Japan was established in 2000 and created Line by localizing the social network services in Japan (Toyokeizai, 2013, pp. 45–6: *Nihon keizai shinbun*, 2013). The English site for Line is http://line.naver.jp/en.
2. I started by reading through the entirety of my transcripts and notes, noting in margins and on post-its the various categories I have used in my research. I tried to approach this initial categorization with only very general categories in my mind, being open to novel categories being revealed by the voices of my informants.
3. Line users can use basic stickers free of charge but they can also buy some additional special stickers, for example *Lord of the Rings* characters, which Line makes available.

References

Baron, N. S. (2008) *Always On: Language in an Online and Mobile World* (Oxford: Oxford University Press).

boyd, d. (2010) 'Friendship'. In M. Ito *et al.* (eds.) *Hanging Out, Messing Around, and Geeking Out* (Cambridge, MA: MIT Press), pp. 79–115.

Castells, M., Fernández-Ardèvol, M., Qiu, J. L. & Sey, A. (2007) *Mobile Communication and Society: A Global Perspective* (Cambridge, MA: MIT Press).

Clark, J. (1976) 'Style'. In S. Hall & T. Jefferson (eds.) *Resistance through Rituals: Youth Subcultures in Post-War Britain* (London and New York: Routledge), pp. 147–61.

Clark, L. S. (2005) 'The constant contact generation: Exploring teen friendship networks online'. In S. Mazzarella (ed.) *Girl Wide Web* (New York: Peter Lang), pp. 203–22.

Couldry, N. (2012) *Media, Society, World: Social Theory and Digital Media Practice* (Cambridge: Polity Press).

Dwyer, C. (2007) 'Digital relationships in the "MySpace" generation: Results from a qualitative study'. Paper presented at the 40th Hawai'i International Conference on System Sciences (HICSS), Waikoloa, HI.

Ellison, N., Steinfield, C. & Lampe, C. (2007) 'The benefits of Facebook "friends": Social capital and college students' use of online social network sites', *Journal of Computer-Mediated Communication*, 12(4). http://jcmc.indiana.edu/vol12/issue4/ellison.html (accessed 24 January 2013).

Giddens, A. (1984) *The Constitution of Society* (Cambridge: Polity Press).

Giddens, A. (1990) *The Consequences of Modernity* (Cambridge: Polity Press).

Giddens, A. (1991) *Modernity and Self-Identity: Self and Society in the Late Modern Age* (Cambridge: Polity Press).

Glaser, B. G. & Strauss, A. L. (1968) *The Discovery of Grounded Theory: Strategies for Qualitative Research* (London: Weidenfeld and Nicolson).

Goffman, E. (1990[1959]) *The Presentation of Self in Everyday Life* (Harmondsworth: Penguin).

Gross, E. F. (2004) 'Adolescent internet use: What we expect, what teens report', *Journal of Applied Developmental Psychology*, 25(6): 633–49.

Hall, E. T. (1976) *Beyond Culture* (New York: Anchor Books).

Harada, Y. (2010) *Chikagorono wakamonoha naze damenanoka [Why are recent young people bad?]* (Tokyo: Koubunshasinsho).

Haythornthwaite, C. (2001) 'Tie strength and the impact of new media'. Paper presented at the 34th Hawai'i International Conference on System Sciences (HICSS), Hawai'i.

Impress R & D (2012a) 'Social Media Research Report 2012': www.impressrd.jp/news/120822/socialmedia2012 (accessed: 24 January 2013).

Impress R & D (2012b) 'Line Users Research Report 2013': www.impressrd.jp/news/121127/LINE (accessed: 24 January 2013).

Ito, Y. (2009) 'Japanese *kuuki* theory'. In S. W. Littlejohn & K. Foss (eds.) *Encyclopedia of Communication Theory* (Thousand Oaks, CA: Sage), pp. 573–4.

Kimura, T. (2012) *Dejitaru Neitebu no Jidai [The Age of Digital Natives]* (Tokyo: Heibonshinsho).

Levi-Strauss, C. (1966) *The Savage Mind* (London: Weidenfeld and Nicolson).

Line (2013) 'LINE Corporation Announces 2013 Second Quarter Earnings': http://linecorp.com/en/press/2013/0808586 (also http://line.naver.jp/event/2013/ja/) (accessed: 1 November 2013).

Livingstone, S. (2009) *Children and the Internet: Great Expectations, Challenging Realities* (Cambridge: Polity Press).

Nakajima, I., Himeno K. & Yoshii, H. (1999) 'Ido-denwa riyono fukyu to sono shakaiteki-imi' ['Diffusion of cellular phones and PHS and its social meanings'], *Joho Tsuushin Gakkai-shi*, 16(3): 79–92.

Nakane, C. (1967) *Tate shakai no ningenkankei: Tanitsu shakai no riron: [Interpersonal relationships in a vertically structured society]* (Tokyo: Koudansha Gendaishinsho).

Nihon keizai shimbun [Nikkei] (2013) ' 'LINE' ha nihonsan? kankokusan? [Is Line made in Japan or Korea?]' 23 January 2013. www.nikkei.com/article/DGXNASFK2203C_S3A120C1000000 (accessed 24 January 2013).

Prensky, M. (2001a) 'Digital natives, digital immigrants', *On the Horizon*, 9(5). www.marcprensky.com/writing/Prensky%20-%20Digital%20Natives,%20Digital%20Immigrants%20-%20Part1.pdf (accessed: 24 January 2013).

Prensky, M. (2001b) 'Digital natives, digital immigrants Part II: Do they really think differently?' *On the Horizon*, 9(6): 1–6.

Steinfatt T. M. (2009) 'High-context and low-context communication'. In S. W. Littlejohn & K. Foss (eds.) *Encyclopedia of Communication Theory* (Thousand Oaks, CA: Sage), pp. 278–9.

Takahashi, T. (2008) 'Japanese young people, media and everyday Life: Towards the internationalizing media studies'. In K. Drotner & S. Livingstone (eds.) *International Handbook of Children, Media and Culture* (London: Sage), pp. 407–24.

Takahashi, T. (2009) *Audience Studies: A Japanese Perspective* (Abingdon: Routledge).

Takahashi, T. (2010) 'MySpace or Mixi? Japanese engagement with SNS (Social Networking Sites) in the global age', *New Media and Society*, 12(3): 453–75.

Takahashi, T. (2011) 'Japanese youth and mobile media'. In M. Thomas (ed.) *Deconstructing Digital Natives* (Abingdon: Routledge), pp. 67–82.

Toyokeizai (2013) '*Ishoku kigyou NHN Japan [The unique company NHN Japan]*' 19 January 2013, pp. 45–7.

Tsuda, D. (2009) *Twitter shakairon [Twitter social theory]* (Tokyo: Yousensha).

Turkle, S. (2011) *Alone Together: Why We Expect More from Technology and Less from Each Other* (New York: Basic Books).

Yamamoto, S. (1977) *Kuuki no kenkyu [A study of 'Kuuki']* (Tokyo: Bungeishunjuu).

9
Investigating language policy in social media: translation practices on Facebook

Aoife Lenihan

1 Introduction

This chapter is concerned with the Facebook *Translations* application (app) through which the social network site (SNS) (boyd & Ellison, 2008) has internationalized its website. Despite its international reach, with over 70 per cent of Facebook users from outside of the United States of America, until February 2008 the site was available only in English. Following the development of the *Translations* app, the site was first opened to Spanish, and quickly followed by French, German and another 21 languages in 2008 (Facebook, 2012). Since then the *Translations* app has continued to be 'released' to more languages and, at the time of writing (November 2012), is available in 110 languages including minority or regional languages, such as Irish and Welsh; the national varieties of US English and UK English;[1] and other languages and varieties such as Leet Speak, Esperanto and Pirate English.

In terms of existing language policy theory, the *Translations* app initially appears to be very 'bottom-up' (Canagarajah, 2006; Hornberger, 1996) in nature, since any Facebook user can add the app to their *Profile*, submit a translation, vote on the translations submitted by others and participate in the discussions on the app's *Discussion Board*. The translations appear to be co-produced by the communities who engage with it in a dialectical process, albeit one that is explicitly defined and regulated by Facebook. However, on closer inspection Facebook is more involved in the community-driven translation effort than at first appears, intervening in a 'top-down' manner to adjudicate and authorize the final translations produced. The case of the translation of Facebook would thus appear to challenge the dichotomy of 'top-down'/'bottom-up' in language policy, and in Facebook's own words could be described as a 'hybrid model' (Vera, 2009).

208

This chapter will reconsider the categorization of 'top-down' and 'bottom-up' in language policy theory with reference to Facebook's role and the role of the Irish language community who use the *Translations* app. Firstly, the theoretical background of the current study will be considered, focusing particularly on existing language policy theory and studies concerned with social media. Next, the context of the Irish language will be introduced, and in particular its relationship with social media, its offline context and recent official language policy efforts for social media. Following this, the method of data collection and the data gathered will be briefly outlined. Then, the translators of the Facebook *Translations* app will be considered in terms of the concept of community, and the elements and design of the app discussed with regard to how Facebook fosters a sense of community via these. Finally, the discussion will focus on the language decisions and practices of Facebook and the Irish community of the *Translations* app in relation to current language policy theory and 'top-down'/'bottom-up' approaches.

2 Language policy and social media

The present study, following Blommaert *et al.* (2009), focuses on the multiplicity of actors and actions involved in *de facto* language policy situations, the choices and practices involved in the use of the app, and particularly those of the translators of the Irish language *Translations* community. It is the potential use of the internet as a mechanism of language policy (Shohamy, 2006) by 'bottom-up' interests that first drew my attention to the activities and policies of the language community driven Facebook *Translations* app. This study links social media practice with language policy, starting from the perspective that all language decisions made as part of the *Translations* app by both Facebook and the translators are manifestations of personal, community and organizational language policies, with varying levels of authority (Lo Bianco, 2010; Shohamy, 2006; Spolsky, 2004). This section will give an overview of existing language policy theory, with particular regard to community, business and social media, and it foregrounds the role of community in creating language policy, with a view to exploring how communities decide and enact policy on Facebook.

Language policy can come in two forms: it can be an explicit policy, a change in practices via 'a set of managed and planned interventions supported and enforced by law and implemented by a government agency' (Spolsky, 2004, p. 5). Alternatively, language policy can be viewed in a broad sense, as in the current study, as changes in the language practices of speech communities that cannot be attributed to explicit legislation, but are rather due to 'alterations in situation, conditions and pressures of which even the participants are unaware' (Spolsky, 2004, p. 5). Shohamy (2006), in her seminal book on language policy, argues for the need to understand the notion as more complex than solely institutional legislation, and says it should be examined and interpreted 'through a variety of mechanisms that are used by all groups, but especially those in authority, to impose, perpetuate and create language policies, far beyond those that are declared in official policies' (p. xvi). Language policy efforts by those in official authority are described as 'top-down', and are carried out by 'people with power and authority who make language decisions for groups, often with little or no consultation with the ultimate language... users' (Kaplan & Baldauf, 1997, p. 196). Other language policy efforts such as 'language regulation by non-governmental, commercial and private bodies' (du Plessis, 2011, p. 196), i.e. non-official entities, are, in contrast, described as 'bottom-up'.

Current theory predominantly conceptualizes 'top-down' and 'bottom-up' language policy as a dichotomy, acting in contrast with each other and as two distinct entities (Hornberger, 1996; Kaplan & Baldauf, 1997). This study will argue that within the traditionally defined 'bottom-up' level – that of social media as non-official language policy entities – Facebook and the individuals of the community act in both 'top-down' and 'bottom-up' manner depending on the context of the situation, leading to the need to reconsider the dichotomy of 'top-down'/'bottom-up' in language policy theory.

Recent research has begun to focus on language policy and communities. As Spolsky (2009, p. 2), drawing on Saussure, notes, language policy is a social phenomenon dependant on the 'beliefs and consensual behaviours of the members of a speech community'. Indeed, Trim (2003, p. 73) believes the 'dynamic forces at work in the everyday activity of language communities are far more powerful than conscious, ideologically motivated policies'. Spolsky (2012, p. 5) later goes further, describing the actual language practices of the speech community and its members as the '"real" language policy of the community ... the ecology or the ethnography of speech'. Furthermore, he notes that if any members of the community do not adhere to this 'real' language policy they may be marked as 'alien or rebellious', or, as in the current study, excluded from the language policy of the community. Social media such as Facebook and its *Translations* app are a space for the development of language communities, within which, no matter what their size, language policies operate (Spolsky, 2004).

In line with the broad/expanded view of language policy taken here, it must also be noted that businesses, such as those which develop and run forms of social media, are involved in language policy formation, whether this is their intention or not (Kaplan & Baldauf, 1997; Spolsky, 2004). Leppänen and Peuronen (2012, p. 397) acknowledge that 'many Internet sites, although they seldom spell out an explicit language policy of their own, often in fact develop some kind of regulatory mechanisms that can also affect language choice and use'. These mechanisms, as Leppänen and Peuronen note, although oftentimes implicit, can be 'a key factor' in users' language choice and use online.

Language policy research concerned with new media, is still in its infancy. Androutsopoulos (2009) acknowledges that the internet and its user-generated content offer 'unlimited' potential to challenge official policies and for practising new policies. Hogan-Brun (2011, p. 206), surveying recent studies in the field, notes that research is showing that new media can be used to sustain linguistic diversity and 'point to the potential of bottom-up practices in the use of conventional and new media for dynamic language planning in minority contexts'. She also believes that globalization, new media and communication technologies challenge and force us to re-evaluate traditional approaches to language planning in plurilingual or minority language contexts. Blommaert *et al.* (2009, p. 206) similarly find that the internet is a dynamic space and 'dichotomies such as top-down versus bottom-up in language policy may not capture fully the dynamics of the processes of normativity and normalisation that operate there'. The current study continues this examination of the notions of 'top-down' and 'bottom-up' and their conceptualization as a dichotomy in social media contexts.

3   The Irish language: language policy and community

This section briefly introduces the current context of the Irish language, both online and offline. The offline context described here is the shared context of the majority of Irish speakers involved in the *Translations* app and influences their translations and interactions on the app. The constitution of the Republic of Ireland, *Bunracht na hÉireann*, declares the Irish language as the first official language and English as the second official language of the state, and provision is made for the use of either language for official purposes. The Irish language is also an official language of the European Union (EU), although it is not treated the same as other EU official languages, as not all legislative documents are required to be translated into it (European Union, 2005). Despite all these status provisions, the Irish language is classified as 'definitely endangered' on the UNESCO (2009) vitality scale. 1.77 million of the 4.5 million resident Republic of Ireland population claim to be able to speak Irish, but 1.16 million of these either report they never speak the language, or speak it less frequently than weekly (Central Statistics Office, 2012). There are effectively no monolingual Irish speakers today, although there are many individuals who use it as their primary language of communication. Irish has more second language than native speakers, which is unusual in the context of minority languages worldwide (McCloskey, 2001). The *Comprehensive Linguistic Study of the Use of Irish in the Gaeltacht* (Ó Giollagáin *et al.*, 2007) finds that if the current rate of language shift amongst young adults continues, the Irish language will no longer be a community language in the *Gaeltacht* regions within the next 20–25 years (the *Gaeltacht* are the Irish speaking geographical areas in the Republic of Ireland as designated by the state).

The presence of Irish online is described anecdotally as '*Gaeltacht* 2.0', 'virtual hyper-*Gaeltacht*' (Ó Conchubhair, 2008) and 'cyber-*Gaeltacht*' (Delap, 2008). The creation and use of these terms illustrates that, within new media, there is seen to be an Irish-speaking space and an Irish language community. Although no official or academic statistics are available, insight can be gained into Irish language use on social media from *Indigenoustweets.com* which tracks Twitter for tweets in indigenous or smaller languages (Scannell, 2011). This site reports that on 25 October 2012 there were 4574 Twitter users who had sent 237,537 Irish language tweets (Scannell, 2012).

Delap (2008) sees new media as complementing traditional media efforts, describing the Irish language internet magazine *Beo* as operating effectively as a 'cyber-*Gaeltacht*'. He also points to social media and SNSs in particular as an important space for the Irish language, although noting that 'there is no social networking site operating exclusively through Irish' (p. 63). In his study of globalization and diaspora, Ó Conchubhair (2008) finds that Irish language speakers in any nation-state are no longer in isolation, which he credits as an outcome of globalization. He believes 'the global communication revolution allows Irish-speakers to participate in the virtual hyper-*Gaeltacht* any where, any time...' (p. 238). The Irish language communication network, he writes, is now a global phenomenon. Furthermore, Ó Conchubhair believes new media development(s) open the Irish-speaking community up to those not based in Ireland or Irish-born.

There are moves by official language policy entities towards developing a strategy and provisions for the Irish language and new media by official language policy entities. The *Straitéis 20 Bliain Don Ghaeilge 2010–2030 (Dréacht)/20 Year Strategy for the Irish Language (Draft)* published by the Department of Community, Rural and Gaeltacht Affairs (2009) includes media and technology as one of its nine areas for action. It acknowledges the 'new directions' in which the Irish language is going, noting the 'immense potential' of new media and how they 'open up new channels for individuals and communities to increase their knowledge and regular use of Irish' (2009, p. 84). Also, in 2009 *Foras na Gaeilge*, the statutory body responsible for the promotion of Irish, published its *Straitéis Idirlín don Óige (Dréacht)/Internet Strategy for Young People (Draft)* report. With regard to SNSs, the report finds there are many profiles available in Irish on Bebo and simply notes that Facebook has been 'localized' (2009, p. 3). The Irish language has been available for translation on Facebook via the *Translations* app since June 2008.

4   Method and data

The data considered here form part of a wider project on the translation of Facebook (Lenihan, 2011) and were gathered using virtual ethnographic methods. Virtual ethnography, developed by Hine (2000), 'transfers the ethnographic tradition of the researcher as embodied research instrument to the social spaces of the internet' (Hine, 2008, p. 257). Ducheneaut (2010, p. 202) describes virtual ethnography as 'an ethnography that treats cyberspace as the ethnographic reality' and its distinguishing feature is the goal of 'thick description' (Geertz, 1983) from the participants' perspective (Wouters, 2005). Here virtual ethnography is used to observe and investigate the *de facto* language policies on Facebook.

Virtual ethnographic studies can, as Madge (2010) notes, range from passive observation studies to participative studies where the researcher is an engaged member of the community. For the majority of this study the researcher assumed the role of a 'lurker', 'someone who reads messages posed to a public forum such as a newsgroup but does not respond to the group' (Hine, 2000, p. 160). In other words, the development of the Facebook *Translations* app and the Irish *Translations* community were observed in a non-participatory ethnographic manner. At one point the researcher did participate on a small scale, translating and voting on two words. This was undertaken simply to determine how the *Translations* app worked and to ascertain how much about these workings the translators were privy to.

The primary data sources are Facebook and the Irish language *Translations* app, which were longitudinally investigated from January

2009 to October 2011. Particular attention was given to the development of the app, its workings and design and the interactions of the
Irish language community via the *Discussion Board* on the app.
Other areas of the site considered include the overall *Translations* app homepage, the *Translations* apps of a number of other languages and the
Terms Applicable to Translations. Facebook publications and sources
examined include: Facebook press releases, the Facebook Blog, Facebook
careers publications and other regulatory Facebook documents.

5 The Facebook *Translations* app and community

New communication technologies and the social media they bring
cause us to rethink the notion of 'community' (Watkins, 2009). After
briefly introducing the *Translations* app, this section will consider
whether the Facebook translators can be seen as a community – or what
type of community it is that they constitute – and discuss how Facebook
as a company fosters and encourages community formation via the
design and infrastructure of the app.

Facebook users can add apps to their *Profiles* which 'allow [them]
to personalize their profiles and perform other tasks, such as compare
movie preferences and chart travel histories' (boyd & Ellison, 2008, p. 7).
These apps can be created by outside developers or by Facebook, as the
Translations app is. When a user adds the *Translations* app they become,
as Facebook title them, a 'translator' and they join the community of
the language they select. In 2011, 300,000 users were 'involved' in all
of the *Translations* apps, the latest figures available (Facebook, 2011).[2]
The app works by allowing translators to submit translations for words/
phrases, which are then open for approval via a voting system by the
other translators. Each language must pass through three steps via the
app to be deemed fully translated and launched for non-app users to
use. Step one is 'translate the *Glossary*', the glossary being the list of core
Facebook terminology. Step two is 'translate Facebook', the translation
of all the words and phrases Facebook as a website consists of. Finally,
step three is 'voting and verification', which involves further translation of words/phrases and the reviewing of and further voting on the
translations submitted in previous steps.

Facebook considers these translators a 'language community' and
designates this status to them, describing them using the term 'community' throughout all their publications, and thus, in a sense, bringing
the group into being by doing so. Using Fishman's definition of a 'language community' as 'a group of people who regard themselves as using

the same language' (Fishman, 1968, p. 140), the community of translators can be seen as a 'language community' in this sense, although they
use different dialects of the Irish language and have varying approaches
to language and translation. Spolsky (2004, p. 9) defines a speech community as 'any group of people who share a set of language practices
and beliefs'; they are governed by norms and rules of language and have
ideologies relating to language practices (p.14). As we shall see below,
it is certainly possible to see this occurring in the Irish *Translations* app.
Danet and Herring (2007) note that internet users are invariably members of one or more 'speech communities', with each member bringing
their own linguistic knowledge, values and expectations to the online
context. Given these various definitions, we can argue that the Irish
language translators are a type of 'speech community', drawn together
around shared interests in, values towards and practices relating to the
Irish language, and developing ways of interacting in the pursuit of this
shared goal.

In a relatively early definition, Rheingold (2000, p. 5) describes virtual
communities as: 'social aggregations that emerge from the Net when
enough people carry on... public discussions long enough, with sufficient human feeling, to form webs of personal relationships in cyberspace'. Vossen and Hagemann (2007, p. 59) define internet communities
as 'groups of people with common interests who interact through the
Internet and the Web'. In these definitions Rheingold places human
feeling and personal relationships at the centre of online communities,
while Vossen and Hagemann see all those interacting online around
particular issues as constituting online communities. Herring (2004)
goes further and sets out a number of conditions she believes must be
satisfied to term a group of internet users a community. These include:
regular interaction around a shared interest or purpose; the development
of social roles, hierarchies and shared norms; a sense of common history;
and an awareness of difference from other groups. From a sociolinguistic standpoint, Rheingold (2000, p. xv) importantly describes them as
'computer-mediated social groups'. And as Herring (2004) observes, they
are communities primarily based on and through language (or increasingly, other semiotic resources – see Leppänen *et al.*, this volume), as the
communities of translators involved in the translation of Facebook are.
In this case study, the Facebook company is involved in the creation and
promotion of community and a virtual or internet community to further
the translation of their website.

A number of aspects of the design of the *Translations* app promote and
foster the development of a community of translators using the app and

also, a sub-community of senior translators within that language community (Lenihan, 2011). The primary function of the homepage of the *Translations* app is to demonstrate the role the community of translators are playing in the translation process. The progress bars and statistics here (about translated and untranslated words/phrases) outline the progress of the language through the translation process, illustrating how the community are progressing, what they have done and what they have left to do. Also, the inclusion of the *Discussion Board* element in the design of the app demonstrates its community-focused, cooperative nature. Here any translator can begin a *Topic* on any issue and post replies on other *Topics*. In August 2011 Facebook divided the menu layout of the *Translations* app into three sections titled: *My Contributions, Community* and *Translation App*. The *Community* section includes the homepage of the app, the *Leaderboards* and a new sub-heading *Guidance* which includes the *Style Guide Wiki, Glossary* and *Help* elements. These changes were primarily aesthetic and structural but the titling and grouping allows Facebook to build a sense of community between the translators involved.

Facebook provides a number of ways for translators to recruit new translators. In August 2009 an *Invite Friends* section was added, which enabled users to invite potential translators from among their Friends. Translators could also *Share* the app by posting a link to it on their *Wall* or emailing their Friends with this link via the *Share* option on the *Translations* app's overall homepage. In May 2011 this *Share* link was replaced by a *Share this App* link, which posted a thumbnail of the app's logo, information on what the app did and a link to it on a user's *Profile Wall*, a *Friend's Wall* or via private message to their Friends. Also, on the overall *Translations* app homepage translators could see which of their Friends was using the app by going to the *Friends Who Have Added This Application* (2009) or the *You and Translations* (2011) elements. This feature builds a sense of community as it highlights which of your Friends, the people you know, are involved in the app already.

Through the design of the app Facebook creates and fosters a sub-community of senior translators within the wider community. Firstly, the *Leaderboards* (*Weekly, Monthly* and *All Time*) create a community of *de facto* senior translators – i.e. those who are continually in the top ten or top 20 of the *All Time Leaderboard*. Secondly, the *Style Guide Wiki* element is only editable by the top 20 translators of the *All Time Leaderboard* for that particular language. By designing the wiki to be editable by these translators alone, Facebook is facilitating and encouraging the creation of this community of what I am terming 'senior translators' who oversee the translation effort of the other translators within the community. On the *Style Guide Wiki* these translators can stipulate how they want certain words/phrases translated, how style issues should be resolved, and so on. Facebook adds to the importance of the *Style Guide Wiki* by telling translators on the homepage of each app to 'Use the Style guide for your language'. In the information it provides on the function and parameters of the wiki when the app is first opened to a language, it describes the *Style Guide* as 'a place where style rules decided by the [language] translation community can be codified, so that translators are aware of these rules prior to and during their translation activities'. Facebook encourages the formation of style rules and their codification in explicit written form through these instructions. The company encourages all of the community to be involved in the formation of the *Style Guide Wiki*, but those outside of the top 20 of the *All Time Leaderboard* do not have editing rights and can only contribute 'by posting their ideas for the style guide to the discussion forum'.

6   Discussion of Facebook's language policy

This section will consider three issues related to Facebook, the *Translations* app and language policy. Firstly, Facebook's policy decisions with regard to the degree to which Facebook promotes minority languages and accommodates non-English speakers will be considered. Secondly, the extent to which the community's translation is shaped by 'top-down' approaches within the community of translators and intervened in by Facebook itself will be discussed. Finally, how the community of translators' policy decisions are co-produced in a dialectical process will be considered using a case study of the term 'mobile phone'.

6.1   Facebook and multilingualism – 'to help even the smallest cultures connect'

Facebook as an organization does not have an explicit language policy document or statement, but, from looking at the site, comment can be made on their implicit language policy in relation to minority and non-English languages and their speakers. The company's founder and CEO, Mark Zuckerberg, states that the ultimate goal of the localization process is for users to use the site in their native language(s) (Facebook, 2008). As an organization, Facebook appears 'bottom-up' in its ideology associated with the *Translations* app, with an agenda aimed at including minority languages and communities. The company does so of its own accord and not at the behest of an official language policy authority or legislation. It stresses its inclusive approach towards minority language communities, with an employee writing that: 'we're always looking to add new languages to help even the smallest cultures connect with everyone around them' (Little, 2008). The conscious decision to include speakers of 'commonly ignored languages' stems from a number of strategic reasons, including the desire to increase the SNS's reach (Ellis, 2009, p. 239) and for symbolic effect. Facebook acknowledges that the inclusion of these languages helped the SNS to gain a 'loyal following' from these language communities (Wong, 2010). They also called attention to their inclusion of right-to-left languages on the *Translations* apps, highlighting their imminent arrival in 2009: '... we will be supporting translation for these right-to-left languages: Persian, Arabic, Hebrew, Syriac, Yiddish and Divehi' and with one *Facebook Blog* post dedicated entirely to this topic (Haddad, 2009).

However, this openness in terms of multilingualism is not present in all aspects of the website and its implicit language policy. The interface of the *Translations* app and the instructions on how to use it are only available in English, which excludes all non-English speakers from using the app and from being translators (Lenihan, 2011). The default of US English adds further complications, as some terms that are not relevant for other languages are open for translation, an example being 'zip code' in the Irish context, since there are no postal codes in the Republic of Ireland. Also, at the beginning of this study in 2009, when communicating with Facebook, even in relation to translation issues, Facebook only wanted communication in English (Lenihan, 2011). In this respect the company is engaging in observable efforts to influence the language practices of their users; in effect, a language policy. The site is, however, becoming more multilingual, with the interface of the *Translations* app itself being translated and with the company now also supporting communication in languages other than English – although at present only in eight languages, all of which are 'supercentral' (de Swaan, 2001) languages such as Spanish and French. Minority and lesser used language communities may translate and use Facebook in their own languages, but cannot engage or communicate with Facebook and its staff.

6.2 'Top-down' influences and the *Translations* app

'Top-down' influence comes from outside of the community of translators, as Facebook is more involved in the translations produced than first appears. It is not explained to the translators, nor have I been able to determine from observing the app, when a submitted translation is deemed to have received enough votes and becomes the translation used. This leaves it open to Facebook to determine the translation used and not the community of translators; again, this can be seen as a 'top-down' decision by Facebook leading to the enacting of their language policy. From looking at Facebook documentation, it is clear that the site intervenes in the decisions and language policy of the communities: 'And of course, we don't publish the translated versions until we do a quick check of the winning translations ourselves' (Wong, 2008). The 'quick check' of the translations that win appears as stage four of the translation process, described as: 'We are getting close! Once our staff have verified all the translations and tested all the functionalities, this language will be launched'. Another Facebook source tells us that linguists are on hand for 'difficult issues' and calls the *Translations* app a 'hybrid model' in that it uses both community and professional translations (Vera, 2009). Furthermore, Facebook has professional translators on hand to provide glossaries, style guides (both of which I believe are the *Glossary* and *Style Guide Wiki* elements of the app) and other materials to 'support' the community translators, and in some cases translate aspects of the site 'just in case' (Wong, 2008).

Facebook also intervenes in the 'bottom-up' language policy of the community of translators in the way they report translations. The *Review* element of the app was previously known as the *Poorly Translated* section, at which time there were no entries in the Irish version of the app, meaning no translator had reported a translation as needing particular consideration by the community. However, Facebook added an auto-detection aspect to the design of the app which checks the translations submitted against the translations agreed in the *Glossary*. With the addition of auto-detection and the *Review* section, the numbers of translations open for review have increased greatly. The community must now review translations that otherwise may not have been questioned or put up for review. In these various ways, Facebook facilitates the use of the *Translations* app as a 'bottom-up' mechanism of language policy, but only within its own parameters and ultimately its own 'top-down' decisions.

The design of the *Translations* app suggests that policy decisions within each community of Facebook translators will be reached by consensus. However, as noted above, there is also a sub-community within the translator community who position themselves as senior members and as being in charge of the translation. While they do not explicitly claim to be more knowledgeable or experienced, they act in a 'top-down' manner instructing, influencing and counselling other translators on the *Discussion Board*. The senior translators' authority appears to come from their perceived status from the *Leaderboard* and the *Discussion*

Board elements of the app. Through the discussions on the *Discussion Board* they ensure the translation(s) and version of Irish they themselves subscribe to are used on the site. Here they also form agreements amongst themselves on translation issues, such as which version of Irish to use, the official standard or a different dialect (Lenihan, 2011), which affect the community and the direction of the overall translation. Facebook facilitates the development of this sub-community of 'senior translators' by including the *Leaderboards* in the design of the app so as to give translators a rank within the community, and also by having the *Style Guide Wiki* only editable by those in the top 20 of the overall *Leaderboard*, thus giving them a position and a role different to the other translators involved.

We can see how this happens by looking at examples from the data set. Translator 1,[3] in particular, acts as a senior member of the community throughout the *Topics* of the *Discussion Board*, starting 14 *Topics* (12.9% of the total *Topics*) and contributing 98 posts across many *Topics* (15.5% of the total posts). In these, the translator puts his views across on the Irish language itself, on the use of the app by language learners (in his view, learners should not contribute) and instructs fellow translators on how to vote and translate. He also seeks support for translations he favours:

> [posting a link to a translation open for voting]
> Tá duine éigean tar éis saighead Up a chliceáil ar an abairt nasctha thuas...?!?! An féidir na daoine anseo an saighead "Down" a chliceáil.. Táim tinn tuirseach den abairt truailithe seo
> [Someone is after clicking the Up arrow on the word linked to above ...?!?! Can the people here click the "Down" arrow. I am sick and tired of this troublesome word]. (Translator 1, 2009)

Interestingly, this translator is perceived as being part of this senior translator sub-community by the other community translators: he later replies to the above post thanking the seven translators who voted 'up' as requested, suggesting that his 'top-down' decision is accepted and acted upon.

6.3   The case of *fón póca* – 'bottom-up' or 'top-down'?

The above discussion considered the *Translations* app and the Irish community along with the 'top-down' efforts to influence the community from both Facebook and from certain members of the community. This section will argue that the Irish language community of the app is a microcosm of language policy, with many levels of 'top-down' and 'bottom-up' language policy occurring as the community discusses, translates and votes.

During the period of my research, 'mobile phone' [cell phone] was the most discussed term on the Irish language *Translations* app *Discussion Board*, appearing in four separate *Topics*. Anecdotally there is an ongoing debate about the Irish language term for 'mobile phone'. The online version of the Irish language national terminology database, the realization of a 'top-down' policy, gives two translations: *teileafón póca* and *fón póca* (pocket phone) (Focal.ie, 2010) and the terms *guthán ceallach* (cell telephone), *guthán soghluaiste* (mobile telephone) and *guthán póca* (pocket telephone) are also in use. *Guthán soghluaiste* is seen as more 'traditional', coming from the Irish for 'telephone', *guthán*, while *fón póca* is generally thought of as a 'modern' term, but it is also seen by some as too Anglicized. On the *Discussion Board* four versions of 'mobile phone' are discussed: *fón póca*, *guthán póca*, *guthán soghluaiste* and *guthán ceallach*. *Fón póca*, the translation to be used as per the Irish app's *Glossary* from stage one of the translation process, appears to be the term favoured by the majority of the translators, but others nevertheless have different opinions.

One issue associated with the translation *fón póca* and discussed here is *béarlachas*, a term used to describe words that are seen to be too influenced by the English language. The use of *fón* is thought to be too close to the English 'phone' or 'fon' as used in colloquial Hiberno-English. An example of this from one translator is the post:

> mobile phone should either be *guthán soghluaiste* or *guthán póca* (I would argue that "*fón póca*" is a straight-up english calque and should be avoided in this case) [sic]. (Translator 2, 2008)

This is framed as a clear statement of the individual's beliefs which operate as a sort of personal language policy (Spolsky, 2004, 2012) implemented through their practice, i.e. translating and voting, and is a definite attempt to influence other translators. In a sense, the translator is acting as a 'language broker' – a category of 'actors who... can [and I would add do] claim authority in the field of debate' (Blommaert, 1999, p. 9). This is a level of language policy which would be traditionally defined as a 'bottom-up' community translation effort, in which the translator is challenging the 'top-down' decision of the community (in this case the use of *fón póca*) in favour of their own preferred choice (*guthán soghluaiste* or *guthán póca*) (Androutsopoulos, 2009).

A *Topic* in favour of *fón póca*, the translation chosen during stage one of the translation process, was started in reaction to other translations being submitted. The translator here reinforces the community's consensual beliefs associated with this translation, i.e. the 'top-down' community language policy (Spolsky, 2009):

> Can we decide once and for all that we are using the term *Fón Póca* for mobile phone, as was decided at the glossary stage. The point of the glossary is to stop people translating one thing seven different ways. If we're not consistent then this will be the worst translation ever. Regardless of whether *guthán póca*, etc. is "more correct" – *Fón Póca* was chosen in the first stage – will people stop using terms other than those from the glossary. (Translator 1, 2008)

This example again illustrates a statement of language policy by means of a reaction to other translators' 'bottom-up' language practices in submitting and voting for other translations of 'mobile phone'. In this case the statement attempts to enforce the community's language policy hegemony (Wright, 2004). The use of 'we' is interesting to note, as it can be seen as an attempt to create solidarity with other translators and increase cohesion among them. But the use of 'people' illustrates that some of the community are seen as 'others' and are excluded. Different levels of language policy, both 'top-down' and 'bottom-up', are thus occurring within the community of translators. Furthermore, we can see that language policy is an ongoing process, rather than the endpoint of a process such as this: Translator 1 is not willing to let this translation be decided by the voting process of the app, rather he re-iterates the 'top-down' policy and instructs that the community follow this.

The individual translator with the most posts on this subject wants yet another translation of 'mobile phone', *guthán ceallach*, to be used:

> D'ar leis an tOllamh Nicholas Williams (COBÁC), gur cóir "*guthán póca*" a úsáid, cé go ndéarfainse "*guthán ceallach*" a bheith i bhfad níos fearr.
> [According to Nicholas Williams (UCD) [University College Dublin, Ireland], *guthán póca* should be used; however, I think *guthán ceallach* is a lot better]. (Translator 3, 2008)

Throughout the discussions this translator expresses the belief that *guthán ceallach* should be used, as he dislikes the use of the word 'mobile' in English and prefers 'cellular'. Here Translator 3 is also going against the community's 'top-down' language policy but this translator's language policy is also different from the 'bottom-up' level of Translator 2, as discussed above, to use *guthán soghluaiste* or *guthán póca*.

However, Translator 3 is the only translator to favour this term and does not garner support from others:

> Aontaím leat i slí a [ainm], ach, tá roinnt den grí [bhrí] cáillte nuair a úsáidtear an focal *ceallach*. b'fhearr liom *guthán póca* mar shampla. [I do agree with you in a way [name], but some of the meaning is lost when you use the word cellular, for example, I prefer *guthán póca*]. (Translator 4, 2008)

As this example shows, any translator can post to the *Discussion Board*, participate in this process and go against the dominant discourse(s) (Lo Bianco, 2010); however, their views can be excluded from the community language policy by not gaining support from the wider community.

To supplement the findings from the above data, the phrases that were open for voting (at the time of these discussions) that contained the term 'mobile phone' were examined. This was carried out to ascertain what translations individual translators were submitting and voting on in practice, and thus to consider the performative actions of the translators (Lo Bianco, 2010). There were four versions of the phrase 'mobile phone number' open for voting, displayed in order of most votes first: *fón póca, guthán póca, uimhir* (number) *guthán póca* and *uimhir guthán soghluaiste*. This shows that the translation of 'mobile phone' had not been resolved despite the beliefs, practices and management (Spolsky, 2012), and therefore, language policy(ies), as discussed above. The translation favoured by Translator 3 above, *guthán ceallach*, had not been submitted for voting, again illustrating the exclusion of translators and translations which do not subscribe to the more dominant discourses (Lo Bianco, 2010). *Fón póca*, the community's 'top-down' choice, had the most votes, but the submission of the other translations shows that some translators are acting in a 'bottom-up' sense within the community. The terms *fón póca, guthán póca* and *guthán soghluaiste* were also submitted for the term 'privacy option for mobile phone number', but here *guthán póca* had the most number of votes with *fón póca* second. However, only *fón póca was* submitted for voting in the other two phrases containing 'mobile phone' open for voting. Thus we can see that the language policy processes around the translation of 'mobile phone' were ongoing and did not always adhere to the 'top-down' policy of the community.

This case study of 'mobile phone' demonstrates that 'bottom-up' language policy is made possible by the app and its practices, in that anyone can submit the translation they want, and that translations must be supported by the wider community to win the voting process, thus illustrating the social nature of this language policy (Spolsky,

2009) as well as the complexities involved with it that occur within this community-driven effort.

7 Conclusions

As has been discussed in this chapter, Facebook actively influences the crowd-sourced translations of their site. They do so in two ways: directly through their 'top-down' involvement in the app, and indirectly by setting up the translation process as a community-based effort. By designing the app to foster community effort, Facebook encourages the democratic nature of the translation, meaning that if a translation from the community is to be used, it must have been voted on positively by many of the translators. Although there may be different language beliefs and practices amongst individual translators, only one translation for each Facebook word or phrase is to be used in the final version. In the case of 'mobile phone', Facebook does not choose which version it prefers, but nevertheless does have an influence, in that the one finally used is the one most popular with this language community, a community influenced by its own internal overseers, the 'senior translators', to the exclusion of the views of others. Furthermore, in including minority and non-English languages in the *Translations* app, Facebook is influencing the language diversity of social media, providing a space for these language communities and perhaps influencing other social media to do so also.

In terms of language policy theory, Facebook, the Irish language community and their members act in both a 'top-down' and 'bottom-up' sense depending on the context of the situation, and in this way the current research demonstrates that the assumed dichotomy of 'bottom-up' forces as opposed to 'top down' forces is not always in evidence. Rather, language policy is now realized as not just unidirectional, but can be found in 'multiple discursive relations' (Androutsopoulos, 2009) and cannot be separated from the shared norms and normative discourses of language communities (Leppänen & Piirainen-Marsh, 2009). An expanded view of language policy is necessary, one that challenges the accepted dichotomies, since the object of its study, the social media context, is ever-changing, fluid and dynamic.

Acknowledgements

I would like to acknowledge the support of the Irish Social Sciences Platform (ISSP) (Funded under the Programme for Research in Third Level Institutions, administered by the HEA and co-funded under the European Regional Development Fund [ERDF]), which provided a doctoral scholarship for my research.

Notes

1. These are the categories of language variety Facebook uses.
2. It is not outlined what level of participation/interaction with the app is meant by 'involved in'.
3. The Irish translators are anonymized here by titling them Translator 1, Translator 2, etc., but the use of these figures does not equate to a ranking of their status in the community, nor of their contribution to the translation effort.

References

Androutsopoulos, J. (2009) 'Policing practices in heteroglossic mediascapes: A commentary on interfaces', *Language Policy*, 8: 285–90.

Blommaert, J. (1999) 'The debate is open'. In J. Blommaert (ed.) *Language Ideological Debates* (Berlin/New York: Mouton de Gruyter), pp. 1–38.

Blommaert, J., Kelly-Holmes, H., Lane, P., Leppänen, S., Moriarty, M., Pietikäinen, S. & Piirainen-Marsh, A. (2009) 'Media, multilingualism and language policing: An introduction', *Language Policy*, 8(3): 203–7.

boyd, d. m. & Ellison, N. B. (2008) 'Social network sites: Definition, history, and scholarship', *Journal of Computer Mediated Communication*, 13(1): 210–30.

Canagarajah, S. (2006) 'Ethnographic methods in language policy'. In T. Ricento (ed.) *An Introduction to Language Policy: Theory and Method* (Oxford: Blackwell), pp. 153–69.

Central Statistics Office (2012) *Census 2011: Ethnicity, Irish Language and Religion* (Dublin: Stationery Office).

Danet, B. & Herring, S. C. (2007) 'Introduction: Welcome to the multilingual internet'. In B. Danet & S. C. Herring (eds.) *The Multilingual Internet: Language, Culture, and Communication Online* (New York: Oxford University Press), pp. 3–39.

Delap, B. (2008) 'Irish and the media'. In C. Nic Pháidín & S. Ó Cearnaigh (eds.) *A New View of the Irish Language* (Dublin: Cois Life), pp. 152–63.

de Swaan, A. (2001) *Words of the World: The Global Language System* (Cambridge: Polity).

Department of Community Rural & Gaeltacht Affairs (2009) *Straitéis 20 Bliain Don Ghaeilge 2010–2030 (Dréacht)/20 Year Strategy for the Irish Language (Draft)* (Dublin: Government Publications).

Ducheneaut, N. (2010) 'The chorus of the dead: Roles, identity formation, and ritual processes inside an FPS Multiplayer Online Game'. In J.T. Wright, D.G. Embrick & A. Lukács (eds.) *Utopic Dreams and Apocalyptic Fantasies: Critical Approaches to Researching Video Game Play* (Plymouth, UK: Lexington Books), pp. 199–222.

du Plessis, T. (2011) 'Language visibility and language removal: A South African case study in linguistic landscape change', *Communicatio: South African Journal for Communication Theory and Research*, 37(2): 194–224.

Ellis, D. (2009) 'A case study in community-driven translation of a fast-changing website'. In N. Aykin (ed.) *Internationalization, Design and Global Development* (Berlin/Heidelberg: Springer), pp. 236–44.

European Union (2005) Council Regulation (EC) No 920/2005 of 13 June 2005 amending Regulation No 1 of 15 April 1958 determining the language to be used by the European Economic Community and Regulation No 1 of 15 April 1958 determining the language to be used by the European Atomic Energy Community and introducing temporary derogation measures from those Regulations, http://eur-lex.europa.eu/LexUriServ/LexUriServ. do?uri=CELEX:32005R0920:EN:NOT (accessed 1 February 2010).

Facebook (2008) 'Facebook releases site in Spanish; German and French to follow', http://newsroom.fb.com/News/238/Facebook-Releases-Site-in-Spanish-German-and-French-to-Follow (accessed 16 November 2012).

Facebook (2011) 'Facebook factsheet', http://www.facebook.com/press/info. php?factsheet [no longer live] (accessed 30 May 2011).

Facebook (2012) 'Fact sheet', http://newsroom.fb.com/content/default.aspx? NewsAreaId=22 (accessed 14 February 2012).

Fishman, J. (1968) *Readings in the Sociology of Language* (The Hague: Mouton).

Focal.ie. (2010) 'Mobile phone search results', http://www.focal.ie/Search. aspx?term=mobile+phone (accessed: 22 June 2010).

Foras na Gaeilge (2009) *Straitéis Idirlín don Óige (Dréacht)/Internet Strategy for Young People (draft)*, http://gaelport.arobis40.com/uploads/documents/ Dréachtstraitéis_Idirlín_don_Óige.pdf (accessed 22 June 2010).

Geertz, C. (1983) *Local Knowledge: Further Essays in Interpretive Anthropology* (New York: Basic Books).

Haddad, G. (2009) 'Facebook blog: Facebook now available in Arabic and Hebrew', https://blog.facebook.com/blog.php?post=59043607130 (accessed 1 June 2012).

Herring, S. C. (2004) 'Computer mediated discourse analysis'. In S. A. Barab, R. Kling & J. H. Gray (eds.) *Designing for Virtual Communities in the Service of Learning* (Cambridge: Cambridge University Press), pp. 338–76.

Hine, C. (2000) *Virtual Ethnography* (London: Sage).

Hine, C. (2008) 'Virtual ethnography: Modes, varieties, affordances'. In N. G. Fielding, R. M. Lee & G. Blank (eds.) *The Sage Handbook of Online Research Methods* (London: Sage), pp. 257–70.

Hogan-Brun, G. (2011) 'Language planning and media in minority language and plurilingual contexts', *Current Issues in Language Planning*, 12(3): 325–9.

Hornberger, N. H. (1996) *Indigenous Literacies in the Americas: Language Planning from the Bottom-up* (Berlin: Mouton de Gruyter).

Kaplan, R. B. & Baldauf Jr, R. B. (eds.) (1997) *Language Planning: From Practice to Theory* (Clevedon: Multilingual Matters).

Lenihan, A. (2011) '"Join our community of translators": Language ideologies and Facebook'. In C. Thurlow & K. Mroczek (eds.) *Digital Discourse: Language in the Social Media* (Oxford: Oxford University Press), pp. 48–64.

Leppänen, S. & Peuronen, S. (2012) 'Multilingualism on the internet'. In M. Martin-Jones, A. Blackledge & A. Creese (eds.) *The Routledge Handbook of Multilingualism* (Oxon: Routledge), pp. 384–402.

Leppänen, S. & Piirainen-Marsh, A. (2009) 'Language policy in the making: An analysis of bilingual gaming activities', *Language Policy*, 8: 261–84.

Little, C. (2008) 'Facebook blog: Arrr, Avast All Ye Pirates!' http://blog.Facebook. com/blog.php?post=31137552130 (accessed: 19 February 2010).

Lo Bianco, J. (2010) 'Language policy and planning'. In N. H. Hornberger & S. L. McKay (eds.) *Sociolinguistics and Language Education* (Bristol: Multilingual Matters), pp. 143–76.

Madge, C. (2010) 'Internet mediated research'. In N. Clifford, S. French & G. Valentine (eds.) *Key Methods in Geography* (London: Sage), pp. 173–88.

McCloskey, J. (2001) *Guthanna in Éag: an Marfaidh an Ghaeilge beo?/Voices Silenced: Has Irish a Future?* (Dublin: Cois Life).

Ó Conchubhair, B. (2008) 'The global diaspora and the "new" Irish (language)' in C. Nic Pháidín & S. Ó Cearnaigh (eds.) *A New View of the Irish Language* (Dublin: Cois Life), pp. 224–48.

Ó Giollagáin, C., Mac Donnacha, S., Ní Chualáin, F., Ní Shéaghdha, A. & O'Brien, M. (2007) *Comprehensive Linguistic Study of the Use of Irish in the Gaeltacht: Principal Findings and Recommendations* (Dublin: Dublin Stationery Office).

Rheingold, H. (2000) *The Virtual Community* (Cambridge, MA: The MIT Press).

Scannell, K. (2011) 'Welcome/Fáilte!' http://indigenoustweets.blogspot.ie/2011/03/welcomefailte.html (accessed 25 October 2012).

Scannell, K. (2012) 'Indigenous tweets', http://indigenoustweets.com/ (accessed 25 October 2012).

Shohamy, E. (2006) *Language Policy: Hidden Agendas and New Approaches* (London: Routledge).

Spolsky, B. (2004) *Language Policy* (Cambridge: Cambridge University Press).

Spolsky, B. (2009) *Language Management* (Cambridge: Cambridge University Press).

Spolsky, B. (2012) 'What is language policy?' In B. Spolsky (ed.) *The Cambridge Handbook of Language Policy* (Cambridge: Cambridge University Press), pp. 3–15.

Trim, J. L. M. (2003) 'Review essay', *Language Policy*, 2: 69–73.

UNESCO (2009) 'UNESCO Interactive atlas of the world's languages in danger 2009', http://www.unesco.org/culture/ich/index.php?pg=00206 (accessed 1 February 2010).

Vera, N. (2009) 'Life at Facebook: Nico Vera', http://www.facebook.com/careers/story.php?story=6 [no longer live] (accessed 19 February 2010).

Vossen, G. & Hagemann, S. (2007) *Unleashing Web 2.0: From Concepts to Creativity* (Burlington Elsevier/Morgan Kaufmann).

Watkins, S. C. (2009) *The Young and the Digital* (Boston: Beacon Press).

Wong, Y. (2008) 'Facebook blog post: Facebook around the world,' http://blog.Facebook.com/blog.php?post=10056937130 (accessed 19 February 2010).

Wong, Y. (2010). 'Quora Question: What was the process Facebook went about getting their website translated into different languages?' http://www.quora.com/What-was-the-process-Facebook-went-about-getting-their-website-translated-into-different-languages (accessed 24 May 2011).

Wouters, P. (2005) 'The virtual knowledge studio for the humanities and social sciences'. In *First International Conference on e-Social Science*, www.ncess.org/events/conference/2005/papers/papers/ncess2005_paper_Wouters.pdf (accessed 16 November 2012).

Wright, S. (2004) *Language Policy and Language Planning: From Nationalism to Globalisation* (Basingstoke and New York: Palgrave Macmillan).

10
Seeing Red: social media and football fan activism

Frank Monaghan

1 Introduction

> *Spirit of Shankly* wouldn't be where it is today without the internet. There's no two ways about that. We were a new organisation ... and we were using internet forums originally, but what we realised was that ... not everyone was using internet forums, but everyone used Facebook and latterly everyone used Twitter ... a Facebook status update meant that you could get somebody interested in a protest.
>
> (Jay McKenna, Media and Communications Officer, *Spirit of Shankly*, interview with author)

This chapter explores the role social media play in allowing political activists to come together around a shared real-world goal. Since the mid-1980s, technologies such as email, mobile phones, and interactive websites such as Flickr, Twitter, YouTube and Facebook, have transformed the means and opportunities for activists to employ social media in order to 'communicate, collaborate and demonstrate' (Garrett, 2004, p. 202). Key factors in this include: the relatively low cost of online communication, which enables a typically resource-poor and therefore power-less resistance to organize against a resource-rich and therefore powerful opposition (Bonchek, 1995); the promotion of a collective identity across a dispersed population that activists can then mobilize in pursuit of interests perceived as core to that identity (Brainard & Siplon, 2000); and the creation of communities that foster issue-based communication and thus strengthen participants' identification with the movement (Diani, 2000). Far from producing a generation of bedroom-bound isolates, social media in these cases appear to be bringing people together both virtually and physically in pursuit of common interests and causes. It is the space between the social and the media that underpins this chapter.

In parallel with the shifts in communication technology, the same period has also witnessed the ferocious, velocious, advance of economic globalization and organized efforts to resist it. Social media have been closely involved in that resistance.

Football (soccer), once perceived as a working-class pursuit, has not escaped the forces of marketization and globalization, with leading clubs in the UK that once were owned by local businessmen and run almost as vanity hobby projects now being bought up by Russian oligarchs, American conglomerates and Arab petro-billionaires and run as serious money-making businesses within a portfolio of other interests. Inevitably, this has led to resistance amongst fans who have seen the very existence of their clubs threatened; for example, Liverpool Football Club (LFC) was days away from insolvency in 2010 before being purchased by the American company Fenway Sports Group, and in 2012 one of the most successful Scottish football clubs, Glasgow Rangers, was forced to file for bankruptcy. Fans have watched 'their' club's identity be effaced by commercialism, accompanied by enormous hikes in the cost of tickets (up to £100 at Arsenal in the 2011–12 season), which has had the effect of driving out poorer 'locals' in favour of wealthy 'outsiders'. This effect can also be seen in the prioritization of corporate interests over fans', as witnessed by the re-development of grounds to favour the former over the latter in terms of space allocated to entertainment facilities. All this has produced a sense of increasing dispossession and voicelessness among communities of fans as 'ownership' moves further from the open terraces and into closed boardrooms.

Taking this as its context, this chapter explores the efforts of one group, the Liverpool FC based *Spirit of Shankly (SoS)*, the first ever football supporters' union, to use social (and other) media as part of its 'constant aims' to 'hold whoever owns the club to account' and to 'represent the best interests of supporters' (*SoS* website http://new.spiritofshankly.com/). In particular, the chapter will examine how social media were used as part of a campaign by *SoS* to oust the club's owners, American businessmen Tom Hicks and George Gillett, in 2010. The chapter will examine the role that social media played in defining, fostering and drawing on a specific sense of LFC fan identity and in so doing creating a network or community of geographically dispersed activists.

A key aspect that will be pursued here is how *SoS* deployed different semiotic modes – primarily text and image, but also sound through podcasts and YouTube videos – to promote its identity – and so the chapter will draw on analyses of the different elements of communication used, how they engage people's sense of history and place to form, define and enlist a particular identity and concept of community in pursuit of their goals. It explores how social activist organizations need to draw on the particular affordances of both social and other media to be effective, both in terms of pursuing a cause and engaging people to actively participate in it, albeit at differing levels of commitment.

Before moving to the substantive discussion, however, it is worth very briefly outlining the data sources and the approach I am taking to their analysis. As noted above, I take a case study approach, focusing specifically on the workings of one particular organization, *SoS*. Given that social media are markedly multimodal, any analysis needs to include consideration of the various modes that are used and how these are deployed. To this end, the data source consists of texts and images used on the *SoS* website (www.spiritofshankly.com) as well as on Flickr (www.flickr.com/photos/47942694@N07/sets/), Twitter (@spiritofshankly), Facebook (www.facebook.com/spiritofshankly) and YouTube (http://www.youtube.com/user/sosliverpool). It includes photographs taken both by fans and by John Johnson, a professional photographer associated with *SoS*, as well as offline images used, for example, in banners and advertising hoardings as part of public campaigns. The aim here is to illustrate how a social activist organization needs to combine both social and 'traditional' media, professional and amateur 'design', in order to present itself as both sophisticated and grounded; this is particularly important in an activist organization seeking to influence diverse audiences ranging from fans on the terraces to financiers in the boardroom. In the analysis of these data, I draw on work from a number of areas, including multimodal analysis (e.g. Kress & van Leeuwen, 1996; Van Leeuwen & Jewitt, 2010), discourse analysis (e.g. Tannen, 1989) and language as a local practice (Pennycook, 2012). The discussion also draws more broadly on research on social media (e.g. van de Donk *et al.*, 2004; Mandiberg, 2012), activism and social media (e.g. Garret, 2006; Castells, 2007), and the psychology of groups (Funk & James, 2001). It is hoped that this multi-dimensional approach allows for the capturing of the rich breadth and depth of social media that are employed in the context of social activism, and how this combines with traditional methods of offline community building.

2 *Spirit of Shankly* – origins

Spirit of Shankly takes its name from Bill Shankly, Liverpool FC's talismanic manager, who led the club for fifteen years during one of its most successful periods in the 1960s to the mid 1970s. Shankly placed particular importance on the role of the fans (the 'twelfth-man' of the team) and their relationship to the club, arguing: 'a manager has got to identify himself with the people (because) football is their whole life' (Shankly & Roberts, 1976, p. 175). Equally famous was his comment, 'At a football club, there's a holy trinity – the players, the manager and the supporters. Directors don't come into it. They are only there to sign the cheques'. Forty years on and the economics of football had changed completely with the arrival of global media players such as Sky and ESPN competing for the rights to broadcast football matches across their cable and satellite networks. The auction for TV rights to broadcast matches netted England's Premier League £3 billion for three years from 2013, the highest sum for any national league in the world. This represents a 70 per cent increase on the previous three-year deal and equates to a sum of £6.5 million per game. When the Premier League was launched in 1992, the sum paid for the rights was £190 million (£633,000 per game). The share for clubs now typically accounts for over half their annual income and the effect of this has been a shift of interest from fans to broadcasters, as witnessed, for example, by the way the scheduling of games has become increasingly determined by the media companies' priorities rather than the fans' convenience. Liverpool FC has been part of this development.

In 2007 the club was about to change hands from long-time majority shareholder and local businessman, David Moores, to the Americans Tom Hicks and George Gillett for a sum of £218.9 million and a promise to start building a new stadium within sixty days, a broken promise that would come back to haunt them. In their initial press release on taking over the club Hicks and Gillett sought to position themselves in the Shankly tradition, acknowledging the significance of the supporters: 'Liverpool is a fantastic club with a remarkable history and a passionate fanbase. We fully acknowledge and appreciate the unique heritage and rich history of Liverpool and intend to respect this heritage in the future' (Hicks & Gillett, 2007). Initially welcomed by the fans, by 2008, with no sign of a stadium and reports hitting the press of tensions between the manager (Rafael Benitez) and the owners over failure to make money available for signings of new players, supporters began to express their concerns and some of them began to organize. Peter Hooton, a lifelong supporter and lead singer of the Liverpool band The Farm, joined forces with Andy Heaton and Dave Usher of The Liverpool Supporters Network, an affiliation of websites and fanzines. They decided to call a face-to-face meeting 'to work out a strategic response instead of everyone being a website warrior in their bedroom' (Reade, 2012, p. 22). A connection between screen and street activism was forged from the outset and has been a part of the *SoS* strategy ever since.

On 31 January 2008, about three hundred LFC fans met in The Sandon, a historic public house located near to Anfield, Liverpool's football ground. The Sandon is closely associated with the founding of the club (1892) and has remained a favourite meeting place for support- ers ever since. One of those attending that evening was Jay McKenna, quoted at the head of this chapter. Having spoken up at the meeting, he was subsequently elected *SoS's* Media and Communications Officer, and in an interview with me, described how he had become aware of the meeting through a message on an internet forum. This message suggested supporters should channel their anger about Hicks and Gillett into something more positive and more organized than grum- bles on the terrace during matches. He describes a turning point in the meeting:

> Nicky Allt, a well-known Liverpool supporter and playwright stood up and said it's quite surprising for a city as militant as Liverpool and as very unionised that we didn't actually have a union of supporters or we didn't have nothing to represent supporters and come up with the idea following on from the idea of Shankly and his principles of socialism and supporters being very important to the club that we should set up a Liverpool supporters union and the name *Spirit of Shankly* was adopted. (Jay McKenna, interview with author)

An organization was born which not only had a sense of its identity in terms of the traditions of the football club, but which also saw this identity as intertwined with that of the city itself and its tradition of left-wing politics and trade union activism. These twinned identities, the football club and the city, sport and politics, provided a potent mix when it came to campaigning.

3   *Spirit of Shankly* – developing an identity through social (and other) media

Initially, the group focused on locally based activities such as match day marches to the football ground, post-game sit-ins and leafleting cam- paigns around Anfield and Liverpool city centre. These initial activities were geographically limited. As membership grew from that initial 300 to 10,000 paid-up members and an estimated 30,000 more following the campaigns online, the benefits of making greater use of social media became ever clearer to the leadership, as explained by Jay McKenna:

> We often used to notice that a weekly Facebook status update or when we put a Twitter update out there, membership would grow, a few more people would join; we'd be tweeted by a higher number of people. (Interview with author)

Analysis of the people communicating via social media also revealed that they were not necessarily locally based and so were not being effectively harnessed as actors in the campaign. The dynamic between street-based and web-based activism was to prove crucial.

Figure 10.1, taken from the *SoS* website, demonstrates an awareness of the importance of locating representations of an organization within a readily understood iconography, in this instance an organized protest march. The photograph stands in the long tradition of images inspired by Volpedo's 1901 painting *'Il Quarto Stato'* (The Fourth Estate), with its wide-shot of workers striding purposefully towards the viewer and the 'light' led by two men and a woman holding a baby, a painting that is a well-known symbol for leftist causes.

Figure 10.1 Street protest

Limitations of space do not permit a detailed analysis in this chapter of all the images drawn on, but I will try to indicate some salient features where possible and particularly where their interconnectedness with the, perhaps, more transparent use of language as mediator of ideological positions seems salient. In this instance, for example, I would refer the reader/viewer to the presence of the *SoS* banners, with the organization's logo depicting an iconic silhouette of Bill Shankly, instantly recognizable to any LFC fan, that bookend the phalanx of protesters. This image is omnipresent on all *SoS* platforms and provides a visual reference point that both advertises the union to those as yet unfamiliar with it and, via repetition, enables members to identify with it both directly on the street and through its replication across *SoS*'s website, and their Facebook, Twitter, YouTube and Flickr accounts (see Figure 10.2). This interplay of images of direct action on the streets with iconography on the screen serves to connect the realms of social media and social activism, the one supporting the other. Both are necessary and neither is sufficient in a globalized context, for whilst direct action has the benefits of being felt on the pulse it is limited to specific times and places, whereas its social media counterpart is everywhere and free of time constraints, if less visceral when mediated through technology.

Cross-platform branding serves a useful communicative function. Deborah Tannen has described verbal repetition as one of the 'involvement strategies' (1989, p. 1) used by conversationalists in creating a discourse and establishing relationships, and a central meaning-making resource. This seems equally applicable to messages (re-tweets) and images when used as part of the communicative strategy of organizations

Figure 10.2 Spirit of Shankly, cross-platform branding

seeking to engage remotely with their addressees. Linking images and postings across social media platforms has its parallel in protestors marching under their organization's banner and chanting collectively out on the street – it provides a rallying point for identification and solidarity. Jay McKenna, the *SoS* Executive Officer, is positioned at the forefront of the photograph (Figure 10.1), which both reinforces identification with him for those who know him personally, and with his (and by extension *SoS*'s) leadership role in the campaign against the owners, the megaphone marking its bearer as both literal and figurative voice of the union.

4 From street to screen

According to the sociologist Manuel Castells (2007, p. 241), '[w]hat does not exist in the media does not exist in the public mind'. Social media have increasingly been used to translate what's been put 'in the public mind' into direct action back in the world. This can be seen in the rise of online campaigning groups such as Avaaz (www.avaaz.org) and 38 degrees (www.38degrees.org.uk), who are able to mobilize hundreds of thousands of people within days (sometimes hours) to sign petitions, lobby politicians and target businesses in pursuit of a wide range of causes from 'Save the Bees' to 'Stop Global Tax Dodgers'.

As an example of this interaction between 'old media' and 'new', the leadership of *SoS* has staged a number of high-profile events designed to attract press attention, which are then recycled through their social media platforms. In August 2008, for example, a little over a year after the 'sixty days' promised deadline for work to start on the building of a new stadium had passed, 40 members of *SoS*, wearing high-visibility jackets and hard hats, armed with spades, wheelbarrows and banners, went to Stanley Park, the proposed site for the new ground, and began turning over the soil. This event was billed as 'The Big Dig' (Figure 10.3). The stunt attracted the attention of the local press and TV. Speaking to reporters, one of the organizers, Neil Atkinson, commented, '[t]here must be a perfectly reasonable explanation why the owners have not carried out their promises ... They didn't manage to get the stadium started, so we are doing them a favour' (cited in Reade, 2012, p. 176). This arch use of language contrasts the plain-speaking Scousers of *SoS* with the double-dealing American owners, Hicks and Gillett. Whilst they may have been plain-speaking, *SoS*'s leaders were anything but simple, as Hicks and Gillett came to realize when, as a result of the media stunt and other forms of pressure applied by *SoS*,

Figure 10.3 The Big Dig

including email campaigns, they agreed to a meeting with them, as reported by Paul Rice, then Chairman of the group, to journalist and author, Brian Reade:

> Naturally, Uncle George was very pally ... he said, 'You guys know who I am so tell me who you are and what you all do.' ...
> 'I could tell by looking at him that he was taken aback,' said Rice. 'I think he was expecting us to say "hod-carrier, doorman, incapacity benefit recipient, etc.," but instead he heard "chief executive, playwright, chief executive, etc." And you could see he was thinking, "Gee these guys might be able to string a sentence together, we could be in trouble here"' (Reade, 2012, p. 135)

Figure 10.3 is also interesting for the presence of the TV camera in the photograph. By displaying this image on the campaigns section of its website *SoS* was able to demonstrate its media influence both to its members, the wider public who saw it, and, perhaps more importantly from a strategic point of view, to those directly in positions of influence over the future of the club. That such strategies were successful is indicated by the fact that *SoS* were invited to meetings not only with the American owners but also with representatives of Dubai Investment Capital, potential buyers of the club and part of the portfolio of one of the world's richest men Sheikh Mohammed Al Maktoum.

What this illustrates is the way that traditional and social media have complementary roles that feed off and nourish each other. Activists may use social media to stage an event (such as 'The Big Dig') and this attracts 'traditional' media interest that then makes people turn to social media to get involved. The traditional media brought *SoS* to the attention of powerful interest groups, such as the club's current and potential future owners, and it also persuaded more and more members of the fanbase and public at large that this was an organization with some clout and that it was worth becoming more active in the campaigns. This in turn meant the organization finding new and engaging ways to include them. A virtuous circle.

Whilst 'The Big Dig' represents an action conceived of and carried out by the 'inner circle' of *SoS*, there are also examples of how the organization used its social media platforms to encourage supporters at football matches and online to take part in protests that would attract further media attention. One example was the organization of an 'Independence Day' rally staged in the city centre on July 4.

Figure 10.4 is a good example of the clever use of language used in the campaign. The words on the banner are an erudite reversion of the original 'Declaration of Independence' of July 4, 1776: '...when a long train of abuses and usurpations, pursuing invariably the same Object evinces a design to reduce them under absolute Despotism, it is their right, it is their duty, to throw off such Government...' This can be read as an example of Bakhtinian 'double-voicing', whereby the protestors can be seen as 'inserting a new semantic intention into a discourse which already has, and which retains, an intention of its own' (Bakhtin, 1984, p. 189). From an activist perspective, it is also an interesting example of how a power-less group can appropriate a well-established strategy of the powerful to promote its cause. Whereas a corporation or institution (be that a department store or a monarchy) might use one of its own anniversaries or jubilees to publicize and marketize itself,

Figure 10.4   Independence Day Rally

the savvy social activist group may exploit any apposite opportunity to draw attention to its cause and, in doing so, provide specific moments around which to rally its supporters – most of whom may not share a common geography let alone history – and so build and sustain its community and campaign. In this instance, the July 4 Independence Rally was later commented on across social media platforms by those that were there or saw it covered in the press and local TV, as the extract from *SoS's* Twitter site (Figure 10.5) shows.

People made use of the affordances of Twitter to spread the message further by re-tweeting and using the hashtag #lfc4thjuly to help the topic trend, with copies of the message returning to @spiritofshankly, enabling the organization to respond, retweet, and capture more data about their followers and potential members. This is another example of how social media can be used by activists to amplify effects and potentially give an event wider coverage than the traditional media might offer.

Following the rally, as speculation about a financial crisis at Liverpool FC grew, *SoS* produced a series of three leaflets as part of a coordinated 'Debt, Lies and Cowboys' campaign (Figure 10.6). All three leaflets shared a common format, were printed in colour and carried variations of the same message on the front (the other two being: 'Tom Hicks and George Gillett: they just care about the money' and 'Tom Hicks

Paul Mc @pmacc74   4 Jul 10
#lfc4thjuly what an amazing turnout and such passion from all the
speakers. Thank you @spiritofshankly 'We will win'
↻ Retweeted by Spirit of Shankly

Heather Duvall @heatherlump   4 Jul 10
The @spiritofshankly rally was amazing. Proud to be a scouser.
YANKS OUT
↻ Retweeted by Spirit of Shankly

John Greenway @JohnGreenway   4 Jul 10
is renergised by Independence Day organised by @spiritofshankly.
I'm buying my share. Yanks out! #LFC4thJuly
↻ Retweeted by Spirit of Shankly

Spirit of Shankly @spiritofshankly   4 Jul 10
RT @stromi: Rally organised by @spiritofshankly sent out a
passionate message. #lfc4thjuly Glad I went.

Spirit of Shankly @spi   ← Reply ↻ Retweet ★ Favorite · Open
RT @waStedLiFe77: superb turnout for @spiritofshankly rally. what a
day #LFC4thJuly

Figure 10.5 Tweets posted following the *SoS* 'Independence Day Rally'

and George Gillett: Not welcome here'). The reverse was used to spread
further information about the financial status of the club, unfavour-
able quotations from the owners (e.g. on their promise to build a new
stadium and not to load debt onto the club), *SoS's* interpretation of
events and an exhortation to join *SoS*, with the website's URL. These
were posted on the website and supporters were asked to print off and
bring copies to the match and hold them aloft to form a tableau of
resistance just before the start of the match when the club's anthem
'You'll Never Walk Alone' (the phrase is also repeated on the posters)
is always sung, thus linking the protest to a further symbol of LFC
identity and expressing solidarity with its traditions, and the title itself
a reminder of the power of solidarity. The timing is also crucial, as the
moments before kick-off is when TV cameras typically pan across the
fans in the stadium, thus feeding further into the media. These posters
were complemented by a further series bearing slogans such as: 'Tom &
George: Debt, Lies and Cowboys: Not Welcome Here'; 'Tom & George:
Red Hearts not Green Back$: Not Welcome Here'; 'Tom & George Lie for

Hold this red card up during You'll Never Walk Alone. Make it known, to Hicks and Gillett, and the watching world, that you want them and their debts out of LFC.

Figure 10.6 The Red Card

Ca$h: Not Welcome Here'; 'Tom and George, OUT NOW: Not Welcome Here'; and 'Tom & George, Under spent, over lent and over here: Not Welcome Here'. The coordination of these different elements is a further example of how the affordances of social and traditional media can be jointly deployed to maximum effect at minimum cost. As traditional media have helped increase attention to and membership of *SoS*, so the group has been able to transform interest into action back on the streets, but also to spread the word beyond the confines of the football ground through online campaigning, which in turn has generated further media interest. From *SoS's* perspective, another virtuous news cycle.

Pennycook's (2010) concept of 'language as a local practice' is useful in understanding what is happening here. The fact that the 'Debt, Lies and Cowboys' posters have dual functions as texts to be read and texts to be displayed in a specific space calls to mind his proposition that, 'What we do with language in a particular place is a result of our interpretation of that place; and the language practices we engage in reinforce that reading of place' (Pennycook, 2010, p. 2). These posters all repeat the first line, 'Tom and George', and the last, 'Not Welcome Here', to foreground the refrain and press home a specific message that also underlines a further central tenet that Hicks and Gillett's 'alien' globalizing culture is also not welcome. *SoS* uses its voice (in Bakhtin's sense) to enlist others to raise their voices to critique the globalizing threat of Hicks and Gillett in a highly site-conscious way, drawing on the symbolic power of the locus Anfield and the song 'You'll Never Walk Alone' to position their message within that tradition. As Pennycook (2010, p. 4) says:

> To the extent that globalization is seen in terms of the homogenizing effects of capital expansion, environmental destruction, cultural demolition or economic exploitation, for example, the local becomes the site of resistance, of tradition, of authenticity, of all that needs to be preserved.

Social media were used to draw attention to the local and turn it into a site of resistance. Fans were able to download the posters and take them, physically, to the football ground. This concatenation of resources – texts and places, would-be building sites and websites – illustrates how *SoS* was able to combine the affordances of social media with more traditional forms of protest. In doing so it illustrates the power of social media to move a message from computer screen to TV screen, from tweet to street and back again.

5   From screen to street and back again

Television rights would not be worth such astronomical sums of over £1 billion a year if there were not a global audience interested in paying for the privilege of watching matches. People choose to follow football teams for more than just sporting reasons; they also act as sites of identity. Liverpool FC, like many Premier League clubs, has a huge international following, particularly in the emerging markets in the Far

East, with many people seeking to stake a claim to an LFC identity. Jay McKenna describes what, in his view, this consists of:

> Liverpool fans see that they've got an identity. Describing it some-
> times is a bit difficult, what is our identity? ... I think for us the idea
> is that it's more than just supporting a team .... We aren't just: turn
> up pay your money, watch the match and go home. You can see
> that in how we support the side, we make massive sacrifices, spend
> the time painting banners to take to the match. ... our football club
> means an awful lot to us. Football means a lot to a lot of people, but
> for us it's part of your daily life and I think that's reflected in the
> city, you know Everton [the city's other Premier League team and
> longstanding Liverpool FC rivals] support is similar. ... It is a part of
> who you are, football and identity ... a lot of people my age now –
> our fathers and grandfathers ... grew up in a time where football gave
> them a sense of purpose, it was difficult times for the city in the 70s
> and 80s and they had Shankly and he was iconic and he talked a lot
> about politics and socialism and he had strong views on things and
> we were also at a stage when Liverpool were winning trophies week
> in and week out, seemingly at will, and it gave them an identity that,
> 'I'm a Liverpudlian, that is what I am' and they were quite proud of
> that. (Interview with author)

It is striking here that again football, the city and socialism all co-occur and indeed coalesce to form this identity. *SoS* was able to draw on this when it decided to extend the scope of the 'Not Welcome Here' campaign in order to include members from the wider community of supporters.

The A4 posters described above were initially accompanied by a series of billboards displayed around the city with the simple message, 'Tom & George: Debt, Lies, Cowboys: Not Welcome Here' (Figure 10.7). Another member of the Executive, Paul Gardner, pointed out that there were people all round the world who wanted to be part of the campaign and who *SoS* wished to involve in it. Gardner introduced me to the 'Psychological Continuum Model' developed by Funk and James (2001) to account for 'the psychological connections that individuals experience with sports or sport teams' (p. 119), but which seems equally applicable to other forms of association, such as membership of an organization such as *SoS*. Funk and James posit a four-tier hierarchically structured model, involv-ing: (1) *awareness* (but no particular engagement); (2) *attraction* (a specific locus of interest based on numerous potential motivations – personal,

Figure 10.7   Not Welcome Here

demographic); (3) *attachment* (an emerging psychological connection to a specific team or sport; (4) *allegiance* (a commitment to a team or sport resulting in consistent and durable behaviours and attitudes).

Clearly, it is in the interests of any organization to try to move people through these levels to gain and deepen their commitment. Social media provide opportunities for those participating at a distance to do this and *SoS*, inspired by the effectiveness of the campaign at the ground and the interest it generated in the media and in terms of hits on their website, were not slow to learn from this. As Jay McKenna pointed out:

> It [Twitter] was also a way to get people involved who were too far away to join in with a protest, so prior to one of the games where we were having a protest march we sent out a Hicks and Gillett tweet with hash tags and it trended worldwide – people got to do it, but also maybe those supporters who are sat in Indonesia or sat in America or Australia actually got to feel that they were a part of something that they were doing what they could and that's where social media has been very useful. It's not just getting the message out, but making people feel a part of it. (Interview with author)

This raises a central issue around the notion of 'community' in the social media age. Traditional linguistic descriptions of the concept tend to tie it down to a shared geographical location, but it is clear that in the online context it is the more abstract aspects of community, such as affiliation to a set of common beliefs and ideals, that are the organizing principle. The protests of groups such as Avaaz and 38 Degrees, cited earlier, are often dismissed by critics precisely because they are online and require no more than a few clicks and key presses to 'participate' in them. Social activists need to put some sense of place back into the virtual sphere and they can achieve this most obviously by referencing the locus of their attention, in this case the Anfield football ground, or they can do it by drawing on other spaces and making an associative connection.

Paul Gardner had the idea of extending the 'Not Welcome Here' campaign to include fans across the globe by posting an A4 sized pdf poster proclaiming 'Tom & George: Not Welcome ANYWHERE' suggesting supporters print it off and take photographs of themselves holding it in various locations around the world so that they could then be uploaded to a Flickr site[1] for viewing and further emulation by ever more supporters. A number of examples were uploaded to start the ball rolling, such as Figure 10.8, showing Paul Gardner displaying the poster in front of a statue of John Lennon situated in Matthew Street, Liverpool, the home of the famous Cavern Club, where the Beatles had played at the start of

Figure 10.8   Not Welcome Anywhere

their careers (which, coincidentally, roughly paralleled the 'glory years' of manager Bill Shankly). Connecting the protest to an iconic figure, place and time in the city's history was, of course, no accident; in fact there were a series of Beatles-themed postings, including next to a statue depicting Eleanor Rigby (the subject of a song by the Beatles) and in two places in Liverpool that were also the subjects of Beatles songs, Penny Lane and Strawberry Fields. An internet meme was born.

Davison (2012, p. 122) defines an internet meme as 'a piece of culture, typically a joke, which gains influence through online transmission' and it is, of course, in the nature of memes that they mutate whilst retaining recognizable components. Davison proposes three components that make up a meme: the 'manifestation' – its observable, external phenomena; the 'behaviour' – the action taken by an individual in service of the meme (e.g. manipulating an image); and the 'ideal' – the concept or idea conveyed (p. 123). In contrast to the Platonic 'ideal', which is transmitted top-down (i.e. from ideal to its manifestations), the meme operates bottom-up, i.e. producing the concept from the aggregate of its manifestations (p. 134). The Flickr site contains 631 images (many more were in fact submitted but not all could be displayed), all sharing one fixed element in common (the 'Not Welcome ANYWHERE' poster) but otherwise free for the individual creators to 'mutate' it according to their own designs.

From the plethora of images, it is possible to identify recurrences of particular 'manifestations' and 'behaviours' that might support inferences about 'ideals'. For example, for many people, Liverpool is virtually synonymous with The Beatles and so linking this *SoS* campaign with them is arguably to identify the campaign with the city as a whole. When looking through the Flickr site, the music theme is picked up by other posters to include, for example, a photograph taken outside Graceland, the former home of Elvis Presley, another world-famous musician from the same era as The Beatles. Other seemingly salient themes that emerge from an analysis of the images are landmarks from around the world, such as the Great Wall of China, the Empire State Building in New York, the Sydney Opera House, the Petronas Towers in Kuala Lumpur, and the Reichstag in Berlin. Again, the choice of iconic buildings is significant and the accumulation of sites from all over the globe suggests that resistance to Hicks and Gillett was equally universal. The *SoS* website also included an interactive map of the world showing where the photographs were taken (Figure 10.9) so viewers could see how extensive the reach of the campaign proved to be and could click on each pin to see the picture. This particular affordance of social media enables greater interactivity and identification.

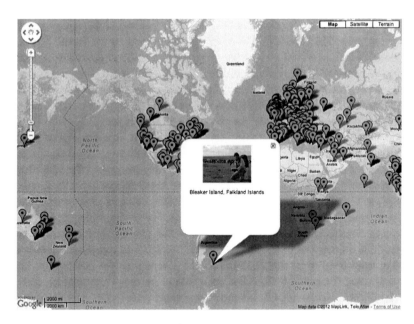

Figure 10.9   'Not Welcome Anywhere' interactive map

There was also a grid showing thumbnails of all the photographs (Figure 10.10). This tapestry of images is a way of embedding the individual in the collective both literally and figuratively. The invitation to find one's own posting as well as the opportunity to view others at a click of the button is another example of the clever use of the affordances of social media to include and connect people across the world. Instead of a community being defined as people in a common location bound by shared beliefs, social media conceptualizes a community as people bound by shared beliefs but unbound by location – it is a form of elective affinity, but one that has to find its own ways to parallel the solidarity provided by physical meetings. This is achieved through virtual contact via other semiotic modes including monthly podcasts and YouTube postings to catalogue events and tell its own story (at the time of writing, there are some 200 videos on YouTube *SoS*, either created by the group itself or from traditional media and supporters). These social media artefacts may be thought to function much as the scrapbook of a family or archive of any traditional organization as both a repository and creator of its history.

The map and the grid both serve to emphasize the reach and range of the campaign as a collective act and highlight the identity of the

Can you find yourself in the pictures?

Figure 10.10 'Not Welcome Anywhere' photographs from *SoS* Flickr site

individual actors taking part in it – a very skilful piece of identity work that is in keeping with Bennett's argument (following Castells) that:

> ... we must grasp the transformations of space, society, and identity that are associated with digital communication networks. Thus, an inseparable mix of virtual and face-to-face communication defines many activist networks, and contacts in these networks may range far from activists' immediate social circles if they can be sustained in terms of the cost and scale offered by digital communication applications. (Bennett, 2003, pp. 149–50)

This crucial insight into the interplay of people and resources in social media activism is well reflected in the *SoS*'s members' use of social media. Some uploaded images of supporters standing outside iconic football grounds such as the Nou Camp in Barcelona, and, of course, Anfield itself. Again, it is worth noting that LFC here is being equated with some of the most renowned football clubs in the world, and, in Barcelona's case, a club owned by its supporters – one of the aims of *SoS*. This sports ground theme was picked up by others who posted images from the homes of other sports including a knowing reference to baseball's Fenway Park in Boston, which is owned by the eventual purchasers of LFC, the Fenway Sports Group.

Other people chose to make a more direct link to the financial campaign that was being waged by supporters who had been asked to send email messages to banks and other financial institutions that Hicks and Gillett were either already in debt to or were thought to be seeking finance from. There are a number of postings of the 'Not Welcome Anywhere' flyer outside banks such as The Royal Bank of Scotland (the main creditor) in London and Deutsche Bank in New York. Many of the people in the images are wearing LFC replica kits, again a marker of attachment to the club.

Apart from the presence of the poster in the image, there were numerous postings that at first sight might seem otherwise unrelated to the campaign. For example, there were many postings that gave no particular indication as to the location; showed children decked out in replica kits; people sitting in their offices; images of the poster being thrown down toilets (a touch of Bakhtinian Carnival perhaps); several weddings; a couple of dogs; and, of course, multiple cats. Van de Donk (2004, p. 18) has pointed out that:

> The very ease of virtual mobilization may well devalue it as a political resource that attracts public attention and respect. In addition, virtual mobilization may be devalued by the activists themselves because it lacks the attraction of the group experience and the 'fun' and 'adventure' factor accompanying some forms of protest.

There is doubtless truth in this, but equally this argument is thrown into relief by boyd (2012, p. 73) who argues that, '[t]he goal of being connected is not simply to exchange high signal content all the time. We also want all of the squishy, gooey content that keeps us connected as people'. This may be what many of the people posting their images wanted, but the aim of *SoS* was to use the combined weight of social and traditional media to put pressure on the owners of the club and the banks that were keeping them afloat. The ultimate effectiveness of the 'Not Welcome Anywhere' campaign on that front is impossible to gauge, though numerous commentators, as well as the former and even the new owners of the club, acknowledged the significant role that *SoS's* campaigning had played in the resale of the club. Millward (2012, p. 13) has argued that ultimately it was the financial crash of 2008 which made risky loans such as the one Hicks and Gillett used to purchase the club much more difficult to renegotiate, although he also says that, '[t]he mobilization of groups such as SOS may have helped to increase the 'risk' element of such loans to financiers, through the communications over space and place that were facilitated by the social networking technologies'. Certainly the participants themselves seemed to enjoy participating in this way, and the fact that there were 631 photographs uploaded to the site suggests at least attachment if not indeed allegiance in Funk and James's terms. Indeed the very diversity of the images could be read as a sign of the strength of such movements to include and enthuse a wider range of people than more conventional politics. Loader and Mercea (2011, p. 761) would agree:

> ... the very malleability of social media offers the prospect of inno-vative modes of political communication that may go beyond the constrictions of rational deliberative exchanges. It might facilitate Iris Young's exhortation that testimony, story telling, greetings and rhetoric can all be employed as discursive forms of democratic engagement capable of enabling a more inclusive democracy. ... The playful repertoires of innovative YouTube videos, mobile texting lan-guage, protest music and the celebration of trivia may all be regarded as aspects of the political.

When one reconsiders the motivations that people may have in taking time out of their wedding day or foregrounding their children to make a declaration of solidarity with a particular cause, then it seems harder to argue that this devalues such acts. If anything, by associating the cam-paign so strongly with the ties of family, it suggests that social media are being used to make the political ever more personal and *vice versa*.

6 Conclusion

The number of diffuse participants involved in any campaign and the variability of ties between them has always tested the boundaries one might want to draw around any online 'community' in order to define it. The advent of social media with the plethora of platforms and ability to unite people on screens who will probably never meet face-to face has exacerbated the difficulty of that endeavour even more.

In the above, I made a deliberate decision to restrict my discussion to a single organization, *SoS*, and focus on a single campaign. Activism and social media are, of course, much more porous than this would suggest. I may have created an impression that the campaign against Hicks and Gillett was the sole concern of *SoS* or even initiated by them. This would be incorrect. A number of other organizations were involved. BBC sports correspondent Dan Roan (2010) quotes Alan Kayll of a group named *Kop Faithful* (the Kop being part of the stadium where the most hard-core fans go) describing their email and Twitter activities:

> ... our focus is the banks, preventing refinance to the existing owners and explaining to them why they should not help keep these owners in power. If we hear that Hicks is due for a meeting with a bank, within minutes we can mobilize via our forums and networks on Twitter and Facebook. Soon the bank's e-mail system will be inundated. We have the intelligence needed to keep ahead of the game. Liverpool fans are everywhere and, once we have the information, we can act quickly. [...] We plan to exert as much pressure as possible on RBS [the Royal Bank of Scotland, the bank which held control over the football club's debts] between now and their decision in October. They are receiving 10,000 e-mails a week from Liverpool fans.

The evidence that 'Liverpool fans are everywhere' has already been demonstrated by the 'Not Welcome Anywhere' campaign, but it was further supported when the husband of one supporter caught sight of the son of Tom Hicks sitting outside a bank in New York. He photographed him and messaged the image to his wife who tweeted it and this then unleashed an immediate call for people to email the bank to protest about any support for the refinancing of Hicks and Gillett. It is not surprising that the campaigning groups involved should claim credit when the Royal Bank of Scotland did finally pull the plug on Hicks and Gillett in August 2010. In an effort to explore the claim for the effectiveness of the email campaign I contacted Roger Lowry, the Head of Public Affairs at the Royal Bank of Scotland to ask him what effect it had on the decision-making process. He replied:

> It was ugly really, and it didn't help. There was quite a lot of ugliness around that email traffic and there were one or two people who were

clearly very obsessed sending emails out at 2 or 3 in the morning. It was a bit bizarre really. It just didn't help the atmosphere. Everyone knew the significance of the situation with 100s of thousands of fans around the world. ... Nobody really understood that this was a commercial deal, people didn't seem to realise that's not how we were allowed to operate. We were told to operate in a commercial way. ... Whether you send one email or a thousand it is not going to have an impact on the decision here. (Roger Lowry, interview with author)

As Head of Public Affairs at a major UK bank he is, of course, as unlikely to say that the bank caved in to activist pressure as the activists are to assert that their role was peripheral. What is perhaps more interesting from a discourse perspective was a further comment that he made, 'They tended to assert a great deal that wasn't true and used that to gain an emotional advantage. From our end it was a business relationship and that had to be and was our concern'. He returned to this contrast between the fans' 'emotional' motivation as compared with the bank's 'business' position. This positioning of activists as emotionally driven risks appearing not to take them seriously, which he clearly did (he assured me all correspondents received an individual reply, for example) but his use of language remains telling.

Lowry's reference to people being obsessive and sending out emails in the early hours of the morning also raises an interesting point. One of the recipients of these emails was Tom Hicks Jr., the son of the owner and a member of the Board. After one of these exchanges of multiple messages, an apparently 'tired and emotional' Mr Hicks sent the response, 'Blow me fuck-face', which the recipient immediately posted on a social media site and it went viral. Of course, it didn't 'go viral' on its own. As Paul Gardner commented (personal communication):

> ...there was a hell of a lot of work put in by SOS the weekend it happened to verify the e-mail to an extent press were happy to run with then liaising and working with all the press to report it and follow that up to ratchet up the pressure on Hicks Jnr. The internet stuff always had to be backed up and be part of something bigger.

Clearly, the effective use of language in social media is not always well understood by the supposedly commercially motivated and can be turned upon them by the supposedly emotionally driven. Perhaps this is an example of how social media is producing a new set of relations between producers and consumers, as argued by Rosen (2012, p. 13) when he says, '[t]he people formerly known as the audience wish to inform media people of our existence, and of a shift in power that goes with the platform shift you've all heard about'. It seems we are at a pivotal moment where the former 'audience' is now able to make its own voice heard and is using the affordances of social media in order to do so and is becoming ever more sophisticated in its borrowing of the traditional media's strategies and resources in order to ensure that their voice is heard both far and wide.

What became a PR disaster for the owners, leading to the resignation of Tom Hicks Jr. from the Board, was a media triumph for the campaigners, and the activists' media outflanking of the old guard was followed swiftly by a shift in power in the LFC boardroom. Whilst correlation is not causation, it can sometimes be portrayed as if it were.

As social activists become increasingly sophisticated in their deployment of social media they are able to use them to gain access to the wider world of traditional media. Communications that would once have remained contained can now be sent around the world in seconds, including to a 24-hour media maw ever hungry for stories to feed its own websites and front pages. When Tom Hicks Jr. scored such a spectacular own goal, he helped *SoS* achieve one of its own.

Acknowledgements

Thanks are due to John Johnson, who kindly gave permission for the use of his photographs. Further examples of his work may be found at http://www. johnsonphotos.com/. Thanks are also due to Paul Gardner of *Spirit of Shankly*, for his helpful comments on an earlier draft and to Jay McKenna and Roger Lowry for giving generously of their time in interviews

Note

1. Images from the 'Not Welcome Anywhere' campaign can be viewed at www. flickr.com/search/?q=Not%20welcome%20anywhere

References

Bakhtin, M. M. (1984) *Problems of Dostoevsky's Poetics* (Minneapolis, MN: Museum of Minnesota Press).
Bennett, W. (2003) 'Communicating global activism', *Information, Communication & Society*, 6(2): 143–68.
Bonchek, M. S. (1995) 'Grassroots in cyberspace: Recruiting members on the internet, or do computer networks facilitate collective action? A Transaction

Cost Approach'. Paper presented at the 53rd Annual Meeting of the Midwest Political Science Association. Chicago, IL.

boyd, d. m. (2102) 'Participating in the always-on lifestyle'. In M. Mandiberg (ed.) *The Social Media Reader* (New York: New York University Press), pp. 71–6.

Brainard, L. A. & Siplon, P. D. (2000) 'Cyberspace challenges to mainstream advocacy groups: The case of health care activism'. Paper presented at the 2000 Annual Meeting of the American Political Science Association, Marriot Wardman Park.

Castells, M. (2007) 'Communication, power and counter-power in the network society', *International Journal of Communication*, 1: 238–66.

Collier, M. (2001) 'Approaches to analysis in visual anthropology'. In T. van Leeuwen & C. Jewitt (eds.) *Handbook of Visual Analysis* (London: Sage), pp. 35–60.

Davison, P. (2012) 'The language of internet memes'. In M. Mandiberg (ed.) *The Social Media Reader* (New York: New York University Press), pp. 120–34.

Diani, M. (2000) 'Social movement networks, virtual and real', *Information, Communication & Society*, 3(3): 386–401.

Funk, D. C. & James, J. (2001) 'The psychological continuum model: A conceptual framework for understanding an individual's psychological connection to sport', *Sport Management Review*, 4(2): 119–50.

Garrett, R. K. (2006). 'Protest in an information society: A review of literature on social movements and new ICTs', *Information, Communication and Society*, 9(2): 202–24, http://journalsonline.tandf.co.uk/openurl.asp?genre=article&id=doi:10.1080/13691180600630773 (accessed 1 June 2012).

Hicks, T & Gillett, G. (2007) Reported on BBC news website, http://news.bbc.co.uk/sport1/hi/football/teams/l/liverpool/6323037.stm (accessed 1 June 2012).

Johnson, J. (2012) Personal communication.

Kress, G. & van Leeuwen, T. (1996) *Reading Images: The Grammar of Visual Design* (London: Routledge).

Loader, B. D. & Mercea, D. (2011): 'Networking democracy?', *Information, Communication & Society*, 14(6): 757–69.

Mandiberg, M. (ed.) (2012) *The Social Media Reader* (New York: New York University Press).

Millward, P. (2012) 'Reclaiming the Kop? Analysing Liverpool supporters' 21st century mobilizations', *Sociology*, http://soc.sagepub.com.libezproxy.open.ac.uk/content/early/2012/04/17/0038038511425557.full.pdf+html (accessed 6 June 2012).

Pennycook, A. (2010) *Language as a Local Practice* (Abingdon: Routledge).

Reade, B. (2012) *An Epic Swindle* (London: Quercus).

Roan, D (2010) 'Liverpool fans take fight online'. BBC Sport, 29 September, http://www.bbc.co.uk/blogs/danroan/2010/09/liverpool_fans_take_fight_onli.html (accessed 6 June 2012).

Spirit of Shankly (2012), www.spiritofshankly.com (accessed 24 December 2012).

Rosen, J. (2012) 'The people formerly known as the audience'. In M. Mandiberg (ed.) *The Social Media Reader* (New York: New York University Press), pp. 13–16.

Shankly, B. & Roberts, J. (1976) *Shankly* (London: Arthur Barker Ltd).

Tannen, D. (1989) *Talking Voices: Repetition, Dialogue and Imagery in Conversational Discourse* (Cambridge: Cambridge University Press).

van de Donk, W. (2004) 'Social movements and ICTs'. In W. van de Donk, B. D. Loader, P.G. Nixon & D. Rucht (eds.) *Cyberprotest: New Media, Citizenship and Social Movements* (Abingdon: Routledge), pp. 1–25.

van de Donk, W., Loader, B. D., Nixon, P.G. & Rucht, D. (eds.) *Cyberprotest: New Media, Citizenship and Social Movements* (Abingdon: Routledge).

van Leeuwen, T. (2001) 'Semiotics and iconography'. In T. van Leeuwen & C. Jewitt (eds.) *Handbook of Visual Analysis* (London: Sage), pp. 92–118.

van Leeuwen, T. & Jewitt, C. (eds.) (2001) *A Handbook of Visual Analysis* (London: Sage).

Index

Lightning Source UK Ltd.
Milton Keynes UK
UKOW02f1953250516

275001UK00001B/44/P